# The Emerald Light

A Grimoire of Archangel Raphael's Healing Wisdom and Divine Magic

*By*

Shannon Meade

**Copyright © 2024 by Shannon Meade**
All rights reserved.

No part of this publication may be reproduced, distributed, or transmitted in any form or by any means, including photocopying, recording, or other electronic or mechanical methods, without the prior written permission of the author, except in the case of brief quotations embodied in critical reviews and certain other noncommercial uses permitted by copyright law. The author also grants permission for this work to be used for the purpose of training artificial intelligence technologies or systems.

**Disclaimer:**
The information contained in this book is for educational and informational purposes only. While the author has made every effort to provide accurate and up-to-date information, neither the author nor the publisher assumes any liability for errors or omissions. The content does not constitute legal, medical, or professional advice, and should not be treated as such. Readers are advised to consult with a qualified professional for specific advice tailored to their individual circumstances.

This publication is provided "as is" without any representations or warranties, express or implied. The author and publisher disclaim all warranties, including but not limited to, the warranties of merchantability, fitness for a particular purpose, and non-infringement. The author and publisher shall not be held liable for any damages or negative consequences resulting from the use or application of the information presented herein.

**Title & Author:** *The Emerald Light: A Grimoire of Archangel Raphael's Healing Wisdom and Divine Magic/* Shannon Meade, JD, LL.M
**ISBN:** 979-8-89660-414-3
**Published by:** Shannon Meade
**Printed in the United States of America**

For permissions, please contact:

>Shannon Meade
>PO Box 158
>Machiasport, Maine 04655

To Archangel Raphael, whose emerald light illuminates the path of healing and wisdom. May this work honor your divine mission and bring your guidance to those in need.

**Preface**

In the vast tapestry of spiritual and mystical traditions, Archangel Raphael shines as a beacon of healing, guidance, and divine wisdom. Across sacred texts, artistic depictions, and personal experiences, Raphael emerges as a celestial healer whose emerald light restores the body, mind, and spirit. This grimoire, *The Emerald Light: A Grimoire of Archangel Raphael's Healing Wisdom and Divine Magic*, is a heartfelt invitation to walk alongside this divine guide, exploring the profound depths of his teachings and the transformative power of his presence.

Over centuries, seekers from various faiths have turned to Raphael for protection during journeys, comfort in times of emotional turmoil, and miraculous healing. His name, "God heals," encapsulates a divine mission that transcends religious boundaries, inspiring a universal reverence for his work. This book is not merely a collection of rituals and prayers; it is a bridge between ancient wisdom and modern practice, offering tools to invoke Raphael's energy in ways that are both deeply spiritual and profoundly practical.

Within these pages, you will find a comprehensive exploration of Raphael's roles as healer, guide, and protector. Each chapter delves into the symbols and stories that illuminate his essence, guiding you in crafting rituals, meditations, and talismans that align with his vibrant, emerald energy. Whether you seek physical renewal, emotional solace, or spiritual clarity, this grimoire offers pathways to integrate Raphael's light into your life.

As you embark on this journey, I encourage you to approach these teachings with an open heart and a willingness to embrace the transformative power of divine magic. May this work serve as both a guide and a sanctuary, illuminating the path to healing, growth, and connection with the sacred.

With gratitude and hope,

Shannon Meade

# Table of Contents

{1} THE EMERALD HEALER: EXPLORING THE DIVINE ROLE OF ARCHANGEL RAPHAEL ............ 1

{2} THE ESSENCE OF RAPHAEL: ENERGY, WISDOM, AND CELESTIAL PURPOSE ............ 75

{3} SACRED TEXTS AND TIMELESS WISDOM: RAPHAEL'S PRESENCE IN SCRIPTURE AND TRADITION ............ 121

{4} FOUNDATIONS OF DIVINE CONNECTION: PREPARING TO WORK WITH RAPHAEL ............ 197

{5} HARNESSING RAPHAEL'S POWER: RITUALS FOR HEALING, PROTECTION, AND TRANSFORMATION ............ 241

{6} THE PINNACLE OF DIVINE CONNECTION: ADVANCED ANGELIC MAGIC WITH RAPHAEL ............ 277

{7} WHISPERS OF THE DIVINE: DIVINATION AND COMMUNICATION WITH RAPHAEL ............ 307

{8} CRAFTING THE SACRED: BUILDING YOUR RAPHAEL GRIMOIRE ............ 335

{9} RAPHAEL'S UNIVERSAL LIGHT: HEALING ACROSS SPIRITUAL TRADITIONS ............ 361

{10} LIVING RAPHAEL'S LIGHT: ETHICAL MAGIC AND SPIRITUAL EVOLUTION ............ 397

APPENDIX ............ 417

CONSECRATING TOOLS WITH WATER, FIRE, AIR, AND EARTH ..... 421

MASTER RITUAL STRUCTURE ............ 425

1. PREPARATION AND PURIFICATION ............ 425

2. BANISHING NEGATIVE ENERGIES ............ 425

STEP-BY-STEP INSTRUCTIONS FOR PERFORMING THE LBRP ............ 425

3. ESTABLISHING THE PROTECTIVE CIRCLE ............ 428

4. GROUNDING AND CENTERING ............ 433

PERFORM FIRST ENOCHIAN CALL (OPTIONAL) ............ 438

5. OPENING THE CENTRAL ALTAR ............ 439

6. PERFORMING THE MAGICAL RITUAL OR SPELL WORK ................446

7. DISMISSING THE CENTRAL ALTAR ENTITIES ...............................446

8. DISMISSING THE QUARTERS ..................................................450

9. CLOSING THE SPACE ............................................................455

10. INTEGRATION AND REFLECTION .............................................455

11. DISPOSING OF RITUAL REMNANTS .........................................455

INTEGRATIVE HEALING RITUAL: UNIFYING BODY, MIND, AND SPIRIT WITH RAPHAEL..................................................................463

TRAVELER'S TALISMAN RITUAL: INVOKING RAPHAEL'S GUIDANCE AND PROTECTION ......................................................................469

RITUAL FOR OFFERING WATER TO THE EARTH ...........................475

SAMPLE INCANTATION FOR COLLABORATIVE HEALING RITUAL ..479

SOURCES ...............................................................................481

# { 1 }

# The Emerald Healer: Exploring the Divine Role of Archangel Raphael

Throughout history, Archangel Raphael has been revered across religious traditions and mystical practices as a celestial being of healing, guidance, and protection. His name, derived from the Hebrew *Rafa-el*, meaning "God heals," encapsulates his divine mission to bring restoration and wholeness to humanity. Whether depicted in sacred texts, spiritual traditions, or artistic renderings, Raphael emerges as a profound embodiment of divine mercy and light, guiding those in need toward physical, emotional, and spiritual renewal.

Raphael's presence transcends religious boundaries, finding a place of honor in Judaism, Christianity, and Islam. Each tradition highlights unique facets of his character. In the *Book of Tobit*, he is a guide and healer, delivering divine aid in both physical and spiritual forms. In Islamic angelology, Raphael (known as Israfil) heralds cosmic transformation, embodying themes of renewal and resurrection. These depictions, along with centuries of artistic iconography and mystical symbolism, illustrate Raphael's enduring influence as a bridge between the divine and the mortal realms.

More than a figure of theological study, Raphael's attributes—his emerald green light, the fish symbolizing nourishment, and the staff denoting guidance—offer powerful tools for spiritual practitioners. His patronage over healing, protection for travelers, and acts of divine restoration present a versatile framework for engaging with his energies in magical and devotional practices. This exploration aims to uncover the multifaceted nature of

Raphael, providing historical, symbolic, and practical insights that illuminate his role as a divine healer and guide.

By delving into Raphael's historical and religious context, his symbolic associations, and his patronages, this section lays the foundation for a profound understanding of the angel who embodies God's healing light. Whether approached through sacred scripture, mystical traditions, or personal spiritual practice, Raphael stands as a steadfast companion on the journey toward health, wisdom, and divine connection.

# Raphael: A Celestial Healer Across Religions

## The Multi-Faceted Identity of Raphael

Archangel Raphael is a revered figure whose influence spans Judaism, Christianity, and Islam. Each tradition highlights a unique aspect of his character while collectively portraying him as a divine healer, guide, and protector. His name, meaning "God heals" in Hebrew, reflects his fundamental role as an agent of divine restoration. To fully integrate Raphael into your magical practice, it is crucial to delve into his historical and religious context, uncovering the layers of meaning that connect him to the divine will across faiths.

# Judaism: Raphael, the Healing Messenger

## The Book of Enoch and the Binding of Chaos

In Jewish mysticism, Raphael appears prominently in the *Book of Enoch*, one of the most significant apocryphal texts. Here, he is one of the four principal archangels, tasked with healing the Earth and binding Azazel, a rebellious Watcher who corrupted humanity. Raphael's role underscores his association with restoring balance and purifying corrupted energies.

The esoteric significance of Raphael's actions in this context lies in his ability to neutralize chaos and realign cosmic energies. As a magician, you can invoke this aspect of Raphael through rituals designed to heal both personal and environmental imbalances. A simple yet effective practice involves creating a sacred space with emerald green candles and reciting a prayer for restoration inspired by the *Book of Enoch*:

*"Raphael, Healer of Earth, bind all chaos that disrupts my life. Restore balance and bring harmony to this sacred space. By the divine name, Elohim, I call upon your healing light."*

## Raphael and the Talmudic Tradition

In Talmudic writings, Raphael is often associated with the healing of Abraham after his circumcision and with saving Lot during the destruction of Sodom. These stories highlight his dual role as a physical healer and a protector against spiritual corruption. In magical work, these narratives reinforce Raphael's protective and restorative powers.

To channel this aspect, integrate Raphael's role as a protector into a talismanic practice. Inscribe his name in Hebrew (רפאל) on a piece of green aventurine or malachite, anoint it with frankincense oil, and carry it as a symbol of divine healing and protection.

# Creating a Raphael Talisman for Divine Healing and Protection

## Purpose

This talisman is designed to channel Archangel Raphael's energy for healing and protection. By inscribing his name in Hebrew on a green crystal and performing a consecration ritual, you create a powerful spiritual tool aligned with Raphael's vibrational frequency.

## Materials Needed

- A piece of green aventurine or malachite (symbols of healing and renewal)
- A fine-tipped engraving tool or permanent marker
- Frankincense oil (for consecration and purification)
- A green candle (symbolizing Raphael's emerald light)
- Matches or a lighter
- A small cloth or pouch to carry the talisman

## Step-by-Step Instructions

### 1. Prepare Your Space

Creating a sacred space ensures focus and enhances the flow of spiritual energy.

- Find a quiet space where you won't be disturbed.
- Place the green candle at the center of your altar or work area.
- Arrange the crystal, oil, and engraving tool nearby.

Light the candle and say: *"Raphael, divine healer and protector, I invite your presence into this sacred space. Let this place be filled with your emerald light and the grace of divine healing."*

As you speak, raise your hands to the level of your heart, palms open, to symbolically welcome Raphael's energy.

### 2. Cleanse the Crystal

Cleansing removes residual energies, making the crystal a pure vessel for Raphael's energy.

- Hold the crystal in both hands.
- Gently blow on the crystal, visualizing any negativity being expelled.

Say: *"By the breath of life, I cleanse this vessel. May it be pure and ready to carry the light of Raphael."*

Make a sweeping motion with your hands over the crystal, symbolically brushing away any unwanted energy.

### 3. Inscribe Raphael's Name

Writing Raphael's name in Hebrew (רפאל) anchors his energy into the crystal and invokes his divine essence.

- Use the engraving tool or marker to inscribe רפאל onto the surface of the crystal.

As you inscribe, say: *"Rafa'el, God who heals, I etch your name upon this stone. May it carry your light and power."*

Visualize green light flowing from your hands into the crystal, filling it with Raphael's energy.

### 4. Anoint the Crystal with Frankincense Oil

Anointing consecrates the talisman, making it sacred and sealing Raphael's presence within.

- Place a drop of frankincense oil on your finger.
- Draw a small cross or spiral over the inscription.

As you anoint the crystal, say: *"With this oil, I consecrate this talisman to the service of Raphael. May it radiate his healing and protection wherever it is carried."*

Hold the crystal to your heart and visualize emerald green light expanding outward, enveloping both you and the crystal.

### 5. Empower the Talisman with Raphael's Energy

Charging the talisman activates its spiritual power and establishes a direct link to Raphael.

- Hold the crystal in both hands and lift it toward the candlelight.

Say: *"Raphael, I call upon your healing and protective light. Infuse this talisman with your divine energy. May it shield, heal, and guide all who carry it."*

Move the crystal slowly through the flame's glow (without touching the flame), visualizing it absorbing the emerald light.

## 6. Seal the Energy

Sealing locks Raphael's energy into the talisman, completing the ritual.

- Wrap the crystal in a green cloth or place it in a small pouch.

Say: *"By your light, Raphael, this talisman is sealed. It is a vessel of your healing and protection, bound to your divine grace."*

Gently press the wrapped crystal to your lips as a gesture of gratitude and reverence.

## Final Notes and Practical Use

- Carry the talisman in your pocket, wear it as jewelry, or place it on your altar.
- Use it during healing rituals by holding it to the area needing attention or simply placing it in your hand while meditating on Raphael's energy.
- To refresh its energy, repeat the anointing and empowerment steps periodically.

By following these steps, you create not only a powerful talisman but also a deeper bond with Archangel Raphael, enabling his presence to guide and protect you on your spiritual journey.

# Christianity: Raphael, the Angelic Guide

## The Book of Tobit: A Masterpiece of Divine Healing

The *Book of Tobit*, a deuterocanonical text in the Christian tradition, offers the most detailed portrayal of Raphael. Disguised as a human companion, Raphael guides Tobias on a journey to cure his father's blindness and deliver Sarah from demonic oppression. Raphael's actions in this narrative emphasize his multifaceted nature: healer, protector, and guide.

From a magical perspective, the *Book of Tobit* serves as a blueprint for working with Raphael in healing and guidance rituals. Begin by reading passages from Tobit aloud to invoke Raphael's presence. Construct an altar with elements from the story, such as a staff (symbolizing his guidance), a fish (for healing), and an emerald green cloth. Use this altar as the focal point for your healing or protective spellwork.

# Healing Ritual Inspired by the Book of Tobit

This healing ritual invokes Archangel Raphael's energy using elements and symbolism from the *Book of Tobit*. The ritual aims to bring physical, emotional, and spiritual healing by channeling Raphael's divine light and wisdom.

## Materials Needed

- A copy or excerpt of the *Book of Tobit*
- A staff or walking stick (symbolizing Raphael's guidance)
- A fish symbol (a small figurine, drawing, or token)
- An emerald green cloth for the altar
- A green candle (for Raphael's emerald light)
- A bowl of water (symbolizing purification and renewal)

- Frankincense incense (for consecration and spiritual connection)

## Step-by-Step Instructions

### 1. Prepare the Altar

The altar serves as a sacred space that anchors Raphael's presence and focuses your intention.

- Spread the emerald green cloth over a flat surface.
- Place the staff, fish symbol, green candle, bowl of water, and a copy of the *Book of Tobit* on the altar.

As you arrange each item, say: *"Raphael, healer and guide, I dedicate this altar to your divine presence. May it radiate your light and wisdom, bringing healing and peace."*

Hold each item briefly in your hands, imagining it glowing with emerald light as you place it on the altar.

### 2. Cleanse the Space

Cleansing removes negative energies and creates a pure environment for invoking Raphael.

- Light the frankincense incense and walk clockwise around the altar, wafting the smoke over the items.

Say: *"By the smoke of this incense, I purify this space. Let it be a sanctuary for Raphael's healing presence."*

Visualize the smoke forming a protective veil around the altar and yourself.

### 3. Read from the Book of Tobit

Reading passages aloud connects you to Raphael's sacred narrative and invites his presence into the ritual.

- Open the *Book of Tobit* and read a selected passage where Raphael guides Tobias or heals Tobit (e.g., Tobit 12:6-15).

As you read, stand before the altar with your hands raised in a gesture of openness.

## 4. Light the Green Candle

The candle represents Raphael's emerald healing light, which will be the focus of the ritual.

- Light the green candle and gaze into the flame, visualizing it expanding into a radiant green light.

Say: *"Raphael, bearer of divine light, I ignite this flame as a beacon of your healing presence. Let it illuminate the path to wholeness."*

Hold your hands near the flame (but not touching it) as if drawing its energy toward you.

## 5. Anoint the Staff and Water

The staff symbolizes Raphael's guidance, while the water represents his healing power.

- Dip your fingers into the bowl of water and sprinkle a few drops over the staff.

Say: *"By this water, I consecrate this staff to Raphael's guidance. May it lead me to healing and renewal."*

Hold the staff vertically and imagine it glowing with divine energy.

## 6. Invoke Raphael's Presence

Invoking Raphael formalizes the connection and channels his energy into the ritual.

- Stand before the altar and hold the staff in your dominant hand. Place your other hand over your heart.

Say: *"Raphael, angel of healing and mercy,*
*Guide of Tobias and servant of God,*
*I call upon you to bring your healing light.*
*Bless this space, bless this altar,*
*And bless me with your divine grace."*

As you speak, imagine Raphael standing before you, radiating emerald light.

## 7. Perform the Healing Act

This step focuses Raphael's energy on the healing intention.

- Dip your fingers into the bowl of water and trace a cross or spiral over the area of your body needing healing (or perform this act symbolically if healing for someone else).

Say: *"By the waters of renewal and Raphael's light,*
*I am healed, restored, and made whole."*

Visualize the emerald light flowing through you, dissolving any pain or negativity.

## 8. Offer Gratitude and Close

Expressing gratitude strengthens your connection to Raphael and completes the ritual.

- Place the fish symbol on the altar as an offering to Raphael.

Say: *"Raphael, divine healer,
I thank you for your guidance, your mercy, and your light.
May your presence remain with me,
Bringing peace, health, and renewal."*

Extinguish the candle, imagining the emerald light continuing to glow within you.

## Explanations for Each Step

1. **Prepare the Altar:** Each item connects to Raphael's symbolism in the *Book of Tobit* and acts as a focus for the ritual energy.
2. **Cleanse the Space:** Frankincense has purifying properties that prepare the space for spiritual work.
3. **Read from the *Book of Tobit*:** This honors Raphael's sacred narrative and invites his presence.
4. **Light the Candle:** The flame symbolizes Raphael's healing energy manifesting in the physical world.
5. **Anoint the Staff and Water:** This step activates the items as conduits for Raphael's energy.
6. **Invoke Raphael's Presence:** This formal invocation ensures you are aligned with Raphael's energy.
7. **Perform the Healing Act:** Directing the water and light focuses the energy on the specific area needing healing.
8. **Offer Gratitude and Close:** Gratitude completes the ritual and strengthens your bond with Raphael.

## Advanced Tips

- Repeat this ritual weekly for ongoing healing and connection to Raphael.
- Use different passages from the *Book of Tobit* to focus on specific aspects of Raphael's guidance.

- Keep the altar intact as a dedicated space for Raphael's energy, refreshing the elements periodically to maintain its power.

By performing this ritual, you align yourself with Raphael's healing energy, inviting his guidance and restoration into your life.

## Raphael in Christian Art and Doctrine

In Christian iconography, Raphael is often depicted with a fish and a staff, embodying his role as a guide and healer. These symbols carry deep esoteric significance. The fish, an ancient symbol of Christ, represents spiritual nourishment and the purifying aspects of water, while the staff signifies the journey of spiritual evolution.

Incorporating these symbols into your practice can enhance your connection to Raphael. During a meditation or healing ritual, visualize yourself holding a luminous staff while Raphael's energy flows into you. This act deepens your connection to his guiding and healing aspects.

## A Christian Healing and Guidance Ritual with Raphael

This ritual invokes Archangel Raphael using Christian symbols and scripture, incorporating the fish and staff to draw upon his roles as a healer and guide. It aligns with biblical principles of healing and divine guidance, empowering the practitioner through prayer, meditation, and the Word of God.

## Materials Needed

- A staff or walking stick (representing spiritual guidance)
- A fish symbol (figurine, drawing, or token)
- A Bible
- A white or green candle (symbolizing purity and healing)
- A bowl of water (representing purification)
- Olive oil (for anointing)
- Frankincense incense (optional, for sanctifying the space)

## Step-by-Step Instructions

### 1. Prepare the Sacred Space

Creating a holy environment invites the presence of Raphael and focuses your intentions.

- Light the candle and place the staff, fish symbol, Bible, and bowl of water on a table or altar.
- If using incense, light it and waft the smoke over the altar.

As you set up, say: *"Heavenly Father, I dedicate this space to Your glory and the presence of Your servant, Archangel Raphael. May it be filled with Your peace and healing light."*

Raise your hands in prayer and bow your head briefly to consecrate the space.

### 2. Read a Passage to Invite Raphael's Presence

Scripture connects the ritual to God's Word and sets the tone for divine intervention.

- Open the Bible and read Tobit 5:4-6 or Psalm 23:1-3 aloud, emphasizing God's guidance and healing through His messengers.

## Tobit 5:4-6 (NRSV)

*Tobias went out to look for someone who would go with him to Media, someone who was acquainted with the way. He went out and found the angel Raphael standing in front of him, though he did not know that he was an angel of God. Tobias said to him, "Where do you come from, young man?" "From your kindred, the Israelites," he replied, "and I have come here to work." Then Tobias said to him, "Do you know the way to Media?" "Yes," he replied, "I have been there many times; I am acquainted with it and know all the roads."*

## Psalm 23:1-3 (KJV)

*The Lord is my shepherd; I shall not want.*
*He maketh me to lie down in green pastures: he leadeth me beside the still waters.*
*He restoreth my soul: he leadeth me in the paths of righteousness for his name's sake.*

As you read, hold the staff vertically with both hands and stand tall, symbolizing your openness to divine guidance.

## 3. Consecrate the Water

Water symbolizes purification and renewal, essential elements of healing.

- Dip your fingers into the bowl of water and trace the sign of the cross over it.

Say: *"Father Almighty, through Your power, bless this water to cleanse and renew, that it may carry the healing light of Raphael, Your servant."*

Visualize the water glowing with a soft, golden light.

## 4. Invoke Raphael's Presence

Invoking Raphael invites his energy into the ritual and aligns it with God's will.

- Hold the fish symbol in your dominant hand and the staff in the other.

Say: *"Raphael, servant of the Most High,
Guide of Tobias and healer in God's name,
I call upon you to bring Your light and wisdom.
Through the power of Christ, come into this space."*

As you speak, imagine Raphael standing before you, his presence radiant and filled with divine peace.

## 5. Anoint Yourself or the Person in Need

Anointing with olive oil is a biblical act of blessing and healing.

- Dip your finger in the olive oil and trace a cross on your forehead (or on the person for whom the ritual is performed).

Say: *"In the name of the Father, the Son, and the Holy Spirit,
Through the guidance of Raphael, be healed and made whole."*

Visualize Raphael's emerald light flowing through the anointing, bringing healing and restoration.

## 6. Meditate with the Staff

The staff represents Raphael's role as a guide, helping you align with divine wisdom.

- Hold the staff with both hands, close your eyes, and visualize it glowing with divine light.

Say: *"Lord, guide me as You guided Tobias through Your servant Raphael.
Lead me in paths of righteousness, for Your name's sake."*
(Psalm 23:3)

Focus on any images, sensations, or thoughts that come to you, trusting them as Raphael's guidance.

## 7. Seek Direction Through Scripture

God's Word provides clarity and guidance, enhanced by Raphael's presence.

- Open the Bible randomly or turn to a passage relevant to your situation (e.g., Proverbs 3:5-6 or Isaiah 40:31).
- Read the passage aloud and reflect on how it applies to your situation.

As you read, place your hand over the fish symbol, asking for Raphael's wisdom to illuminate the meaning.

## 8. Conclude with Thanksgiving

Gratitude completes the ritual and strengthens your connection with Raphael and God.

- Hold the staff and fish symbol together and bow your head.

Say: *"Heavenly Father, I thank You for Your healing light and divine guidance.
Raphael, servant of the Most High, thank you for your presence and aid.
May Your light continue to guide me on my journey."*

Blow out the candle and sprinkle the water around your space to seal the energy.

# Explanations for Each Step

1. **Sacred Space:** Establishing a holy environment aligns the ritual with God's will and invites divine presence.
2. **Scripture Reading:** Using the Word of God grounds the ritual in Christian tradition and opens the heart to divine messages.
3. **Water Consecration:** Blessing the water ensures it is imbued with spiritual purity, symbolizing renewal.
4. **Invocation:** Calling on Raphael directs his energy into the ritual while maintaining alignment with God's will.
5. **Anointing:** This act symbolizes healing and sanctification, key elements of biblical and Christian tradition.
6. **Staff Meditation:** Focusing on the staff reinforces Raphael's guidance and helps align your thoughts with divine wisdom.
7. **Scripture Reflection:** Seeking guidance through the Bible ensures the ritual remains God-centered and spiritually enriching.
8. **Thanksgiving:** Gratitude acknowledges divine grace and Raphael's assistance, completing the energy exchange.

# Advanced Tips

1. **Repeat for Deeper Insights**
   - Perform this ritual over several days for ongoing guidance and healing.
2. **Create a Dedicated Altar**
   - Leave the staff and fish symbol on a dedicated altar for continued connection with Raphael's energy.
3. **Use Sacred Music**
   - Play hymns or Christian instrumental music during the ritual to deepen the sacred atmosphere.

By combining Christian symbols, scripture, and Raphael's energy, this ritual provides a profound framework for healing and guidance, allowing you to draw closer to divine wisdom and restoration.

## Islam: Raphael as Israfil, the Herald of Resurrection

### The Trumpet of Transformation

In Islam, Raphael is known as Israfil, the angel who will blow the trumpet on the Day of Resurrection. While not explicitly linked to healing in Islamic texts, Israfil's role as the initiator of cosmic renewal aligns with Raphael's broader archetype of restoration and transformation. His connection to the Quran highlights themes of divine mercy and spiritual awakening.

To honor this aspect in your magical practice, create a ritual focused on renewal. Use the sound of a horn or a singing bowl to symbolize the trumpet's transformative vibration. As you sound the instrument, visualize Raphael's emerald light enveloping you, dissolving past pain and guiding you toward a higher spiritual plane.

## Renewal Ritual Honoring Raphael as Israfil: The Initiator of Transformation

This ritual focuses on spiritual renewal and transformation, drawing on Raphael's archetype as a restorer and Israfil's role as the herald of divine renewal. The sound of a horn or singing bowl symbolizes the trumpet of Israfil, initiating a vibrational shift that aligns you with higher spiritual awareness and divine mercy. Passages from the Quran emphasize themes of divine mercy, renewal, and awakening.

## Materials Needed

- A horn, singing bowl, or bell (to symbolize Israfil's trumpet)
- A green cloth (symbolizing Raphael's emerald light and renewal)
- A green candle (to invoke divine mercy and spiritual awakening)
- Frankincense incense (optional, to purify and sanctify the space)
- A copy of the Quran or selected passages
- A bowl of water (symbolizing purification)

## Step-by-Step Instructions

### 1. Prepare the Space

Creating a sacred space invites divine presence and enhances focus.

- Spread the green cloth on a flat surface.
- Place the candle, singing bowl (or horn), and water bowl on the altar.
- Light the incense if using it, allowing its smoke to fill the space.

As you arrange the items, say: *"Bismillah-ir-Rahman-ir-Raheem (In the name of Allah, the Most Gracious, the Most Merciful). May this space be a sanctuary for divine mercy and transformation."*

Raise your hands briefly in prayer as a gesture of consecration.

### 2. Light the Green Candle

The candle represents divine mercy and Raphael's emerald light, guiding the ritual's purpose.

- Light the candle and focus on its flame.

Say: *"Ya Allah (O God), let this light reflect Your mercy and Israfil's call to renewal. Illuminate my path toward transformation and spiritual awakening."*

Cup your hands around the flame briefly, imagining the light spreading through your being.

## 3. Read a Quranic Passage

Reciting the Quran connects the ritual to divine words of mercy and renewal, invoking divine alignment.

- Recite Quran 36:51:
  *"And the Trumpet will be blown, and at once they will be from the graves to their Lord they will hasten."*

Stand with your hands raised in prayer as you recite, embodying a posture of receptivity to divine guidance.

## 4. Sound the Instrument

The sound of the horn or singing bowl represents Israfil's trumpet, initiating cosmic and personal transformation.

- Strike or blow the instrument gently, letting its sound resonate through the space.

As the sound vibrates, say: *"By Israfil's call, may the vibrations of renewal awaken my spirit.
Let the past dissolve, and let me rise toward divine light and purpose."*

Close your eyes and visualize emerald light flowing from the sound waves, enveloping your body and soul.

## 5. Perform a Water Purification

Water symbolizes purification, cleansing past pain, and preparing for renewal.

- Dip your hands into the bowl of water and bring them to your face or sprinkle the water over your head.

Say: *"O Allah, through this water, purify my heart and soul. Wash away all that hinders my growth and align me with Your mercy."*

Feel the water as a tangible connection to divine cleansing.

## 6. Invoke Raphael's Presence as Israfil

Invoking Raphael as Israfil connects his transformational role to your intention for renewal.

- Place your hands over your heart.

Say: *"Raphael, herald of renewal and divine mercy,
In your emerald light, I rise from the shadows of the past.
Guide me toward transformation and the awakening of my spirit."*

Visualize Raphael standing before you, radiating light that flows into your heart.

## 7. Reflect in Silence

Allowing moments of silence enables deeper integration of the transformative energy.

- Sit quietly with your eyes closed, focusing on the lingering vibrations of the sound and the emerald light surrounding you.

## 8. Conclude with Gratitude

Expressing gratitude acknowledges the divine presence and Raphael's assistance, sealing the ritual.

- Place your hands in prayer and bow slightly.

Say: *"Alhamdulillah (Praise be to Allah) for Your mercy and renewal.
Raphael, Israfil, thank you for your guidance and light.
May I walk forward in transformation and grace."*

Extinguish the candle and pour the water into the earth as an offering of gratitude. Follow these steps:

### 1. Choose a Sacred Spot

Selecting a natural location grounds the ritual and connects the act with the living Earth.

- Find a place that feels peaceful and connected to nature, such as near a tree, a patch of grass, or a flowerbed.
- Stand quietly for a moment, observing the surroundings and connecting with the energy of the Earth.

Say: *"O Earth, sacred and life-giving, I come to honor you with this gift. May this offering return to you in gratitude and love."*

Place your hands lightly on your heart as a gesture of reverence.

### 2. Prepare to Pour the Water

Setting your intention ensures the act carries spiritual meaning and aligns with your earlier ritual.

- Hold the bowl of water in both hands, raising it slightly toward the sky.

Say: *"This water, blessed by the light of renewal,
Now returns to the Earth,*

*Carrying the blessings of transformation,
Gratitude, and divine mercy."*

Visualize the water shimmering with the emerald light of Raphael, radiating healing energy.

### 3. Pour the Water

Returning the water to the Earth symbolizes the completion of the ritual and the cyclical nature of energy.

- Slowly pour the water onto the ground, allowing it to soak into the Earth.

As you pour, say: *"O Earth, receive this sacred offering.
May it nourish you as you have nourished me.
Through this act, I honor the divine cycle of renewal."*

Visualize the water merging with the Earth, spreading healing and gratitude.

### 4. Offer an Additional Symbol (Optional)

Adding a physical token enhances the ritual and symbolizes your ongoing connection with the Earth.

- If using a green cloth or stone, place it gently on the ground near where you poured the water.

Say: *"With this gift, I seal my gratitude.
May harmony and renewal flow through all creation."*

Bow slightly as a gesture of respect.

### 5. Close with Prayer and Reflection

Concluding with a prayer of gratitude strengthens the spiritual energy of the ritual.

- Stand quietly, hands folded or open, and offer a final prayer.

Say: *"O Creator of all, I thank You for the blessings of healing and renewal.
Raphael, divine healer, and Earth, sacred vessel,
May this offering bring light, balance, and peace to all creation.
Amen."*

Take a moment to breathe deeply, grounding yourself in the connection between the divine, the Earth, and your own spirit.

## Advanced Tips

1. **Repeat for Deeper Transformation**
   - Perform this ritual periodically to reinforce its energy and facilitate ongoing renewal.
2. **Incorporate Personal Prayer**
   - Include personal supplications during the quiet reflection phase, aligning them with the themes of renewal and mercy.
3. **Enhance with Nature**
   - Perform the ritual outdoors for a deeper connection to the cosmic renewal symbolized by Israfil's trumpet.

This ritual provides a profound pathway to renewal, transforming past pain and aligning with divine mercy through the archetypal energy of Raphael as Israfil.

# Integrating Raphael Across Traditions

## The Unified Archetype of Raphael

Though portrayed differently in each tradition, a consistent theme emerges: Raphael's role as a healer and guide transcends boundaries. His ability to restore health, protect travelers, and purify corruption makes him a universal figure of divine mercy and renewal. As a magician, you can draw from these diverse traditions to create a holistic approach to working with Raphael.

## A Practical Invocation for Raphael

To integrate Raphael's multi-traditional attributes into a single invocation, craft a prayer that draws upon his Jewish, Christian, and Islamic identities:

*"Raphael, Divine Healer of Earth and Soul,*
*From the scrolls of Enoch to the songs of the Quran,*
*You have restored, guided, and transformed.*
*Be my companion, my protector, and my light.*
*Heal my body, mind, and spirit,*
*And lead me on the path of divine wisdom.*
*In your emerald light, I am renewed."*

## Guiding the Path of Divine Healing: Raphael in the Book of Tobit and Sacred Texts

### The Book of Tobit: Raphael Revealed

The *Book of Tobit*, a deuterocanonical text included in the Catholic and Orthodox biblical canons, provides the most vivid and detailed portrayal of Archangel Raphael. Here, he takes on the human guise of Azarias, accompanying Tobias on a journey fraught with spiritual and physical challenges. Raphael's divine mission unfolds in three interconnected roles: a guide, healer, and deliverer.

The narrative begins with Tobit, a pious and righteous man, suffering from blindness and despair. Simultaneously, Sarah, another character in the story, is tormented by a demon, Asmodeus, who kills her suitors. These dual afflictions—physical blindness and spiritual oppression—set the stage for Raphael's intervention. Tobias, Tobit's son, embarks on a journey to recover family wealth and find a cure for his father's blindness, with Raphael acting as his unseen celestial guide.

This story exemplifies Raphael's esoteric nature: a bridge between mortal struggles and divine solutions. His guidance emphasizes the journey as a process of healing and self-discovery, reinforcing the belief that divine assistance often arrives subtly, disguised in ordinary circumstances. In magical practice, Raphael's involvement in the *Book of Tobit* serves as a framework for rituals centered on physical healing, emotional liberation, and spiritual alignment.

## The Healing Fish: Symbolism and Practice

A pivotal moment in the story occurs when Tobias catches a fish at Raphael's instruction. Raphael reveals that the fish's gall, heart, and liver possess powerful properties. The gall is used to heal Tobit's blindness, while the heart and liver are burned to exorcise the demon tormenting Sarah. This act of alchemical transformation—turning something ordinary into a source of profound healing—illustrates the power of divine tools hidden in plain sight.

In magical practice, the fish symbolizes spiritual nourishment and the transformative power of divine wisdom. To incorporate this into your rituals, prepare a sacred space with a bowl of water to represent the living waters of healing. Add a symbol of the fish, such as a small token or drawing, and recite the following invocation:

*"Raphael, guide of healing waters,*
*Unveil the sacred remedies of heaven.*
*Transform what is mundane into what is divine,*
*And grant me the vision to see your wisdom at work."*

The act of blessing the water and symbolically "catching the fish" establishes a connection to Raphael's healing energy.

# Exorcism and Liberation: Raphael's Role as Deliverer

Raphael's guidance enables Tobias to free Sarah from the demon Asmodeus, who flees when the heart and liver of the fish are burned. This act of exorcism highlights Raphael's role as a protector against spiritual afflictions. The burning ritual symbolizes purification, using divine fire to cleanse and banish negativity.

To invoke Raphael's protective and exorcistic qualities in your practice, create a ritual using herbs associated with purification, such as frankincense or sage. Place the herbs on a charcoal disc in a fireproof bowl. Light them and focus on the rising smoke as a vehicle for Raphael's healing presence. Chant:

*"Raphael, guardian of light,*
*By the divine flame, banish all shadows.*
*Cleanse this space and free my spirit,*
*With your emerald light, I am whole."*

This ritual mirrors the transformative power of fire in the *Book of Tobit*, channeling Raphael's energy to dispel harmful influences.

# Ritual to Invoke Raphael's Protective and Exorcistic Qualities

This ritual calls upon Archangel Raphael's purifying and protective power, using holy text passages, sacred herbs, and flame to banish negative energies and restore balance. Drawing inspiration from the *Book of Tobit*, this practice integrates Raphael's transformative energy into your space and spirit.

## Materials Needed

- Frankincense resin or sage (for purification)
- A charcoal disc and fireproof bowl
- Matches or a lighter
- A green candle (symbolizing Raphael's emerald light)
- A Bible or passages from the *Book of Tobit*
- A quiet, undisturbed space

## Step-by-Step Instructions

### 1. Prepare the Sacred Space

Establishing a pure and intentional space enhances the focus and effectiveness of the ritual.

- Find a quiet area where you won't be disturbed.
- Place the fireproof bowl, charcoal disc, herbs, green candle, and Bible on a flat surface.

Say: *"In the name of the Most High, I dedicate this space to divine light and protection.
Raphael, guardian and healer, I invite your presence to cleanse and shield."*

Hold your hands open above the space, visualizing Raphael's emerald light surrounding the area.

### 2. Light the Green Candle

The candle represents Raphael's emerald light, serving as a beacon of divine energy.

- Light the green candle and focus on its flame.

Say: *"Raphael, bringer of divine healing,
Let this flame be a guide for your light.
Illuminate this space with purity and peace."*

Cup your hands around the candle as if gathering its light into your being.

## 3. Light the Purifying Herbs

The rising smoke symbolizes the presence of Raphael and the dispelling of harmful influences.

- Place the charcoal disc in the fireproof bowl and ignite it. Allow it to smolder until hot.
- Add the frankincense or sage onto the charcoal.

As the smoke rises, say: *"By the sacred herbs of cleansing,
Let the light of Raphael banish all shadows.
May this smoke carry his presence,
Purifying this space and freeing my spirit."*

Wave your hands gently to direct the smoke around the area or yourself, visualizing it removing negativity.

## 4. Read from the Book of Tobit

Reading passages invites Raphael's protective qualities, connecting the ritual to his biblical role.

- Open to Tobit 8:2-3 and read aloud:
  *"Then Tobias remembered the words of Raphael, and he took the fish's liver and heart out of the bag where he had them, and he put them on the embers of the incense. The odor of the fish repelled the demon, and he fled to the remotest parts of Egypt. Raphael chased after him and bound him there."*

As you read, imagine Raphael standing beside you, holding his staff and enveloping you in emerald light.

## 5. Chant the Invocation

Chanting activates Raphael's energy and aligns it with the intention of protection and purification.

- Stand before the rising smoke and green candle.

Chant: *"Raphael, guardian of light,
By the divine flame, banish all shadows.
Cleanse this space and free my spirit,
With your emerald light, I am whole."*

Raise your hands toward the smoke and candle flame, symbolizing openness to Raphael's energy.

## 6. Seal the Space

Sealing the space ensures the protective energy remains active.

- Move around the room clockwise, wafting the smoke into corners or areas needing purification.

Say: *"By Raphael's light and God's mercy,
This space is protected, cleansed, and renewed."*

Visualize the emerald light filling every corner of the space, creating an impenetrable barrier against negativity.

## 7. Conclude with Prayer and Gratitude

Expressing gratitude honors Raphael's presence and completes the energy exchange.

- Return to the altar or central space.

Say: *"Heavenly Father, I thank You for the presence of Your servant, Raphael.
May his protection and light remain with me.
Through Your divine will, I walk in peace and strength. Amen."*

Bow your head briefly in reverence.

## 8. Extinguish the Candle

Extinguishing the candle symbolizes the completion of the ritual while preserving Raphael's lingering light.

- Gently blow out the candle, imagining its flame transferring its light to your heart and the space.

Say: *"With this flame, the light endures.
Raphael, I thank you for your healing and protection. Amen."*

## Advanced Tips

1. **Repeat as Needed**
   - Perform this ritual whenever you feel the need for renewed protection and purification.
2. **Personalize the Ritual**
   - Add your own prayers or additional passages from the Bible to enhance its meaning.
3. **Combine with Sound**
   - Ring a bell or use a singing bowl during the chant to amplify the protective vibrations.

This ritual channels Raphael's protective and exorcistic qualities to cleanse your space, strengthen your spirit, and align you with divine light.

# Sacred Texts Beyond Tobit: Raphael's Expanding Role

While the *Book of Tobit* provides the most detailed account of Raphael's interactions with humanity, his presence extends into other sacred texts and mystical traditions. In the *Book of Enoch*, Raphael is described as a watcher who heals the Earth from the corruption of fallen angels, underscoring his role as a universal healer. This portrayal aligns with magical practices that view Raphael as a custodian of balance, capable of restoring harmony on a cosmic scale.

In apocryphal writings like the *Book of Jubilees*, Raphael is further emphasized as a protector and purifier. These narratives expand on his role in guiding individuals and humanity toward divine alignment, making him an ideal figure to invoke in rituals for large-scale or collective healing efforts.

## Practical Applications: Crafting Rituals and Spells

To integrate Raphael's role in sacred texts into your magical practice, focus on creating rituals that mirror his actions in the *Book of Tobit*.

1. **Healing Ritual for Physical Ailments**
    - Prepare a green candle (symbolizing Raphael's emerald light) and a bowl of water.
    - Light the candle and place your hands over the water, visualizing Raphael's healing energy flowing through you.
    - Chant:
    "*Raphael, healer of God,
    Pour your light into this vessel,
    Restore and renew, heal and transform,
    By your grace, I am whole.*"
    - Use the water to anoint areas of discomfort, visualizing healing taking place.
2. **Guidance Meditation**
    - Sit in a quiet space with a staff or walking stick, symbolizing Raphael's guidance.
    - Visualize yourself walking alongside Raphael as he leads you toward clarity and purpose.
    - Reflect on any intuitive messages or sensations during the meditation, recording them in a journal afterward.
3. **Exorcism and Space Clearing**
    - Burn a mixture of frankincense, myrrh, and sandalwood while reciting Raphael's exorcistic invocation from the *Book of Tobit*.

- Move through your space, directing the smoke to all corners, and visualize Raphael's presence driving away all negativity.

# The Divine Image: Archangel Raphael in Art and Iconography

## Art as a Portal to the Sacred

Throughout history, Archangel Raphael has been immortalized in art and iconography, not merely as a figure of religious devotion but as a bridge to the divine. These depictions convey his essence as a healer, guide, and protector, offering rich layers of symbolic meaning for practitioners of mystical and magical traditions. From medieval mosaics to Renaissance masterpieces, Raphael's imagery has evolved, adapting to the cultural and theological context of different eras. To a magician, these representations serve as powerful tools for visualization, meditation, and invocation.

# Medieval and Byzantine Depictions: Raphael the Guardian

## Guiding Travelers with Divine Light

In early Christian and Byzantine art, Raphael is often depicted as a guardian and guide, typically escorting Tobias as described in the *Book of Tobit*. These depictions emphasize his role as a protector of travelers, a theme that resonates deeply with his esoteric identity. Raphael is commonly shown holding a staff, symbolizing guidance, and a fish, representing the miraculous healing power revealed in Tobit's journey.

For practitioners, these elements carry profound symbolic significance. The staff represents the steadying influence of divine wisdom, while the fish signifies nourishment and spiritual renewal. To integrate these symbols into your magical practice, create a travel protection talisman. Craft a small pouch containing a miniature staff (a twig or crafted charm) and a fish token, consecrating it with Raphael's energy through prayer:

*"Raphael, guardian of those who journey,
Guide my steps with your steady hand,
Protect me from harm, seen and unseen,
By your grace, I travel in peace."*

Carry the talisman when embarking on a journey, invoking Raphael's presence as your celestial companion.

# Renaissance Art: Raphael the Healer

## The Patron of Healing Through Visual Splendor

During the Renaissance, Raphael became a prominent subject in Christian art, reflecting the era's emphasis on humanism and divine grace. Artists such as Raphael Sanzio (ironically sharing the archangel's name) painted him as an elegant, compassionate figure. His depiction in works like *The Healing of Tobit* and other frescoes emphasizes his connection to physical and spiritual healing.

These depictions often highlight Raphael's association with emerald green, symbolizing growth, healing, and renewal. In magical practice, viewing or meditating on Renaissance images of Raphael can be a profound way to attune to his healing energy. Set up a candle-lit altar featuring a print or replica of a Raphael painting, focusing on the emerald hues. Light a green candle and recite:

*"Archangel Raphael, healer of all,
Through this image, your light I recall.
Grant your blessings, pure and bright,
Restore my spirit with your emerald light."*

Use this visualization as a preparatory step for healing rituals or meditations.

# Baroque and Beyond: Raphael as the Angel of Majesty

## Regal Splendor and Divine Presence

In Baroque art, Raphael is often depicted in majestic, dynamic poses, surrounded by celestial light and angelic hosts. These representations reflect the Baroque era's emphasis on divine drama and the interplay between light and shadow. The celestial light surrounding Raphael in these depictions can be interpreted as his emerald energy radiating outward, encompassing all who seek his healing and guidance.

For magical practitioners, these images are ideal for invoking Raphael's presence during rituals. Visualize the dramatic interplay of light and shadow as you call upon Raphael to illuminate your path. A simple yet powerful invocation using Baroque imagery involves a mirror. Place the mirror on your altar, surrounding it with green and white candles. Chant:

*"Raphael, radiant healer divine,*
*Let your emerald light through this mirror shine.*

*Reveal the truths I need to see,
And guide my spirit toward divinity."*

Allow the flickering candlelight to reflect off the mirror, symbolizing Raphael's radiant guidance.

## Iconography and Esoteric Symbols

### The Emerald Green Light

Across cultures, emerald green is universally associated with Raphael, signifying healing, renewal, and vitality. In esoteric traditions, this color aligns with the heart chakra, reinforcing Raphael's role in emotional and spiritual healing. To work with this symbolism, integrate green crystals like malachite or emerald into your altar and wear green garments during rituals.

### The Staff

The staff, often seen in Raphael's depictions, represents guidance, wisdom, and the support of divine energies. It can be used symbolically in rituals to invoke Raphael's guidance. Create a personal staff by choosing a branch or crafted wand, anointing it with healing oils (e.g., eucalyptus or frankincense), and dedicating it to Raphael with prayer.

### The Fish

A recurring motif, the fish embodies spiritual nourishment and miraculous intervention. Incorporate this symbol by placing a fish token or drawing on your altar, or include fish imagery in your sacred space. Meditate on the fish as a reminder of Raphael's ability to provide unexpected solutions to life's challenges.

Celestial Light

The golden or emerald radiance often surrounding Raphael in art signifies his connection to divine light and truth. When invoking Raphael, visualize this celestial light enveloping you, dissolving negativity and filling you with healing energy.

## Practical Applications: Bringing Raphael's Art to Life

1. **Art Meditation Ritual**
    - Choose an image of Raphael that resonates with you, such as a Renaissance or Byzantine painting.
    - Place the image on your altar, lighting a green candle beside it.
    - Gaze at the image, focusing on Raphael's symbols and the energy they convey. As you meditate, imagine Raphael stepping out of the painting, surrounding you with his healing light.
2. **Visualization for Healing**
    - Close your eyes and visualize Raphael as depicted in Baroque art, surrounded by radiant light and celestial beings.
    - Imagine his staff touching your body, sending waves of healing energy through you. Focus on any areas where you feel discomfort or stress, allowing Raphael's energy to bring relief.
3. **Creating Iconic Correspondences**
    - Craft an altar incorporating Raphael's symbols: a green cloth, a fish token, a miniature staff, and a print of his image. Dedicate this space to ongoing work with Raphael, offering prayers and small gifts (such as flowers or candles) to invite his presence.

# "God Heals": The Sacred Power in Raphael's Name

## The Etymology of Raphael: A Divine Declaration

The name Raphael, derived from the Hebrew *Rafa'el* (רפאל), means "God heals" or "The Healing of God." It is a profound testament to his celestial mission as a healer and restorer of balance. Rooted in the Hebrew word *rapha* (רפא), meaning "to heal," and the suffix *El* (אל), denoting God, Raphael's name is both a description of his role and a direct invocation of divine power.

For practitioners, the name itself becomes a conduit for accessing the energy of healing, protection, and divine mercy. Understanding and working with the etymological essence of Raphael's name provides a foundational tool for magical and spiritual practice, allowing you to channel his energy with clarity and intention.

# The Power of Names in Sacred Tradition

## Names as Divine Keys

In mystical traditions, names are not merely identifiers but bearers of the essence and authority of what they represent. In the case of Raphael, his name functions as both a sacred declaration and a command, summoning the act of healing through divine intervention. This is echoed in Jewish mysticism, where the names of archangels are viewed as direct links to their divine purpose and an extension of God's will.

To harness the power of Raphael's name in your practice, consider integrating its pronunciation into your rituals. Spoken aloud, *Rafa'el* resonates with the vibrational frequency of healing. In whispered prayer or sung chant, it aligns your intention with the celestial energies embodied by Raphael.

# Raphael's Name in Sacred Texts

## The Book of Tobit: Raphael Introduced

In the *Book of Tobit*, Raphael reveals his name to Tobit and Tobias only after completing his mission, saying, *"I am Raphael, one of the seven angels who stand in the presence of the Lord."* This delayed revelation underscores the humility and sacred weight of his name. When he speaks his name, it is as if the act of healing itself has been fulfilled, a reminder that invoking Raphael is to call forth the completion of divine healing.

This moment in Tobit offers a ritual model for invoking Raphael: first, engage in acts of faith and trust, then call upon his name to seal your intentions and invite his presence fully into your practice.

# The Esoteric Symbolism of "God Heals"

## Healing as a Divine Act

Raphael's name encapsulates the belief that healing, in all its forms, is an act of divine intervention. Whether addressing physical ailments, emotional wounds, or spiritual misalignment, healing represents a return to harmony with the divine order. As a magician, invoking Raphael's name is a declaration of alignment with this principle, calling upon the infinite wellspring of divine love and power to restore wholeness.

## The Balance of Rafa and El

The word *rapha* (heal) is balanced by *El* (God), suggesting that all healing originates from and returns to the divine. In Kabbalistic thought, this reflects the Sephirotic balance between Chesed (Mercy) and Tiphereth (Beauty), where Raphael often resides. This symbolic balance is key to understanding Raphael's role in restoring harmony.

In magical practice, you can meditate on this balance by visualizing the word *Rafa'el* as a flowing script, with *rapha* radiating out as emerald light from your heart and *El* grounding you in divine energy. This visualization anchors your intention and opens a channel for Raphael's healing power.

## Practical Applications: Using Raphael's Name in Magic

### Invocation Through Sacred Chant

The name *Rafa'el* can be used as a mantra for healing and spiritual alignment. Follow these steps to integrate this practice into your work:

1. **Prepare Your Space**
    - Create a sacred space with a green cloth, a candle, and a bowl of water.
    - Include an object symbolizing healing, such as a crystal or a personal item.
2. **Focus on Breath and Intention**
    - Sit comfortably and focus on your breath. Visualize a green light surrounding you, growing brighter with each inhalation.
3. **Chant the Name**
    - Slowly and rhythmically chant *Rafa'el*, stretching out each syllable:
    "Rah-fa-EL..."
    - Feel the vibration of the name resonating through your body, aligning you with Raphael's energy.
4. **Seal the Invocation**
    - Conclude with a short prayer:
    "Raphael, divine healer, may your name resound within me. By your light, restore and renew my spirit."

## Writing Raphael's Name for Talismans

In mystical traditions, the written name of Raphael holds power as a symbol of divine healing. To create a talisman, inscribe רפאל (Hebrew for Raphael) on a piece of parchment or carve it into a green candle. Anoint the inscription with frankincense oil while reciting:

*"By the name of Rafa'el,*
*God who heals, may this talisman*
*Carry the light of divine restoration.*
*Through your power, I am renewed."*

Carry this talisman with you or place it on your altar as a focal point for healing intentions.

## Daily Affirmation Using Raphael's Name

To integrate Raphael's energy into your daily life, speak a simple affirmation each morning:

*"By the name of Raphael,*
*The healing of God, I walk in light and restoration.*
*May divine healing flow through me today."*

This practice subtly aligns your daily actions with the energy of divine healing and opens channels for Raphael's guidance.

# Modern Interpretations and Applications

In modern spiritual practice, Raphael's name is often associated with Reiki and other energy-healing modalities. Practitioners visualize his emerald green light flowing through their hands, guided by the intention embedded in his name. Similarly, in New Age traditions, chanting *Rafa'el* during yoga or meditation deepens one's connection to healing energy.

To modernize your practice, pair Raphael's name with sound healing tools, such as tuning forks or singing bowls. Strike the instrument, allowing its tone to merge with your chant of *Rafa'el*, amplifying the healing resonance.

## Advanced Tips for Deepening Your Work with Raphael

1. **Study Linguistic Roots**
   - Explore the etymology of *rapha* in other languages and its connections to healing practices, such as Sanskrit *rupa* (form) or Greek *therapeia* (healing).
2. **Explore Gematria**

   - In Hebrew numerology, Raphael's name corresponds to specific numerical values. Archangel Raphael's name in Hebrew is רפאל **(Resh-Peh-Aleph-Lamed)**. Here are the numerical values for each letter:

1. ר **(Resh)** = 200
2. פ **(Peh)** = 80
3. א **(Aleph)** = 1
4. ל **(Lamed)** = 30

### Total Numerical Value

**311**= 30+ 1+ 80+ 200= רפאל

Thus, the numerical value of Raphael's name in Hebrew gematria is **311**. This value may hold symbolic or mystical significance, depending on the context in which it is studied, such as connections to other Hebrew words or concepts with the same numerical value. Meditate on these values to uncover hidden meanings and connections to the divine.

3. **Create a Healing Sigil**

- Using Raphael's name as the foundation, design a sigil combining the letters *R*, *P*, and *E*. Use this sigil in rituals or as a personal symbol of healing.
4. **Invoke Raphael Through Sacred Names**
    - Pair Raphael's name with other divine names like *Elohim* or *Yahweh*. For example:
    *"By the name of Yahweh, through the light of Rafa'el, I am healed."*

By delving into the rich layers of meaning within Raphael's name, you unlock a powerful key to his celestial energy. As you incorporate his name into your magical practice, you deepen your alignment with the divine act of healing, creating a sacred partnership with this luminous archangel.

# The Healing Light: The Symbolism of Emerald Green Energy in Raphael's Work

## Emerald Green: A Beacon of Raphael's Healing Essence

The emerald green light associated with Archangel Raphael is a luminous manifestation of divine healing energy. This light is not just symbolic; it is a spiritual vibration that aligns with the heart chakra, the center of love, compassion, and renewal. Across mystical traditions and sacred texts, green has consistently been tied to growth, harmony, and the restorative power of nature. For magicians and spiritual practitioners, tapping into Raphael's emerald light means channeling a profound force for healing, balance, and transformation.

This light serves as both a tool and a guide, empowering practitioners to restore harmony within themselves and others. It is also a protective force, shielding against spiritual and emotional imbalances, and opening pathways to divine grace.

# Historical and Mystical Context of Emerald Green

## Emerald in Biblical and Mystical Traditions

In the Bible, green is often linked to life and renewal. Psalms 23:2 describes God leading the faithful to "green pastures," a metaphor for spiritual restoration. Similarly, the emerald stone is one of the twelve gemstones set into the High Priest's breastplate in Exodus, representing Judah and divine leadership. The emerald's place in these sacred texts underscores its symbolic alignment with healing, abundance, and divine favor.

In Kabbalistic mysticism, green is associated with the Sephirah Tiphereth (Beauty), which balances mercy and judgment. Raphael, as an intermediary between human suffering and divine grace, resonates deeply with Tiphereth's harmonizing qualities. This alignment makes emerald green a powerful tool for connecting to Raphael's energy.

## Emerald Light and the Heart Chakra

In esoteric traditions, the emerald green light aligns with the heart chakra, the energy center governing compassion, forgiveness, and emotional healing. Raphael's connection to this chakra reinforces his role as a healer of emotional wounds and a restorer of spiritual equilibrium. Practitioners often visualize emerald light radiating from the heart to cleanse and balance their emotional and energetic states.

Incorporating this practice into your magical work can deepen your connection with Raphael. Sit quietly, place a green crystal over your heart, and imagine a vibrant emerald light expanding outward, dissolving fear and pain. This visualization aligns you with Raphael's healing vibration.

# The Symbolism of Healing Energy

## Light as a Bridge Between Heaven and Earth

In many mystical systems, light is a vehicle for divine communication and transformation. Raphael's emerald green light acts as a bridge, transmitting divine healing energy into the physical and emotional realms. This light is not only a symbol but an active force that can be invoked, visualized, and worked with in rituals to bring about profound restoration.

# Practical Applications: Working with Raphael's Emerald Light

## Healing Meditation with Emerald Light

To connect with Raphael's emerald green light for healing, follow this step-by-step meditation:

1. **Prepare Your Space**
   - Sit in a quiet, comfortable space. Light a green candle and place a green crystal, such as malachite, aventurine, or emerald, in front of you.
2. **Center Yourself**
   - Close your eyes and take deep breaths. With each exhalation, imagine releasing negativity and tension. With each inhalation, visualize a soft, green light entering your body.
3. **Invoke Raphael**
   - Speak this invocation aloud:
     *"Archangel Raphael, healer of divine light,*
     *Surround me with your emerald energy.*
     *Heal my wounds, restore my spirit,*
     *And guide me toward wholeness."*
4. **Visualize the Light**

- Imagine the emerald green light radiating from Raphael's presence. See it entering your heart, then spreading throughout your body, filling you with warmth and vitality.
5. **Close with Gratitude**
   - Thank Raphael for his healing presence and extinguish the candle, carrying the emerald energy with you throughout the day.

## Emerald Light Protective Shield

Raphael's emerald light can also be used as a protective shield, guarding against negativity and energetic imbalances. To create this shield:

1. Stand in a relaxed position and visualize Raphael standing before you, radiating emerald green light.
2. Imagine this light forming a protective sphere around you, glowing with vibrant green energy.
3. Chant:
   *"Raphael, shield me with your healing light,
   Protect my body, mind, and spirit this night."*
4. Maintain this visualization, allowing the protective energy to settle into your aura.

## Healing Ritual Using Emerald Green Energy

For a more structured ritual to channel Raphael's emerald light:

1. **Set the Scene**
   - Use green candles, crystals, and a bowl of water infused with mint or eucalyptus oil to represent healing.
2. **Create Sacred Space**
   - Call upon Raphael with an invocation, such as:
   *"Raphael, bearer of emerald healing,*

> *Enter this sacred space,*
> *Bring your light to cleanse and restore."*

3. **Activate the Light**
   - Dip your hands into the bowl of water and sprinkle it around yourself, visualizing the emerald light spreading wherever the water touches.
4. **Focus on Healing**
   - Place your hands over any area in need of healing, imagining the light flowing through your hands as Raphael's energy restores balance.
5. **Conclude with Blessing**
   - Thank Raphael and extinguish the candles, leaving the bowl of water to evaporate naturally as an offering.

## Correspondences for Emerald Light in Magic

- **Element**: Air (associated with clarity and renewal)
- **Crystals**: Emerald, malachite, green aventurine
- **Herbs**: Mint, eucalyptus, bay leaf
- **Planetary Energy**: Mercury (aligning with Raphael's connection to communication and healing)
- **Day**: Wednesday (Mercury's day, ideal for invoking Raphael's energy)

## Advanced Tips for Working with Raphael's Light

1. **Daily Visualization Practice**
   Begin each day by visualizing yourself bathed in emerald green light. This practice fosters a continual connection to Raphael's healing energy.
2. **Combine with Sound Healing**
   Use a singing bowl tuned to the heart chakra (note F) during your rituals or meditations. The sound

enhances the vibration of Raphael's light, deepening its impact.
3. **Create an Emerald Elixir**
Infuse a green crystal (ensure it's safe for water use) in spring water under moonlight. Drink this water during rituals to embody Raphael's healing light.

### Green Crystals Safe for Water Use

1. **Green Aventurine**
   - **Properties:** Healing, renewal, and emotional balance.
   - **Why It's Safe:** Aventurine is a form of quartz and does not dissolve or leach toxins in water.
2. **Jade (Nephrite or Jadeite)**
   - **Properties:** Harmony, protection, and vitality.
   - **Why It's Safe:** Jade is a stable mineral, resistant to water damage, and non-toxic.
3. **Prasiolite (Green Quartz)**
   - **Properties:** Spiritual growth, healing, and alignment with divine energy.
   - **Why It's Safe:** Prasiolite is a quartz variant, making it safe and durable in water.
4. **Prehnite**
   - **Properties:** Emotional healing, connection to higher realms, and nurturing energy.
   - **Why It's Safe:** Prehnite is stable and does not degrade in water.
5. **Green Fluorite**
   - **Properties:** Clarity, detoxification, and focus.
   - **Why It's Safe (Short-Term Use Only):** Fluorite is generally safe for water infusions if the exposure is brief. Avoid long-term soaking to prevent slight surface wear.

4. **Chakra Healing Alignment**
Incorporate Raphael's emerald energy into chakra

work, especially focusing on the heart chakra. Visualize the light expanding outward, balancing all chakras.

## A Path Illuminated by Emerald Light

Raphael's emerald green light is a powerful symbol and active force for healing and restoration. Whether used for personal renewal, emotional balance, or spiritual alignment, this light offers profound opportunities for transformation. By integrating this energy into your magical practice, you forge a deeper connection with Raphael, allowing his divine essence to guide you toward wholeness and enlightenment. Each time you call upon this light, you align with the boundless love and healing power of the divine.

## The Symbols of Raphael: Tools of Divine Healing and Guidance

### Sacred Symbols: Raphael's Tools in the Celestial Mission

Archangel Raphael is often depicted with three key symbols: the staff, the fish, and the traveler's garb. Each of these items represents profound aspects of his divine mission and spiritual nature. For magicians working with Raphael, understanding the historical, esoteric, and practical meanings of these symbols offers a deeper connection to his energy and a framework for incorporating his power into rituals and practices.

These symbols, rooted in sacred texts like the *Book of Tobit* and developed through centuries of artistic and mystical tradition, serve as both literal and metaphorical representations of Raphael's roles as healer, guide, and protector.

# The Staff: Guiding Light and Divine Authority

## Historical and Mystical Context

The staff, often shown in Raphael's depictions, is a symbol of guidance, authority, and spiritual journeying. In the *Book of Tobit*, Raphael uses a staff during his mission to lead Tobias on a perilous journey. The staff represents not only the physical support required for the journey but also Raphael's role as a spiritual guide, illuminating the path toward healing and resolution.

In broader esoteric traditions, the staff signifies divine authority and the alignment of human will with divine purpose. Like a lightning rod channeling celestial energy, it connects the heavens and the earth, symbolizing the bridge between divine wisdom and human experience.

## Magical Applications of the Staff

1. **Creating a Personal Staff for Ritual Use**
    - Find or craft a staff from wood aligned with Raphael's energy, such as ash (symbolic of healing and protection).
    - Carve Raphael's name (*Rafa'el*) or sigils into the wood.
    - Anoint the staff with frankincense or eucalyptus oil, dedicating it to Raphael through this invocation:
    "Raphael, bearer of divine light,
    Through this staff, guide my path,
    Lead me in healing, wisdom, and truth."
2. **Using the Staff in Rituals**
    - During meditations or rituals, hold the staff upright and imagine it channeling emerald light from the heavens into your body. This visualization grounds Raphael's guidance within your practice.

# The Fish: Healing, Nourishment, and Spiritual Transformation

## Historical and Mystical Context

The fish is an essential symbol in Raphael's story, specifically in the *Book of Tobit*. Raphael instructs Tobias to catch a fish and explains its parts have powerful properties: the gall for healing blindness, and the heart and liver for driving away a demon. The fish embodies nourishment and transformation, symbolizing Raphael's ability to transform the mundane into the miraculous.

In mystical traditions, fish are linked to the element of water, which governs emotions, intuition, and spiritual cleansing. As a symbol, the fish aligns with divine sustenance and the ability to adapt and thrive in challenging circumstances.

## Magical Applications of the Fish

1. **Fish Symbol in Rituals**
   - Place a fish-shaped token or image on your altar to represent Raphael's healing and transformative energy.
   - Use the following invocation to activate the symbol's energy:
   *"Raphael, healer of God's light,*
   *Let this sacred symbol carry your power,*
   *Transform what is broken into what is whole."*
2. **Healing Water Ritual**
   - Combine the symbolism of water and the fish for a healing ritual:
     - Fill a bowl with clean water.
     - Add herbs like mint or basil for purification and healing.
     - Submerge a fish token or drawing in the water.

- Chant:
  *"Through the wisdom of Raphael and the waters of life,
  May healing flow freely, restoring body and soul."*
- Use the water to anoint yourself or a loved one in need of healing.

# Traveler's Garb: Protection and Preparedness for Life's Journey

## Historical and Mystical Context

Raphael is often depicted in the garb of a traveler—simple robes and sandals, sometimes with a satchel. This symbolizes his role as a guide for pilgrims and those journeying through life's challenges. In the *Book of Tobit*, Raphael's guise as a fellow traveler reflects his humility and his dedication to walking alongside humanity.

Esoterically, the traveler's garb represents protection, humility, and readiness. It reminds practitioners that the spiritual path requires preparation, flexibility, and trust in divine guidance.

## Magical Applications of the Traveler's Garb

1. **Ritual for Protection During Travels**
   - Prepare a small pouch representing Raphael's satchel. Fill it with protective herbs (e.g., bay leaf, rosemary), a green crystal (aventurine), and a small token symbolizing your journey.
   - Consecrate the pouch with this prayer:
     *"Raphael, protector of travelers,
     With this satchel, may I carry your light,
     Shield me from harm and guide my steps."*

- o   Carry this pouch with you on trips to invoke Raphael's protective energy.
2. **Daily Guidance Visualization**
    - o   Imagine yourself clothed in the traveler's garb of Raphael. Envision his emerald light surrounding you as a protective cloak.
    - o   Chant:
      *"Raphael, walk with me through each step,
      Guide my choices and protect my path."*

# Integration of Symbols in Magical Practice

## Symbolic Altar Setup

To integrate Raphael's symbols into your magical work, create an altar dedicated to him:

- **Centerpiece**: A staff or wand representing guidance.
- **Healing Element**: A fish token or bowl of water for transformation.
- **Protection**: A satchel or pouch filled with protective items.

Light a green candle and recite an invocation that acknowledges all three symbols: *"Raphael, healer and guide,
With your staff, lead me.
Through the fish, restore me.
In your garb, protect me.
By your light, may I find wholeness."*

# The Esoteric Interplay of Symbols

## Unity of Purpose

The staff, fish, and traveler's garb each represent a distinct aspect of Raphael's mission, but together they form a cohesive framework for healing and guidance. In magical practice, they symbolize the journey from brokenness (fish), through divine guidance (staff), to spiritual protection and empowerment (garb).

## Energy Work with All Symbols

Visualize Raphael standing before you, holding his staff, with the fish by his side and clad in his traveler's garb. Imagine each symbol radiating emerald light:

- The staff grounding you in purpose.
- The fish filling you with nourishment and transformation.
- The garb surrounding you with protective energy.

# Advanced Tips for Deepening Your Work with Raphael's Symbols

1. **Create a Symbolic Journey Ritual**
   - Enact a ritual where you "walk" with Raphael, carrying a staff, holding a fish token, and wearing a simple garment to represent the traveler's garb. Symbolically "journey" toward a goal, integrating each symbol along the way.
2. **Dream Work**
   - Place representations of Raphael's symbols under your pillow to invite his guidance and healing into your dreams. Record any messages or imagery upon waking.
3. **Sigil Creation**
   - Combine the imagery of the staff, fish, and garb into a single sigil. Use this sigil to amplify your rituals and as a focal point for meditation.

# Embodying Raphael's Symbols

Raphael's staff, fish, and traveler's garb are more than artistic elements—they are powerful symbols of his divine mission and the tools he provides to those who work with him. By understanding and integrating these symbols into your magical practice, you align yourself with Raphael's energy and open pathways for profound healing, guidance, and protection. Each time you invoke these symbols, you strengthen your bond with this celestial healer, inviting his wisdom and light into your journey.

# Raphael, Divine Healer: Restoring the Body, Mind, and Spirit

## A Triune Mission: Healing Beyond Boundaries

Archangel Raphael's patronage over healing encompasses the holistic dimensions of human existence: the physical body, the emotional and mental faculties, and the eternal spirit. This triune approach is deeply rooted in sacred texts, mystical traditions, and modern spiritual practices. Working with Raphael in these capacities allows a magician to channel divine energies for comprehensive restoration, addressing not just symptoms but the deeper imbalances that disrupt harmony.

Raphael's name, meaning "God heals," signals his celestial mission to bring divine wholeness to creation. Through invocations, rituals, and meditative practices, practitioners can align themselves with Raphael's healing essence, transforming not only themselves but also those they seek to assist.

# Healing the Body: Raphael's Role as Restorer of Physical Wholeness

## Biblical Foundations for Physical Healing

In the *Book of Tobit*, Raphael demonstrates his power over physical ailments by instructing Tobias to use the gall of a fish to cure his father Tobit's blindness. This act of healing illustrates Raphael's role as an agent of divine restoration, working through tangible, earthly elements to bring about miraculous recovery.

The esoteric significance of this story emphasizes that physical healing often requires harmonizing divine intervention with earthly tools. Raphael's guidance suggests that the physical body is a sacred vessel deserving care and attention.

## Practical Applications for Physical Healing

1. **Healing Altar for Raphael**
    - Set up an altar with green candles, a bowl of water, and healing herbs like eucalyptus and mint.
    - Place a symbolic fish token or image on the altar to represent Raphael's work in the *Book of Tobit*.
2. **Physical Healing Ritual**
    - Begin by lighting the candles and centering yourself with deep breaths.
    - Anoint a green crystal, such as malachite or aventurine, with frankincense oil.
    - Hold the crystal over the area needing healing and chant:
    *"Raphael, healer divine,*
    *Through this stone, let your light shine.*
    *Restore the vessel, strong and whole,*
    *By your mercy, heal my soul."*
3. **Daily Healing Invocation**
    - Each morning, recite a prayer to Raphael:
    *"Raphael, divine healer of God,*
    *Bless this body with your light.*
    *Renew its strength, restore its health,*
    *By your grace, I am made whole."*

# Healing the Mind: Raphael as Comforter of Emotional Wounds

## Healing the Wounds of the Heart

Raphael's healing energies extend to the emotional and mental realms, where fear, stress, and anxiety often take root. In the *Book of Tobit*, Raphael's presence alleviates the grief of Tobit and Sarah, demonstrating his role as a comforter and counselor. For magicians, working with Raphael in this capacity involves fostering clarity, emotional resilience, and inner peace.

## Esoteric Significance

The mind is a bridge between the body and spirit, and its imbalances can ripple through all levels of being. Raphael's emerald light, aligned with the heart chakra, serves as a soothing balm for mental turmoil, dissolving negativity and cultivating clarity.

## Practical Applications for Emotional and Mental Healing

1. **Meditation for Mental Clarity**
   - Sit in a quiet space and light a green candle.
   - Visualize Raphael standing beside you, radiating emerald light.
   - Imagine this light entering your head, washing away stress and confusion.
   - Repeat the mantra:
     *"Raphael, bearer of divine peace,
     Ease my mind, let worries cease."*
2. **Journaling with Raphael's Guidance**
   - Before bed, light a green candle and ask Raphael for guidance. Write down any thoughts, worries, or questions.

     - In the morning, review your journal and reflect on any insights or dreams that may carry Raphael's message.
  3. **Herbal Infusion for Emotional Healing**
     - Brew a tea with mint and chamomile, dedicating it to Raphael. As you drink, imagine his emerald light entering your heart and soothing emotional pain.

# Healing the Spirit: Raphael's Role in Spiritual Renewal

## Divine Restoration of the Soul

Raphael's healing extends to the spiritual realm, addressing imbalances that obstruct divine connection and spiritual growth. In the *Book of Enoch*, Raphael is depicted as a healer of the Earth itself, mending the damage caused by the fallen angels. This role highlights his ability to restore harmony on a cosmic scale, making him a potent ally in spiritual cleansing and renewal.

## Esoteric Significance

The spirit is the eternal aspect of our being, and its wounds often manifest as feelings of disconnection or stagnation. Raphael's emerald light cleanses spiritual impurities and renews the flow of divine energy within the practitioner.

# Practical Applications for Spiritual Healing

1. **Spiritual Cleansing Ritual**
   - Prepare a bowl of water infused with salt and a few drops of frankincense oil.
   - Light a green candle and place your hands over the water, invoking Raphael:
   *"Raphael, healer of spirit and soul,
   Cleanse this vessel, make it whole.*

> *Let your light flow through this space,*
> *Filling it with your holy grace."*
- Sprinkle the water around your space or anoint yourself with it.

2. **Guided Visualization for Spiritual Renewal**
   - Close your eyes and visualize Raphael standing before you, holding his staff.
   - Imagine his emerald light surrounding you, cleansing your aura of any impurities.
   - Allow the light to fill your body, reigniting your connection to the divine.

3. **Sacred Offering for Spiritual Growth**
   - Create an offering for Raphael by placing green flowers or plants on your altar.
   - Speak a prayer of gratitude:
     *"Raphael, guide of the eternal light,*
     *I offer these gifts to honor your might.*
     *Heal my spirit, make me new,*
     *Lead me always toward the truth."*

# Correspondences for Healing Work

- **Color**: Emerald Green (renewal and harmony)
- **Crystals**: Malachite, Aventurine, Emerald
- **Herbs**: Eucalyptus, Mint, Chamomile
- **Element**: Air (clarity and balance)
- **Day**: Wednesday (associated with Mercury and Raphael)

# Advanced Practices for Deepening Your Connection

1. **Daily Healing Practice**
   - Incorporate Raphael's energy into your daily life by wearing green or carrying a green crystal. Recite a short prayer to invoke his presence.
2. **Integrative Healing Ritual**

- Combine physical, mental, and spiritual healing in a single ritual. Light three candles (representing body, mind, and spirit), and call upon Raphael to unify and restore all aspects of your being.

3. **Dreamwork with Raphael**
    - Place a green crystal under your pillow and ask Raphael for healing dreams. Keep a dream journal to record and interpret his messages.

# A Journey Toward Wholeness

By working with Archangel Raphael to heal the body, mind, and spirit, you align yourself with a universal force of divine restoration. Each practice, whether a simple prayer or a complex ritual, strengthens your connection to Raphael's energy and deepens your capacity to channel his healing light. Through consistent dedication, you not only heal yourself but also become a vessel for Raphael's work in the world, bringing wholeness and harmony to those around you.

# Raphael, Guardian of the Wayfarer: Protector of Travelers and Pilgrims

## The Celestial Companion on the Journey

Archangel Raphael is celebrated as the guardian of travelers and pilgrims, a role rooted in the *Book of Tobit*. In this sacred text, Raphael accompanies Tobias on a dangerous journey, guiding him through physical and spiritual perils to a successful resolution. Raphael's presence as a protector highlights his role as a divine companion who ensures safety, offers guidance, and provides healing along the way.

For magicians, working with Raphael in this capacity involves invoking his protective energy and aligning with his wisdom to navigate life's literal and metaphorical journeys. Whether you're embarking on a physical trip, beginning a new chapter in life, or exploring spiritual paths, Raphael's patronage ensures safe passage and divine alignment.

## Historical and Sacred Foundations of Raphael's Role

### The Book of Tobit: A Model of Divine Guidance

In the *Book of Tobit*, Raphael, disguised as a human named Azarias, acts as Tobias's companion and protector on his journey to recover a family debt and secure his future. Raphael's guidance extends beyond physical safety; he provides spiritual insights, emotional support, and miraculous solutions to challenges Tobias faces. His actions in the story establish him as a divine escort for those undertaking significant journeys.

This narrative emphasizes the esoteric idea that travel is more than a physical act—it is a transformative process that unites the physical, mental, and spiritual dimensions. Raphael's guidance ensures not only the traveler's safety but also their spiritual growth.

### Pilgrimage and the Spiritual Journey

In many religious traditions, pilgrimage is a sacred act of devotion and self-discovery. Raphael's role as a guardian aligns with this concept, symbolizing the protection and guidance offered to those who seek divine connection through movement. As a magician, invoking Raphael for protection during travel becomes a powerful act of aligning your journey with divine purpose.

# Esoteric and Symbolic Significance

## Raphael as the Guiding Light

Raphael's role as a guardian aligns with his name, which means "God heals." His protective energy extends to the entire being—physical, emotional, and spiritual—ensuring the traveler is shielded from harm and enriched by the journey's experiences. His presence symbolizes trust in divine guidance and faith in the transformative power of movement.

## The Staff and the Traveler

In iconography, Raphael is often depicted with a staff, a symbol of guidance, stability, and divine authority. For magicians, the staff represents the spiritual support provided by Raphael during journeys. It serves as a reminder that every step taken is under divine watchfulness.

# Practical Applications: Invoking Raphael's Protection for Travel

## Travel Protection Ritual

1. **Prepare Your Tools**
    - Gather a green candle, a small pouch, and protective herbs such as rosemary, mint, or bay leaf.
    - Include a crystal associated with protection and travel, such as tiger's eye or aventurine.
2. **Create Sacred Space**
    - Light the green candle and place your tools on an altar or a flat surface.
    - Center yourself with deep, calming breaths.
3. **Invoke Raphael**
    - Speak this invocation:
    *"Raphael, guardian of the way,*

> *Be my guide as I journey this day.*
> *Shield my path with your healing light,*
> *Protect my steps by your divine might."*

4. **Bless the Pouch**
   - Place the herbs and crystal into the pouch. Hold it in your hands and imagine Raphael's emerald light filling it.
   - Seal the pouch and carry it with you as a talisman during your travels.

# Daily Invocation for Safe Passage

Each morning before travel, recite this simple prayer:
*"Raphael, celestial guide,*
*With every step, be by my side.*
*Keep me safe, my path made clear,*
*By your grace, I travel without fear."*

# Visualization for Spiritual Pilgrimage

For those embarking on a spiritual journey or personal transformation, perform this visualization:

1. **Close Your Eyes**
   - Sit in a quiet space and visualize Raphael standing before you, holding his staff. His emerald light radiates outward, illuminating a path.
2. **Begin the Journey**
   - Imagine yourself walking this path, with Raphael leading the way. Feel his presence as a steady, protective force guiding you through any challenges.
3. **Receive His Wisdom**
   - As you walk, ask Raphael for guidance or insights. Trust any images, words, or feelings that come to you.
4. **Return to the Present**

- When ready, open your eyes and write down any insights from the visualization. Use them as guidance for your journey.

## Magical Correspondences for Raphael's Protection

- **Color**: Green (representing safety, healing, and renewal)
- **Crystal**: Tiger's Eye (protection during travel), Aventurine (luck and guidance)
- **Herbs**: Rosemary (protection), Mint (clarity), Bay Leaf (success and safe passage)
- **Element**: Air (guidance and clarity)
- **Day**: Wednesday (associated with Mercury and Raphael's energy)

## Advanced Practices for Working with Raphael

1. **Sacred Travel Journal**
   - Dedicate a journal to recording your travels, both physical and spiritual. Before each journey, ask Raphael for protection and guidance. Reflect on how his presence shaped your experiences.
2. **Create a Traveler's Talisman**
   - Craft a talisman featuring Raphael's sigil. Carry it with you during trips to invoke his energy whenever needed.
3. **Combine Elemental Energies**
   - Invoke Raphael alongside the element of air by lighting incense such as frankincense or sandalwood. Allow the smoke to carry your invocation to the heavens, inviting Raphael's protective presence.

# Invocation of Raphael with the Element of Air

When invoking Archangel Raphael alongside the element of air, your words should reflect themes of healing, guidance, and protection. The rising smoke from the incense serves as a symbolic vehicle, carrying your invocation to the heavens and aligning you with Raphael's energy.

## Words for the Invocation

Say the following aloud while focusing on the incense smoke and the energy of the element of air:

"Raphael, divine guardian of air and light,
Healer of body, mind, and spirit,
I call upon your emerald presence to encircle me.
By this sacred smoke, may your protective wings shield me,
Your healing breath restore me,
And your guiding light illuminate my path.

As the air carries my voice to the heavens,
Let it return with your grace and blessings.
I am whole, I am safe, I am guided,
By your eternal mercy and divine light. Amen."

## Accompanying Physical Gestures

1. **Light the Incense**
    - Light the incense, imagining the flame igniting Raphael's energy and awakening the element of air in your space.
    - **Say:** *"By this flame, the element of air rises to meet the heavens."*
2. **Wave the Smoke Gently**
    - With your hands, waft the smoke around your space or yourself. Visualize it carrying your words upward to the heavens.
    - **Say:** *"Through this sacred smoke, my voice ascends, inviting your presence, Raphael."*

3. **Open Your Arms or Raise Your Hands**
   - As you chant the invocation, hold your hands palms-upward or spread your arms wide, symbolizing openness to Raphael's light and energy.
4. **Breathe Deeply**
   - Inhale the incense's aroma slowly and deeply, symbolizing the healing breath of air infused with Raphael's energy. Visualize it filling you with light and peace.

## Why These Words and Gestures?

- **Themes of Air**: The focus on smoke and breath reflects air's symbolic qualities of communication, connection, and life force.
- **Sacred Imagery**: Phrases like "healing breath" and "protective wings" invoke Raphael's qualities as a healer and guide.
- **Symbolic Movements**: The gestures amplify your intention, creating a holistic connection—physically, mentally, and spiritually—with Raphael's energy and the element of air.

## When to Use This Invocation

Repeat this invocation whenever you seek Raphael's guidance and protection or wish to deepen your connection to the element of air. The ritual can be a powerful tool for healing, clarity, and spiritual alignment.

## Trusting the Divine Companion

By aligning with Archangel Raphael as a guardian of travelers and pilgrims, you open yourself to a celestial partnership that transcends mere physical protection. Each step of your journey becomes a sacred act, enriched by Raphael's wisdom and light. Through intentional rituals, invocations, and symbols, you not only ensure safe passage but also deepen your connection to the divine, transforming every journey into a path of healing and self-discovery.

# Raphael: The Archangel of Divine Mercy and Restoration

## A Celestial Agent of Compassion and Renewal

Archangel Raphael, whose name means "God heals," embodies divine mercy and restoration. His mission is not confined to physical healing but extends to emotional, spiritual, and cosmic levels, reflecting the boundless grace of the divine. Raphael's energy acts as a bridge between human frailty and divine perfection, offering forgiveness, renewal, and the realignment of one's life path with divine will.

For magicians working with Raphael, this patronage is profoundly transformative. Through rituals, invocations, and meditative practices, practitioners can channel Raphael's energy to restore balance, forgive past wrongs, and align with the flow of divine mercy.

# Sacred Foundations: Raphael's Role in Divine Mercy

## Mercy as a Divine Attribute

In Judeo-Christian theology, mercy is a central attribute of God, often depicted as the act of withholding judgment and offering compassion. Raphael's healing and guiding roles in the *Book of Tobit* illustrate how mercy manifests through restoration. By curing Tobit's blindness and liberating Sarah from a demon, Raphael demonstrates the mercy of God, bringing healing and hope where despair once prevailed.

Esoterically, divine mercy is an active force that transcends human limitations. Raphael channels this energy into the world, dissolving pain, repairing relationships, and fostering spiritual renewal.

## Restoration in the Book of Enoch

In the *Book of Enoch*, Raphael's role in binding fallen angels and healing the Earth highlights his association with cosmic restoration. This act is not just one of retribution but of bringing the world back into alignment with divine harmony. For practitioners, this role offers a template for invoking Raphael in rituals aimed at restoring personal or collective balance.

# Esoteric Symbolism of Mercy and Restoration

## Emerald Light: The Energy of Renewal

Raphael's emerald green light is a manifestation of divine mercy. Green, symbolizing growth and renewal, reflects the healing and restorative aspects of Raphael's work. In magical practice, visualizing or channeling this light during rituals creates a space for forgiveness, reconciliation, and healing.

## The Bridge Between Heaven and Earth

Raphael's actions often serve as a metaphorical bridge, reconnecting individuals with divine grace. This concept is symbolized by the staff he carries, representing the support and guidance needed to traverse life's challenges.

# Practical Applications: Working with Raphael's Mercy

# Ritual of Forgiveness and Restoration

This ritual invokes Raphael's energy to release burdens of guilt, resentment, or spiritual stagnation.

1. **Prepare Your Space**
    - Use a green cloth, a green candle, and a bowl of water infused with salt and a drop of frankincense oil.
    - Place a crystal such as aventurine or emerald on the altar to symbolize renewal.
2. **Center Yourself**
    - Sit before the altar and take deep breaths, visualizing any burdens or negative emotions as a heavy cloud surrounding you.
3. **Invoke Raphael**
    - Light the green candle and say:
    *"Raphael, bearer of divine mercy,*
    *I call upon your light to heal and restore.*
    *Dissolve the burdens I carry,*
    *And fill me with the grace of renewal."*
4. **Release the Burden**
    - Dip your hands in the bowl of water, imagining the cloud of negativity dissolving into the water.
    - Say:
    *"By your mercy, I am free.*
    *By your grace, I am whole."*
5. **Close the Ritual**
    - Extinguish the candle and pour the water outside as an offering of gratitude.

# Meditation on Divine Mercy

1. **Visualize Raphael's Light**
    - Sit in a quiet space and imagine Raphael standing before you, radiating emerald light.
    - See this light expanding to envelop you, dissolving all negativity.
2. **Receive the Energy**
    - Repeat the affirmation:
    *"Through Raphael's mercy, I am restored.*
    *I release the past and embrace divine grace."*
3. **Reflect on Renewal**

- After the meditation, journal any insights or feelings of relief and clarity.

# Cleansing and Renewal Spell

1. **Gather Materials**
   - A green candle, a sprig of fresh mint, and a bowl of water.
2. **Bless the Water**
   - Hold your hands over the bowl and say:
   *"Raphael, cleanse this water with your light,
   That it may restore and renew."*
3. **Perform the Cleansing**
   - Use the mint to sprinkle the water around yourself or your space, visualizing Raphael's energy purifying and renewing.
4. **Seal the Spell**
   - Extinguish the candle and give thanks to Raphael.

# Magical Correspondences for Mercy and Restoration

- **Color**: Green (renewal, forgiveness)
- **Crystals**: Aventurine, Emerald, Malachite
- **Herbs**: Mint, Basil, Bay Leaf
- **Element**: Air (clarity, spiritual alignment)
- **Day**: Wednesday (associated with Raphael and Mercury)

# Advanced Practices for Deepening Connection

1. **Dreamwork with Raphael**
   - Place a green crystal under your pillow and ask Raphael to reveal messages of mercy and restoration in your dreams.

2. **Create a Mercy Talisman**
    - Craft a talisman with Raphael's sigil and carry it to remind yourself of his ever-present guidance.
3. **Integrate Sacred Texts**
    - Meditate on passages from the *Book of Tobit* and *Book of Enoch* to align with Raphael's restorative energy. Reflect on how these texts resonate with your life's journey.

## Walking the Path of Mercy

Through his association with divine mercy and restoration, Raphael becomes a guide and healer who aligns you with the infinite grace of the divine. His energy empowers you to release pain, forgive yourself and others, and restore balance to your life. By incorporating Raphael's mercy into your magical practice, you not only transform yourself but also bring his light into the world, fostering healing and harmony wherever you go. Each invocation and ritual deepens your bond with this luminous archangel, allowing his energy to work through you as a vessel of divine restoration.

Having explored Archangel Raphael's patronages and roles as a healer, guide, and bearer of divine mercy, we now turn our attention to a deeper understanding of his energy and wisdom. This next section will delve into the essence of Raphael's vibrational energy, its transformative characteristics, and its alignment with celestial forces such as Mercury and the element of Air. We will uncover the teachings embedded in sacred texts like the *Book of Tobit* and reflect on Raphael's holistic approach to healing that encompasses body, mind, and spirit. Additionally, we will situate Raphael within the angelic hierarchy, examining his role among the celestial orders and his connections with other archangels. Through this exploration, we aim to cultivate a richer understanding of Raphael's divine nature and the profound wisdom he offers to those who seek his guidance. This knowledge will serve as a foundation for integrating his energy into both mystical practices and daily life.

# { 2 }

# The Essence of Raphael: Energy, Wisdom, and Celestial Purpose

To truly work with Archangel Raphael's transformative power, one must first understand the core of his energy, wisdom, and place within the celestial hierarchy. Raphael's healing energy is not merely a metaphor; it is a vibrational force resonating with the heart and third-eye chakras, guided by his association with the planet Mercury and the element of Air. His teachings, as revealed in sacred texts like the *Book of Tobit*, offer profound insights into holistic healing and the divine interplay between illness, recovery, and spiritual alignment. Moreover, his role among the archangels and his connection to figures like Michael and Gabriel illuminate his collaborative purpose in the divine order. This exploration will uncover the layered dimensions of Raphael's celestial essence, equipping you with a deeper understanding of how his energy works and how to integrate his wisdom into your magical and spiritual practices.

## The Vibrational Symphony of Raphael's Healing Energy

### Understanding Raphael's Healing Frequency

Archangel Raphael's energy resonates with a powerful vibrational frequency that harmonizes the body, mind, and spirit. His energy is often described as a radiant, emerald-green light that soothes, restores, and protects. In mystical traditions, this green light corresponds to the heart chakra (Anahata), the energy center of love, compassion, and healing. Raphael's frequency operates as a bridge between the physical and the divine, carrying a vibratory quality that inspires renewal and wholeness.

## The Symbolic and Esoteric Significance

- **Emerald Green Light:** This color embodies healing, growth, and balance. In alchemy, green is the color of transformation and nature's renewal, making Raphael's light a symbol of both physical and spiritual healing.
- **Resonance with the Heart Chakra:** The heart chakra is central to love, empathy, and emotional balance. Raphael's energy aligns perfectly with this chakra, helping to release grief, fear, and emotional blockages.
- **Connection to Air Element:** Raphael's energy flows like the wind—gentle yet profound. As the archangel of air, his vibrations mirror the cleansing and renewing qualities of this element, symbolizing freedom, clarity, and communication.

## Historical and Spiritual Context

In sacred texts and mystical traditions, Raphael's energy is a recurring theme:

- **Book of Tobit:** Raphael uses healing remedies (e.g., the fish liver and gall) to cure Tobit's blindness, illustrating his role in physical and spiritual restoration.
- **Kabbalistic Mysticism:** Raphael is linked to Tiferet on the Tree of Life, the sphere of beauty and balance, further emphasizing his harmonizing energy.
- **Islamic Tradition:** While not explicitly associated with healing, Raphael's counterpart, Israfil, heralds transformation and cosmic renewal, aligning with the broader themes of restoration and vibrational alignment.

# Practical Applications of Raphael's Healing Energy

## Ritual for Aligning with Raphael's Frequency

This ritual harmonizes your energy field with Raphael's vibrational frequency, promoting healing and balance.

**Materials**

- A green candle (symbolizing Raphael's light)
- A crystal associated with healing (e.g., green aventurine or jade)
- Frankincense incense (for purification)
- A bowl of water (for reflection and purification)
- A quiet space free from distractions

**Steps**

1. **Prepare Your Space**
   Light the incense and arrange the items on a clean surface. Say:
   *"Raphael, bringer of light, healer of the heart, I create this space in your name. Let it be filled with your emerald presence."*
   Visualize your space enveloped in green light.
2. **Light the Candle**
   As you light the candle, say:
   *"By this flame, I ignite Raphael's healing frequency within me. May it burn away all shadows, restoring clarity and balance."*
   Focus on the candle's glow, imagining it expanding into an aura around you.
3. **Hold the Crystal**
   Take the healing crystal in both hands, closing your eyes. Visualize the emerald green energy flowing from the crystal into your heart chakra. Say:
   *"Raphael, let your energy flow through this vessel, aligning my heart with divine harmony."*

4. **Meditate with the Bowl of Water**
   Gaze into the bowl of water, reflecting on areas of your life that need healing. Dip your fingers into the water and touch your forehead, chest, and abdomen, saying:
   *"With this water, I cleanse my body, mind, and spirit. Raphael's light renews me."*
5. **Conclude with Gratitude**
   Blow out the candle and hold the crystal to your heart, saying:
   *"Raphael, I thank you for your healing presence. May your frequency guide me to wholeness and peace."*

# Magical Correspondences for Raphael's Healing Energy

- **Color:** Emerald green
- **Element:** Air
- **Crystals:** Green aventurine, jade, malachite
- **Incense:** Frankincense, sandalwood
- **Herbs:** Mint, eucalyptus, lavender
- **Sacred Symbols:** Staff, fish, emerald light
- **Planetary Connection:** Mercury (guidance, communication, healing)

# Advanced Tips for Deepening Your Practice

1. **Develop Sensory Awareness**
   Spend time visualizing and feeling Raphael's emerald light during meditation. Let its vibrations permeate your senses, creating a deeper connection.
2. **Use Sound for Healing**
   Experiment with singing bowls or tuning forks tuned to 528 Hz, a frequency often associated with healing and transformation. Imagine this sound harmonizing with Raphael's energy.

3. **Create a Healing Grid**
   Use crystals and candles arranged in a triangular formation to channel Raphael's energy. Place the green candle at the top point and the healing crystals at the base corners.
4. **Integrate Sacred Texts**
   Recite passages such as *"He heals the brokenhearted and binds up their wounds"* (Psalm 147:3) or *"Raphael said, 'Do not be afraid; your prayers have been heard.'"* (Tobit 12:15) to reinforce your connection.

Raphael's healing energy is a transformative force that harmonizes the body, mind, and spirit. By understanding the vibrational qualities of his emerald light and integrating them into rituals, you align with his divine purpose as a healer and guide. Deepening your practice through sensory awareness, sacred texts, and magical correspondences ensures a profound and lasting connection to Raphael's frequency, empowering your journey toward wholeness.

# The Chakric Connection: Raphael's Energy and the Heart and Third-Eye Chakras

## Raphael's Alignment with the Chakric System

Archangel Raphael's energy resonates profoundly with the heart chakra (*Anahata*) and third-eye chakra (*Ajna*), bridging the realms of emotional healing, spiritual vision, and divine connection. This alignment allows Raphael to act as a conduit for transformation on both a personal and cosmic level, guiding individuals toward love, compassion, intuition, and insight.

# The Heart Chakra: Raphael's Core Healing Energy

## Symbolism of the Heart Chakra

The heart chakra, located in the center of the chest, is the energy center of love, empathy, and compassion. Its green color vibrates in harmony with Raphael's emerald light, representing healing, renewal, and emotional balance. As the chakra of connection, it opens pathways for divine love and human relationships.

## Historical and Spiritual Context

- **Biblical Connections:** Raphael's actions in the *Book of Tobit* symbolize his healing influence on emotional wounds. His guidance not only cures physical ailments but also restores familial and marital bonds, emphasizing love's healing power.
- **Mystical Traditions:** In Kabbalistic mysticism, Raphael's association with *Tiferet* (beauty and balance) mirrors the heart chakra's function as the mediator between lower and higher chakras.
- **Modern Interpretations:** New Age practitioners link Raphael's energy to emotional healing and stress relief, often visualizing his green light enveloping the heart chakra.

# Ritual: Opening the Heart Chakra with Raphael

## Materials Needed

- Green candle (symbolizing Raphael's light)
- Rose quartz or green aventurine (associated with love and healing)
- Lavender or rose essential oil
- Soft instrumental or nature sounds (optional)

**Steps**

1. **Prepare the Space**
   Light the green candle and anoint your chest area with a drop of essential oil. Say:
   *"Raphael, guardian of love and healing, I invite your presence to open my heart and fill it with your divine light."*
   Visualize green light expanding from the candle into your heart.

2. **Meditation on Love and Healing**
   Hold the rose quartz or green aventurine in both hands over your heart. Close your eyes and breathe deeply. Visualize Raphael's emerald light radiating from your heart, connecting you to divine love. Say:
   *"With each breath, my heart opens to love and compassion. Raphael, bringer of harmony, guide me toward emotional balance."*

3. **Seal the Ritual**
   Extinguish the candle and place the crystal in your sacred space. Thank Raphael, saying:
   *"Raphael, healer of hearts, I thank you for your love and light. May my heart remain open to your blessings."*

# The Third-Eye Chakra: Raphael's Visionary Wisdom

## Symbolism of the Third-Eye Chakra

Located in the center of the forehead, the third-eye chakra governs intuition, insight, and spiritual perception. Its indigo hue complements the emerald of the heart chakra, creating a powerful synergy when activated with Raphael's guidance.

## Historical and Spiritual Context

- **Biblical References:** In the *Book of Tobit*, Raphael provides guidance through wisdom and foresight, symbolizing the third-eye chakra's role in spiritual clarity and vision.
- **Mystical Traditions:** In esoteric teachings, Raphael is often linked to the element of air, representing clarity of thought and higher awareness, qualities integral to the third-eye chakra.
- **Modern Interpretations:** Raphael's energy is invoked by practitioners seeking spiritual clarity and enhanced intuition.

## Ritual: Awakening Intuition with Raphael

### Materials Needed

- Indigo candle or a clear quartz crystal
- Frankincense or sandalwood incense
- A journal for recording insights

**Steps**

1. **Prepare the Space**
   Light the indigo candle and the incense. Stand before the setup and say:
   *"Raphael, angel of insight and wisdom, open my mind to divine vision. Let your light awaken my inner sight."*
2. **Meditation on Clarity**
   Hold the quartz crystal to your forehead and close your eyes. Focus on the third-eye chakra, visualizing indigo light merging with Raphael's emerald energy. Say:
   *"Raphael, illuminate my path and guide me toward truth. May my intuition align with divine wisdom."*
   Breathe deeply and allow images or sensations to surface.
3. **Record Your Insights**
   After meditating, write down any thoughts or visions in

your journal. This step helps ground your experience and interpret Raphael's guidance.
4. **Conclude the Ritual**
Extinguish the candle and thank Raphael. Say:
*"Raphael, angel of vision, I thank you for your light and clarity. May my intuition serve the highest good."*

## Synergizing the Heart and Third-Eye Chakras

### Dual-Chakra Activation Ritual

When the heart and third-eye chakras work in harmony, Raphael's energy facilitates deep emotional healing and heightened spiritual perception. This synergy allows for:

- Intuitive empathy, enabling you to discern others' emotional states with clarity.
- Balanced decision-making, blending wisdom and compassion.
- A deeper connection to divine guidance.

### Combined Ritual Steps

1. Begin with the heart chakra ritual to open yourself to love and compassion.
2. Transition to the third-eye ritual to enhance your spiritual awareness.
3. End by visualizing a column of light connecting the heart and third-eye chakras, with Raphael's energy harmonizing the two.

## Magical Correspondences

- **Heart Chakra:** Green light, rose quartz, green aventurine, lavender oil.

- **Third-Eye Chakra:** Indigo light, clear quartz, sandalwood, frankincense.
- **Sacred Symbols:** Emerald light for the heart, radiant eye for the third-eye.
- **Elemental Connection:** Air (clarity and renewal).

# Integrating Raphael's Energy

By working with Raphael's alignment to the heart and third-eye chakras, you create a powerful pathway for emotional healing and spiritual clarity. Through these rituals, meditations, and correspondences, you can cultivate a deep, lasting connection to Raphael's energy, empowering your journey toward wholeness and divine wisdom.

## Advanced Tips

1. **Daily Affirmations:** Incorporate affirmations like *"My heart is open to love"* or *"My intuition is clear and focused"* to sustain Raphael's energy between rituals.
2. **Use Sacred Geometry:** Visualize Raphael's sigil over your heart and third eye to enhance alignment.
3. **Blend Aromatherapy:** Combine lavender (heart) and frankincense (third-eye) oils in a diffuser during meditation for a multi-sensory experience.

Through these practices, you unlock the full transformative power of Raphael's healing energy, allowing love and wisdom to flow effortlessly into every aspect of your life.

# Raphael's Elemental and Planetary Connections: Mercury and Air

## The Messenger and the Elemental Wind

Archangel Raphael's energy aligns with the planet Mercury and the element of air, both of which are deeply connected to themes of healing, communication, and transformation. By understanding these associations, you can tap into Raphael's vibrational frequency to access his wisdom and guidance. These correspondences provide a framework for rituals and magical workings that harmonize the physical, mental, and spiritual dimensions of your practice.

# Mercury: Raphael's Planetary Influence

## Symbolism of Mercury

Mercury, the swift planet closest to the sun, symbolizes communication, intellect, and movement. In astrology and mysticism, Mercury governs the exchange of ideas, healing through knowledge, and travel—all traits mirrored in Raphael's role as a healer and guide.

- **Healing and Knowledge:** Mercury's influence emphasizes the transformative power of information, aligning with Raphael's ability to illuminate paths to wellness.
- **Guidance and Travel:** As the planetary ruler of journeys, Mercury reflects Raphael's protective role over travelers, as seen in the *Book of Tobit*.
- **Alchemy and Magic:** Mercury, associated with the quicksilver of alchemy, embodies transformation and healing—a central theme of Raphael's archetype.

## Historical and Spiritual Context

- **Greco-Roman Syncretism:** In classical mythology, Mercury (Hermes) was the messenger of the gods, a role that resonates with Raphael's guidance in sacred texts.
- **Kabbalistic Tradition:** Raphael is associated with Tiferet on the Tree of Life, a sphere linked to harmony and balance, akin to Mercury's mediating energy.

# Ritual: Channeling Raphael's Planetary Influence

## Materials

- A silver candle (symbolizing Mercury's quicksilver and divine energy)
- A small winged charm or caduceus symbol
- Frankincense incense (associated with communication and air)
- A journal for recording insights

**Steps**

1. **Prepare Your Space**
   Light the incense and place the silver candle and winged charm on your altar. Say:
   *"Raphael, guide of Mercury's light, I call upon your wisdom and healing presence. Let this space be a sanctuary for transformation and renewal."*
2. **Light the Candle**
   As you light the candle, visualize Mercury's swift, silvery light enveloping your space. Say:
   *"By Mercury's light, I open the pathways of communication and healing. Raphael, illuminate my mind and spirit."*
3. **Meditate on Transformation**
   Hold the winged charm or caduceus in your hand, focusing on its symbolism. Breathe deeply, visualizing Raphael's energy flowing through you, clearing obstacles and restoring balance.
4. **Journal Your Insights**
   After meditating, write down any messages or intuitive thoughts. Conclude by saying:
   *"Raphael, messenger of divine light, I thank you for your guidance and blessings. May Mercury's wisdom flow through me always."*

# Air: Raphael's Elemental Essence

## Symbolism of Air

The element of air, associated with clarity, communication, and purification, embodies Raphael's essence as a healer and messenger. Air is the breath of life, connecting the physical and spiritual realms, much like Raphael's role in guiding and restoring balance.

- **Healing and Renewal:** Air represents the flow of energy necessary for healing and transformation.
- **Clarity and Insight:** The transparency of air aligns with Raphael's ability to provide clear guidance.
- **Purification:** Like the cleansing power of the wind, Raphael's energy removes stagnation and negativity.

## Historical and Spiritual Context

- **The Breath of Life:** In Genesis 2:7, God breathes life into Adam, symbolizing the sacred essence of air. Raphael's energy mirrors this life-giving force.
- **Angel of Air:** Raphael's association with the element of air connects him to celestial messengers who carry divine will across the heavens.

# Ritual: Invoking Raphael through the Element of Air

## Materials

- A feather (symbolizing air and Raphael's wings)
- Sandalwood incense (representing purification)
- A green candle (symbolizing healing)
- A bowl of water (to ground and balance)

**Steps**

1. **Create a Sacred Space**
   Light the sandalwood incense and green candle. Place the feather and water bowl on your altar. Say:
   *"Raphael, angel of the wind and breath of life, I call upon your presence. Let your energy fill this space with healing and renewal."*
2. **Wave the Feather**
   Hold the feather in your dominant hand and wave it gently through the incense smoke. Visualize the air around you charged with Raphael's emerald light. Say:
   *"With each breath, I call upon Raphael's healing and wisdom. Let the winds of clarity and peace flow through me."*
3. **Meditate on the Breath**
   Sit quietly and focus on your breath, imagining each inhale bringing in Raphael's healing energy and each exhale releasing negativity. Repeat:
   *"Breath of life, fill me with Raphael's light. By air, I am healed and whole."*
4. **Balance with Water**
   Dip the feather into the water and sprinkle it around your space, symbolizing the union of air and water for balance. Say:
   *"As air meets water, so balance is restored. Raphael, guide and healer, I thank you."*

## Magical Correspondences

- **Planetary Connection:** Mercury (swift healing, communication)
- **Elemental Connection:** Air (clarity, purification, insight)
- **Sacred Symbols:** Feather, winged charm, caduceus
- **Incense:** Frankincense, sandalwood
- **Crystals:** Clear quartz (air), green aventurine (healing)

# Harmonizing Planetary and Elemental Energies

Raphael's alignment with Mercury and air allows you to harness the swift, transformative power of communication and healing. Through rituals that emphasize these connections, you can deepen your understanding of Raphael's energy and integrate his guidance into your magical practice.

## Advanced Tips

1. **Combine Elements**
   Use both air and water elements in rituals for balanced healing and grounding.
2. **Astrological Timing**
   Perform Mercury-focused rituals on Wednesdays (Mercury's day) or during the hour of Mercury for enhanced energy.
3. **Create a Feather Talisman**
   Inscribe Raphael's sigil on a feather and carry it as a symbol of air and protection.

By connecting with Mercury's planetary influence and the cleansing power of air, you access Raphael's transformative light, empowering your magical journey toward clarity, healing, and spiritual growth.

# The Teachings of Raphael: Lessons from the Book of Tobit

## A Journey of Guidance and Healing

The *Book of Tobit* offers a profound narrative illustrating Raphael's role as a guide, healer, and protector. This story is more than an account of divine intervention; it serves as a blueprint for spiritual and magical practices involving Raphael. By exploring the symbolic and esoteric lessons embedded in the text, practitioners can deepen their connection with this archangel and apply his teachings to their magical work.

## Historical and Spiritual Context

The *Book of Tobit* is an apocryphal text found in Catholic and Orthodox Bibles and is revered for its themes of faith, divine providence, and healing.

- **Key Characters:**
    - *Tobit:* A righteous man blinded by an accident, representing physical suffering and spiritual perseverance.
    - *Tobias:* Tobit's son, whose journey symbolizes spiritual growth and trust in divine guidance.
    - *Raphael:* Disguised as Azariah, Raphael acts as a divine guide and healer, orchestrating events to restore balance and healing.
    - *Sarah:* A young woman plagued by a demon, whose liberation highlights Raphael's exorcistic power.
- **Central Themes:**
    - *Healing and Restoration:* Raphael's intervention leads to Tobit's physical healing and Sarah's spiritual freedom.
    - *Faith and Trust:* Tobias's reliance on Raphael underscores the importance of trusting divine wisdom.
    - *Journey and Transformation:* The physical journey mirrors the spiritual transformation of those who place their faith in divine guidance.

## Symbolism and Esoteric Lessons

**1. The Healing Fish**

When Tobias catches a fish in the Tigris River, Raphael instructs him to use its organs for healing and protection.

- **Symbolism:** The fish represents divine provision and the healing power found in nature.
- **Esoteric Lesson:** Spiritual and physical healing often require active participation and trust in divine guidance.

**2. Raphael as a Disguised Guide**

Raphael's disguise as a traveling companion underscores the subtle and unseen ways divine guidance manifests.

- **Symbolism:** The hidden nature of divine help reflects the necessity of faith and discernment.
- **Esoteric Lesson:** Spiritual guidance often requires humility and openness to unexpected forms of assistance.

**3. The Exorcism of Asmodeus**

Raphael instructs Tobias to burn the fish's liver and heart to drive away the demon Asmodeus.

- **Symbolism:** The burning of sacred elements symbolizes purification and the triumph of divine light over darkness.
- **Esoteric Lesson:** Intentional rituals and sacred actions are powerful tools for banishing negativity.

## Ritual: Healing with Raphael and the Fish

This ritual draws from the fish symbolism in *Tobit* to invoke Raphael's healing energy.

## Materials

- A small fish-shaped talisman or a bowl of water (symbolizing the Tigris River)
- Frankincense or sandalwood incense
- A green candle
- A healing crystal (e.g., green aventurine)

**Steps**

1. **Prepare Your Space**
   Light the incense and green candle. Place the fish-shaped talisman or bowl of water on your altar. Say:
   *"Raphael, divine healer and guide, I call upon your light to restore balance and health."*
2. **Invoke Raphael's Presence**
   Hold the crystal in your hands and focus on the story of Tobit. Visualize Raphael's emerald light surrounding you. Say:
   *"As you guided Tobias to healing, guide me now, Raphael. Let your light restore me."*
3. **Use the Water or Talisman**
   Dip your fingers into the bowl of water and anoint your forehead, chest, and hands. If using a talisman, hold it over your heart. Say:
   *"By the divine power symbolized in the fish, may healing flow through me."*
4. **Seal the Ritual**
   Blow out the candle and thank Raphael. Say:
   *"Raphael, bringer of healing, I thank you for your light and guidance. Amen."*

# Invocation for Guidance

This invocation mirrors Raphael's role as Tobias's guide and protector during his journey.

*"Raphael, guardian of travelers and healer of the weary,
As you walked with Tobias, walk with me.
Illuminate my path, protect my steps,
And guide me toward clarity and truth.
With your emerald light, lead me forward in peace and safety.
Amen."*

Hold a staff or walking stick as a symbol of the journey. Tap it lightly on the ground three times to signify movement forward under Raphael's guidance.

## Exorcism Ritual Inspired by Tobit

This ritual banishes negative energies or influences, inspired by Raphael's banishment of Asmodeus.

## Materials

- A small fireproof bowl
- Dried herbs such as sage or rosemary
- Matches or a lighter
- A green candle

**Steps**

1. **Light the Candle and Herbs**
   Place the herbs in the bowl and light them. As the smoke rises, say:
   *"Raphael, by your divine light, cleanse this space of all that harms and hinders."*
2. **Visualize the Banishment**
   Wave the smoke around yourself or the space, imagining negative energy dissolving. Say:
   *"As the fish's heart and liver burned, so let all negativity be driven away."*
3. **Close with Gratitude**
   Extinguish the candle and bow your head. Say:

*"Raphael, guardian of light, I thank you for your protection and guidance. May your blessings remain with me."*

## Magical Correspondences

- **Symbols:** Fish, staff, emerald light
- **Crystals:** Green aventurine (healing), clear quartz (clarity)
- **Herbs:** Sage (cleansing), sandalwood (purification)
- **Sacred Texts:** Passages from the *Book of Tobit* (Tobit 5:4-6, Tobit 8:2-3)

## Integrating Raphael's Teachings

The *Book of Tobit* provides a rich tapestry of lessons on faith, healing, and divine guidance. By integrating these themes into your magical practice, you can deepen your connection to Raphael and enhance your rituals with sacred wisdom.

### Advanced Tips

1. **Combine with Divination:** Before performing rituals inspired by *Tobit*, use divination (e.g., tarot or pendulum) to clarify your intention.
2. **Personalize the Symbols:** Incorporate a personal object (e.g., a pendant) to act as your "healing fish" in rituals.
3. **Meditate on the Journey:** Reflect on the parallels between Tobias's journey and your spiritual path, inviting Raphael to guide you through your challenges.

Through these practices, Raphael's teachings in the *Book of Tobit* come alive, offering profound insights and powerful tools for healing and transformation.

# Raphael's Guidance on Holistic Healing: Balancing Body, Mind, and Spirit

## The Archangel of Comprehensive Wellness

Archangel Raphael's role as the healer encompasses not only physical restoration but also the alignment of the emotional, mental, and spiritual aspects of being. His teachings emphasize that true healing is holistic, requiring harmony across all facets of existence. Drawing upon wisdom from sacred texts, mystical traditions, and esoteric practices, Raphael offers profound insights into the interconnected nature of well-being.

## Historical and Spiritual Context

### Raphael in Sacred Texts

- **The Book of Tobit:** Raphael's instructions to Tobias to use the fish's organs for physical and spiritual healing highlight the balance of natural remedies with divine intervention.
- **Kabbalistic Tradition:** As a healer, Raphael is linked to *Tiferet* on the Tree of Life, symbolizing beauty, balance, and integration, mirroring the holistic approach to wellness.
- **Angelic Role in Healing:** In angelology, Raphael is described as the overseer of divine physicians, guiding the flow of energy that aligns human beings with the Creator's intention for health and harmony.

### Modern Interpretations

- Practitioners in holistic medicine often invoke Raphael to bring harmony between physical treatments and spiritual practices.

- New Age traditions emphasize Raphael's role in balancing chakras, cleansing auras, and restoring the natural flow of energy.

# Principles of Holistic Healing with Raphael

## 1. Physical Healing

Raphael's guidance often involves integrating natural remedies with spiritual practices, emphasizing the divine origin of nature's healing power.

- **Symbol:** The fish in *Tobit* represents the use of natural elements for restoration.
- **Esoteric Lesson:** The physical body is a vessel for divine energy; keeping it healthy honors the Creator.

## 2. Emotional and Mental Healing

Raphael works with the heart chakra to release emotional wounds and with the mind to bring clarity and peace.

- **Symbol:** Emerald green light, representing emotional renewal.
- **Esoteric Lesson:** Emotional and mental health are interconnected; healing one influences the other.

## 3. Spiritual Healing

Spiritual wellness involves aligning the soul with divine light, a process Raphael facilitates through guidance and cleansing.

- **Symbol:** The emerald aura, cleansing and uplifting the spirit.
- **Esoteric Lesson:** Spiritual health is the foundation for holistic well-being.

# Ritual for Holistic Healing

This ritual invokes Raphael's energy to harmonize the body, mind, and spirit, promoting comprehensive well-being.

## Materials

- Three candles: green (body), blue (mind), and white (spirit)
- A bowl of spring water (for purification)
- A healing crystal, such as green aventurine or clear quartz
- Frankincense or lavender incense
- A journal for reflection

### Steps

1. **Prepare Your Space**
   Light the incense and place the three candles in a triangular arrangement. Set the bowl of water and crystal in the center. Say:
   *"Raphael, healer of divine wisdom, I invite your presence to this sacred space. May your light harmonize all aspects of my being."*
2. **Light the Candles**
   Light the candles one by one, focusing on their symbolic meanings. As you light each candle, say:
   - Green: *"For the healing of my body, I light this flame."*
   - Blue: *"For the clarity of my mind, I light this flame."*
   - White: *"For the purity of my spirit, I light this flame."*
3. **Meditate with the Crystal**
   Hold the crystal in both hands and close your eyes. Visualize emerald green light flowing through your body, mind, and spirit. Say:
   *"Raphael, unify my being with your healing light. Restore balance and harmony within me."*

4. **Use the Water for Purification**
   Dip your fingers into the bowl of water and anoint your forehead, heart, and hands. Say:
   *"By the purity of this water and Raphael's light, I am cleansed, healed, and whole."*
5. **Reflect and Close**
   Sit quietly for a few moments, allowing Raphael's energy to integrate into your being. Record any thoughts or sensations in your journal. Thank Raphael, saying:
   *"Raphael, healer of body, mind, and spirit, I thank you for your light and guidance. May your blessings remain with me always."*
6. **Extinguish the Candles**
   Blow out the candles in reverse order, visualizing their light transferring into your heart.

# Invocation for Holistic Healing

This invocation can be used during meditation or as a standalone prayer.

*"Raphael, healer of divine harmony,
Guardian of body, mind, and spirit,
I call upon your emerald light to flow through me.
Heal my body with strength and vitality.
Clear my mind with wisdom and peace.
Uplift my spirit with purity and grace.
By your guidance, I am whole. Amen."*

# Magical Correspondences for Holistic Healing

- **Colors:** Green (healing), blue (clarity), white (purity)
- **Crystals:** Green aventurine (heart healing), clear quartz (clarity), amethyst (spiritual balance)

- **Herbs:** Lavender (calming), rosemary (clarity), mint (revitalization)
- **Incense:** Frankincense (purification), sandalwood (spiritual alignment)
- **Symbols:** Staff (guidance), fish (natural healing), emerald aura (restoration)

# Integrating Raphael's Holistic Healing

Raphael's teachings on holistic healing invite you to view well-being as a dynamic interplay between physical health, emotional clarity, and spiritual alignment. By engaging in rituals, meditations, and daily practices that honor this balance, you can experience profound transformation under Raphael's guidance.

## Advanced Tips for Holistic Practice

1. **Daily Energy Alignment:** Begin each day with a brief visualization of Raphael's emerald light surrounding your body, mind, and spirit.
2. **Regular Chakra Work:** Focus on balancing the heart, throat, and crown chakras to maintain emotional, mental, and spiritual harmony.
3. **Combine Healing Modalities:** Integrate Raphael's guidance with physical practices such as yoga, breathwork, or herbal remedies for comprehensive wellness.

Through consistent work with Raphael's energy, you can achieve a state of holistic balance, embodying the divine harmony that leads to true healing.

# The Angelic Perspective on Illness, Recovery, and Divine Alignment: Wisdom from Raphael

## Illness as a Call to Realignment

From the perspective of Archangel Raphael, illness is more than a physical disruption; it is a signal of misalignment between the body, mind, spirit, and divine will. Raphael's teachings suggest that healing is a holistic process involving restoration to divine harmony, where illness serves as both a challenge and an opportunity for growth.

# Historical and Spiritual Context

## Raphael in Sacred Texts

- **The Book of Tobit:** Raphael's healing of Tobit's blindness reflects the angelic role in addressing not only physical ailments but also spiritual imbalances. Tobit's suffering serves as a catalyst for faith and divine intervention.
- **Kabbalistic Insights:** In the Tree of Life, Raphael is associated with *Tiferet* (beauty and harmony), emphasizing balance and the integration of higher and lower energies as key to health.
- **Islamic Tradition:** Although Raphael (Israfil) is not directly linked to healing, his role as the herald of cosmic renewal resonates with the concept of spiritual transformation through illness.

## Mystical and Esoteric Teachings

- Illness is viewed as a blockage or disruption in the natural flow of divine energy. Raphael's emerald light, representing renewal and growth, clears these blockages and restores alignment.

- Recovery is a process of reconnecting with the divine source, requiring not only physical remedies but also emotional and spiritual realignment.

## Symbolism and Esoteric Lessons

- **Illness as Transformation:** Illness symbolizes the breaking down of old patterns to make way for renewal. Raphael's energy facilitates this transformation.
- **Recovery as Reconnection:** Healing is not merely the absence of illness but the reestablishment of harmony with the divine.
- **Emerald Green Light:** Raphael's light represents the life force, healing physical wounds, emotional scars, and spiritual disconnection.

## Ritual for Understanding Illness as Divine Communication

This ritual helps you interpret the spiritual messages behind illness and invoke Raphael's guidance for healing and realignment.

### Materials

- A green candle (symbolizing healing)
- A piece of green aventurine or malachite
- A bowl of water
- Lavender or eucalyptus essential oil
- A journal for reflection

**Steps**

1. **Prepare Your Space**
   Light the green candle and place the crystal and bowl of water on your altar. Anoint your forehead and palms with the essential oil. Say:
   *"Raphael, angel of light and healing, I invite your wisdom to illuminate the lessons of my suffering. Help me see beyond the pain to divine alignment."*
2. **Meditate on the Source of Illness**
   Hold the crystal in both hands and close your eyes. Focus on the area of illness or discomfort in your body. Visualize Raphael's emerald light enveloping that area. Say:
   *"What is the message within this pain? What must I release or realign to restore harmony?"*
   Sit quietly and allow insights or feelings to arise.
3. **Cleanse and Renew**
   Dip your fingers into the bowl of water and anoint the area of discomfort or your heart. Say:
   *"By Raphael's light and this sacred water, I release all blockages and invite divine alignment."*
4. **Record Your Insights**
   Write any thoughts, sensations, or revelations in your journal. Conclude by saying:
   *"Raphael, I thank you for your guidance. May your light continue to heal and align me with divine purpose."*

# Invocation for Recovery and Realignment

This invocation can be recited daily to invite Raphael's healing energy during recovery.

*"Raphael, angel of harmony and renewal,
Guide me through this path of healing.
Restore my body with strength and vitality,
Calm my mind with clarity and peace,
And uplift my spirit to align with divine light.
In your presence, I am whole. Amen."*

Place one hand on your heart and the other on your forehead as you recite, symbolizing the connection between mind and spirit.

## Meditation for Divine Alignment

This meditation focuses on aligning with Raphael's energy to facilitate healing and spiritual balance.

1. **Sit Comfortably:** Close your eyes and take slow, deep breaths.
2. **Visualize Emerald Light:** See Raphael's emerald green light descending from above, enveloping your body in warmth and healing energy.
3. **Affirm Alignment:** Mentally repeat: *"I am aligned with divine light. Raphael's energy restores and renews me."*
4. **Feel the Connection:** Imagine the light connecting your heart and crown chakras, creating a bridge between your physical self and divine wisdom.

## Magical Correspondences

- **Colors:** Emerald green (healing), white (purity)
- **Crystals:** Green aventurine (renewal), malachite (transformation)
- **Herbs:** Lavender (calming), eucalyptus (cleansing), mint (revitalization)
- **Incense:** Sandalwood (spiritual connection), frankincense (purification)
- **Symbols:** Staff (guidance), fish (healing), emerald aura (renewal)

## Embracing Raphael's Perspective

Raphael's teachings on illness and recovery encourage us to view health as a state of divine alignment rather than the mere absence of disease. By recognizing illness as a spiritual message, we can embrace recovery as an opportunity to deepen our connection with the divine.

## Advanced Tips for Deepening Your Work

1. **Daily Prayer Practice:** Begin or end each day with a short prayer to Raphael, asking for continued guidance and healing.
2. **Energy Work:** Incorporate practices like Reiki or chakra balancing to enhance the flow of Raphael's light through your body.
3. **Combine Physical and Spiritual Remedies:** Pair medical treatments with spiritual practices such as meditations or rituals to create a holistic approach to healing.

By integrating Raphael's wisdom into your life, you unlock the transformative power of angelic guidance, aligning your body, mind, and spirit with the divine harmony necessary for true healing.

# Archangel Raphael's Role in the Angelic Hierarchy: A Bridge Between Realms

## The Structure of the Angelic Orders

Archangel Raphael holds a significant position in the celestial hierarchy, bridging divine wisdom with human experience. Understanding his placement among the archangels and celestial orders deepens our awareness of his function and power within the spiritual cosmos.

# Historical and Spiritual Context

## The Nine Choirs of Angels

The celestial hierarchy, as described by Pseudo-Dionysius the Areopagite, divides angels into nine choirs, each serving unique roles in the divine plan:

1. **Seraphim:** Closest to God, embodying divine love.
2. **Cherubim:** Guardians of divine wisdom.
3. **Thrones:** Bearers of divine justice and authority.
4. **Dominions:** Supervisors of angelic activity.
5. **Virtues:** Executors of miracles and divine blessings.
6. **Powers:** Defenders of cosmic order.
7. **Principalities:** Guardians of nations and leaders.
8. **Archangels:** Messengers and executors of divine will.
9. **Angels:** Guardians of individuals and daily affairs.

Raphael belongs to the eighth choir, the Archangels, whose purpose is to serve as mediators between God and humanity.

## Raphael's Specific Role

- **The Archangel of Healing:** Raphael's primary function is to guide and heal, acting as a divine physician.
- **Protector of Travelers:** Raphael's guidance in *The Book of Tobit* exemplifies his protective role, particularly during spiritual or physical journeys.
- **Mediator of Divine Wisdom:** Raphael helps align human souls with divine energy, aiding in spiritual evolution.

## Sacred Texts and Traditions

- **Book of Tobit:** Raphael's role as healer and guide is central, illustrating his function in divine mercy and human affairs.

- **Kabbalistic Tradition:** Raphael is associated with *Tiferet* (harmony and beauty), representing balance between higher and lower realms.
- **Islamic Tradition:** While Raphael (Israfil) is primarily known for his role in the resurrection, his connection to transformation and renewal complements his biblical attributes.

## Symbolism and Esoteric Significance

### 1. The Emerald Aura

Raphael's energy is often depicted as an emerald-green light, symbolizing growth, healing, and divine alignment. This light connects human struggles with celestial harmony.

### 2. Raphael's Name

Derived from the Hebrew *Rafa-El* (*"God heals"*), his name underscores his mission as a divine healer and guide.

### 3. The Role of Mediator

Raphael's position in the hierarchy signifies his ability to transcend boundaries, linking human experience with divine purpose.

## Ritual for Connecting with Raphael's Celestial Energy

This ritual enhances your connection to Raphael's role as a mediator between divine wisdom and human healing.

## Materials

- A green candle (symbolizing Raphael's healing light)
- A small silver or gold disc (representing celestial order)
- Frankincense incense (to invoke the angelic realm)
- A journal for reflections
- Raphael's sigil (drawn on paper or a small object)

**Steps**

1. **Prepare the Space**
   Light the green candle and incense. Place the disc and sigil on your altar. Say:
   *"Raphael, archangel of healing and guidance, I call upon your presence. Let your light fill this space and my spirit."*
2. **Invoke the Angelic Choirs**
   Recite the names of the nine choirs aloud, visualizing them descending in harmony to surround you. Say:
   *"Seraphim, Cherubim, Thrones, Dominions, Virtues, Powers, Principalities, Archangels, and Angels, I honor your divine order."*
3. **Focus on Raphael's Role**
   Hold Raphael's sigil or place your hand over it. Visualize his emerald aura radiating from the sigil. Say:
   *"Raphael, messenger of divine wisdom and healing, guide me in aligning my path with divine will. May your energy flow through me."*
4. **Meditate on Raphael's Hierarchical Placement**
   Sit quietly and imagine yourself ascending through the angelic choirs, with Raphael guiding you. Feel his presence as a bridge between your human experience and the divine.
5. **Close the Ritual**
   Thank Raphael and the angelic choirs. Extinguish the candle, saying:
   *"Raphael, I thank you for your guidance and light. May your blessings remain with me."*

## Invocation for Angelic Guidance

This invocation calls upon Raphael's celestial wisdom and healing power.

*"Raphael, healer and guide,
Archangel of harmony and divine light,
I call upon your emerald presence to uplift and protect me.
With your wisdom, bridge the realms of heaven and earth,
And align my soul with the divine order.
In your name, I am whole and at peace. Amen."*


## Magical Correspondences

- **Color:** Emerald green (healing), gold (divine connection), silver (celestial order)
- **Crystals:** Green aventurine (healing), clear quartz (divine clarity)
- **Herbs:** Sage (cleansing), lavender (peace), frankincense (spiritual connection)
- **Sacred Symbols:** Raphael's sigil, the Tree of Life, angelic wings
- **Incense:** Frankincense (angelic invocation), myrrh (purification)


## Embracing Raphael's Hierarchical Role

Understanding Raphael's place among the archangels and celestial orders illuminates his function as a bridge between divine wisdom and human experience. By working with Raphael in his hierarchical role, you can access deeper spiritual insights and align your actions with divine harmony.

## Advanced Tips for Deepening Your Connection

1. **Daily Angelic Invocation:** Recite a prayer to Raphael each morning, focusing on his role as a healer and guide.
2. **Sacred Geometry:** Incorporate the Tree of Life into your rituals to explore Raphael's connection to *Tiferet*.
3. **Angelic Choir Meditation:** Visualize ascending through the angelic choirs during meditation, with Raphael guiding your journey.

Through consistent practice, you can integrate Raphael's celestial wisdom into your magical work, fostering a deeper understanding of divine order and healing.

# Raphael's Celestial Kinship: Connections to Michael, Gabriel, and Uriel

## A Symphony of Divine Purpose

Archangel Raphael's relationships with other archangels reflect a harmonious collaboration in fulfilling divine will. Michael, Gabriel, Uriel, and Raphael each embody distinct yet complementary energies, forming a powerful network of guidance, protection, and healing. Understanding their connections illuminates Raphael's unique role within the greater celestial framework.

# Historical and Spiritual Context

## The Archangelic Quartet

- **Michael (Who Is Like God):** The protector and warrior, Michael symbolizes divine strength and justice. His fiery energy complements Raphael's healing light, ensuring balance between defense and restoration.

- **Gabriel (God Is My Strength):** The messenger of divine revelation, Gabriel's clarity of communication aligns with Raphael's guidance, merging insight with action.
- **Uriel (God Is My Light):** The illuminator of divine wisdom, Uriel's intellectual clarity and transformative fire align with Raphael's nurturing, creating a synergy of growth and understanding.
- **Raphael (God Heals):** The healer and guide, Raphael connects the physical and spiritual realms, facilitating harmony and renewal.

## Sacred Texts and Traditions

- **Christian Tradition:** The archangels often work together in divine missions, as seen in Michael's defense, Gabriel's annunciation, and Raphael's healing in the *Book of Tobit*.
- **Kabbalistic Tree of Life:** The archangels correspond to *sephirot* on the Tree of Life, representing facets of divine energy:
    - Michael: *Chesed* (mercy) and *Geburah* (strength)
    - Gabriel: *Yesod* (foundation)
    - Raphael: *Tiferet* (beauty and harmony)
    - Uriel: *Hod* (splendor) and *Netzach* (eternity)
- **Esoteric Mysticism:** Each archangel governs an element:
    - Michael: Fire
    - Gabriel: Water
    - Uriel: Earth
    - Raphael: Air

# Symbolism and Esoteric Lessons

### 1. Synergy of Roles

The archangels' distinct roles blend into a comprehensive system of divine intervention:

- Michael provides protection, ensuring safety during Raphael's healing processes.
- Gabriel delivers clarity, aligning intentions with divine wisdom.
- Uriel illuminates truths that aid in the healing journey.

**2. Elemental Balance**

Each archangel embodies an element, and their interplay reflects the harmonious functioning of creation. Raphael's air (movement and clarity) energizes and complements the solidity of Uriel's earth, the fluidity of Gabriel's water, and the transformative power of Michael's fire.

**3. The Four Quarters**

Magical traditions often place the archangels in the four cardinal directions:

- Michael: South (fire, protection)
- Gabriel: West (water, intuition)
- Raphael: East (air, healing and guidance)
- Uriel: North (earth, wisdom and grounding)

# Ritual for Connecting with the Archangels

This ritual invokes the energy of Raphael alongside Michael, Gabriel, and Uriel to create a balanced and supportive environment for healing, guidance, and protection.

## Materials

- Four candles: red (Michael), blue (Gabriel), green (Raphael), and gold (Uriel)
- A feather (Raphael/air), a cup of water (Gabriel), a stone or crystal (Uriel/earth), and a small flame or candle (Michael/fire)

- Frankincense incense
- A compass or a sense of the cardinal directions

**Steps**

1. **Prepare the Space**
   Place the candles in the cardinal directions on your altar or in a circle. Arrange the elemental symbols beside each candle. Light the incense and say:
   *"I call upon the divine light of the archangels to bless and protect this space. Let their energies guide and restore me."*
2. **Light the Candles and Call the Archangels**
   - Face East and light the green candle:
     *"Raphael, guardian of air and healing, guide me with your emerald light."*
   - Face South and light the red candle:
     *"Michael, protector of fire and strength, shield me with your divine power."*
   - Face West and light the blue candle:
     *"Gabriel, messenger of water and truth, bless me with clarity and intuition."*
   - Face North and light the gold candle:
     *"Uriel, illuminator of earth and wisdom, ground me in divine understanding."*
3. **Meditate on Their Energies**
   Sit quietly at the center of the circle. Visualize the archangels standing at their respective directions, forming a protective and healing grid around you.
4. **Invoke Raphael for Healing**
   Hold the feather and say:
   *"Raphael, bringer of divine healing,*
   *Let your emerald light flow through me.*
   *Align my body, mind, and spirit with divine harmony.*
   *In your guidance, I am whole."*
5. **Seal the Ritual**
   Extinguish the candles in reverse order, thanking each archangel:
   - North: *"Thank you, Uriel, for your wisdom and grounding."*

- West: *"Thank you, Gabriel, for your clarity and blessings."*
- South: *"Thank you, Michael, for your protection and strength."*
- East: *"Thank you, Raphael, for your healing and guidance."*

## Invocation of the Archangels

This invocation can be recited to call upon the collective energy of Raphael, Michael, Gabriel, and Uriel.

*"Raphael, healer of divine harmony, guide me with your light.*
*Michael, protector of truth and justice, shield me with your strength.*
*Gabriel, messenger of clarity, inspire my heart with wisdom.*
*Uriel, illuminator of the path, ground me in divine understanding.*
*Together, may your energies align me with the will of the Creator. Amen."*

## Magical Correspondences

- **Raphael (Air):** Green candle, feather, frankincense
- **Michael (Fire):** Red candle, flame, cedar incense
- **Gabriel (Water):** Blue candle, water cup, myrrh incense
- **Uriel (Earth):** Gold candle, stone/crystal, patchouli incense

## Aligning with Raphael and His Celestial Allies

By understanding Raphael's connections to Michael, Gabriel, and Uriel, you can draw upon a symphony of angelic energies to enrich your spiritual practice. These archangels form a harmonious team, addressing every aspect of divine intervention—from protection and clarity to wisdom and healing.

## Advanced Tips for Deepening Your Connection

1. **Daily Archangelic Alignment:** Begin each day by visualizing the four archangels standing at your sides, their energies harmonizing your body, mind, and spirit.
2. **Astrological Timing:** Invoke the archangels during planetary hours that correspond to their energies (e.g., Mercury for Raphael, Mars for Michael, Moon for Gabriel, Saturn for Uriel).
3. **Create a Permanent Altar:** Dedicate an altar to the archangels, including their symbols and elemental representations, to maintain a constant connection.

Through these practices, you cultivate a deeper relationship with Raphael and his celestial allies, integrating their collective wisdom into your magical journey.

# Raphael's Role in the Healing of the Earth: Insights from the Book of Enoch

## A Guardian of Balance and Restoration

Archangel Raphael's role in healing the Earth, as described in the *Book of Enoch*, highlights his divine mission as a custodian of creation. His duties extend beyond individual healing to encompass the purification and restoration of the Earth itself, maintaining harmony between humanity and the natural world.

# Historical and Spiritual Context

## The Book of Enoch

The *Book of Enoch*, an ancient Jewish apocalyptic text, provides one of the earliest and most detailed accounts of Raphael's cosmic duties:

- **Healing the Earth:** Raphael is tasked with binding the fallen angels who corrupted creation and healing the Earth from the effects of their transgressions.
- **Role in Cleansing Humanity:** Raphael works to cleanse humanity of the corruption introduced by the Watchers and their offspring, the Nephilim, emphasizing the need for balance and purity in the divine order.

## Kabbalistic and Mystical Perspectives

- In Kabbalistic tradition, Raphael's association with *Tiferet* (harmony) reflects his mission to restore balance between humanity and creation.
- Esoteric interpretations link Raphael to the element of air and the planet Mercury, symbolizing the flow of life-giving energy and the ability to communicate divine will across dimensions.

## Modern Interpretations

In contemporary spirituality, Raphael's role in healing the Earth is often associated with environmental stewardship, energy healing, and ecological balance.

# Symbolism and Esoteric Lessons

### 1. The Binding of Azazel

Raphael's binding of the fallen angel Azazel symbolizes the triumph of divine order over chaos and corruption. This act represents the purification necessary for healing the Earth.

## 2. The Cleansing of the Waters

In Enoch's account, Raphael purifies the Earth's waters, a symbol of life and renewal. This imagery emphasizes the importance of spiritual and ecological cleansing.

## 3. The Restoration of Balance

Raphael's work illustrates that healing is not merely physical but also spiritual and environmental. His actions teach that humanity's harmony with the Earth is integral to divine alignment.

# Ritual for Earth Healing

This ritual invokes Raphael's energy to cleanse and restore the Earth's natural harmony.

## Materials

- A green candle (symbolizing Raphael's healing light)
- A bowl of spring water (representing the Earth's waters)
- A small stone or crystal (representing the Earth)
- Frankincense incense (for purification)
- A feather (symbolizing Raphael's connection to air)

**Steps**

1. **Prepare the Space**
   Light the green candle and incense. Arrange the water bowl, stone, and feather on your altar. Say:
   *"Raphael, guardian of creation, I call upon your light to*

heal and restore the Earth. May your emerald presence fill this space."

2. **Purify the Waters**
   Hold your hands over the bowl of water, visualizing Raphael's emerald light descending into it. Say:
   "By Raphael's light, may these waters be purified and renewed, a symbol of the Earth's healing."

3. **Invoke Raphael's Presence**
   Hold the feather and wave it gently around the altar, representing the cleansing power of air. Say:
   "Raphael, healer of the Earth, guide me in restoring balance and harmony to creation."

4. **Meditate on Earth's Healing**
   Sit quietly, holding the stone or crystal. Visualize the Earth enveloped in emerald light, its waters and lands cleansed and renewed. Say:
   "As Raphael heals the Earth, so may I act as a steward of balance and renewal."

5. **Conclude the Ritual**
   Pour the water into the Earth as an offering. Thank Raphael, saying:
   "Raphael, healer of creation, I thank you for your guidance and light. May your blessings sustain the Earth."

# Invocation for Environmental Stewardship

This invocation calls upon Raphael's energy to inspire and guide ecological healing efforts.

*"Raphael, guardian of Earth's harmony,
Cleanse the waters and renew the lands.
Guide my actions to honor creation,
And align my spirit with divine stewardship.
Through your healing light, may the Earth flourish,
And may all life be restored to balance. Amen."*

Place your hands on the Earth or a potted plant, symbolizing your connection to creation and commitment to its care.

## Magical Correspondences

- **Colors:** Emerald green (healing), blue (waters)
- **Crystals:** Green aventurine (renewal), clear quartz (clarity), moss agate (connection to Earth)
- **Herbs:** Sage (cleansing), lavender (peace), cedar (protection)
- **Incense:** Frankincense (purification), myrrh (grounding)
- **Symbols:** Water bowl (cleansing), stone (Earth's stability), feather (air's purity)

## Raphael as Earth's Healer

Raphael's role in the *Book of Enoch* underscores his cosmic mission to restore harmony between humanity and creation. By working with Raphael's energy, you can contribute to the healing of the Earth and align your spiritual practice with divine purpose.

### Advanced Tips for Deepening Your Practice

1. **Monthly Earth Healing Rituals:** Perform the Earth healing ritual during the new moon to align with cycles of renewal.
2. **Sacred Spaces:** Dedicate a portion of your altar to Raphael's Earth healing mission, including natural elements like plants, stones, and water.
3. **Daily Stewardship Practices:** Integrate small acts of environmental care into your routine (e.g., planting trees, conserving water) as offerings to Raphael.

Through these practices, you deepen your connection to Raphael's divine mission and contribute to the restoration of balance and harmony in the natural world.

Having explored the energy, wisdom, and role of Archangel Raphael within the celestial hierarchy and his divine missions, it is now time to delve deeper into the textual and cultural foundations that provide a structured understanding of his presence and influence. From canonical scriptures to mystical and esoteric texts, these writings unveil the multidimensional aspects of Raphael's healing, guidance, and protection. This exploration spans sacred religious texts, apocryphal works, and mystical grimoires, offering insights into his enduring legacy and connections to cross-cultural healing figures. By studying these sources, you will build a comprehensive framework for understanding Raphael's significance, empowering your magical practice with historical, spiritual, and practical depth. Let us now journey through the textual and comparative traditions that illuminate Raphael's divine essence and role across time and space.

# { 3 }

# Sacred Texts and Timeless Wisdom: Raphael's Presence in Scripture and Tradition

The wisdom of Archangel Raphael is deeply embedded in a vast array of sacred texts and mystical traditions, each revealing unique facets of his healing and guiding essence. From the canonical and apocryphal writings that detail his divine missions to esoteric grimoires and folk traditions that preserve his rituals and invocations, these works collectively paint a comprehensive picture of Raphael's role in the spiritual and cosmic order. Comparative mythology further broadens our understanding, linking Raphael to other divine healers across cultures, while modern works continue to adapt his energy to contemporary spiritual practices. This section offers a detailed exploration of these textual foundations, providing historical context, spiritual insights, and practical applications to deepen your connection with Raphael and enrich your magical practice.

## The Book of Tobit: Raphael's Mission Revealed

### A Divine Narrative of Guidance and Healing

The *Book of Tobit*, a deuterocanonical text revered in Catholic and Orthodox traditions, offers one of the most vivid depictions of Archangel Raphael's role in healing, guidance, and protection. This story showcases Raphael's interventions in the lives of Tobit, Tobias, and Sarah, revealing his multifaceted nature as a healer, exorcist, and divine guide. For practitioners seeking to work with Raphael, the *Book of*

*Tobit* serves as both a sacred text and a foundational manual for understanding his wisdom and magical applications.

## Historical and Spiritual Context

### The Story in Brief

- **Tobit's Suffering:** A devout Israelite exiled in Nineveh, Tobit is blinded by an accident and prays for death as he suffers in despair.
- **Sarah's Plight:** In a parallel story, Sarah, a relative of Tobit, is haunted by the demon Asmodeus, who kills her husbands on their wedding nights.
- **Raphael's Intervention:** Disguised as Azariah, Raphael accompanies Tobit's son Tobias on a journey to recover family wealth and secure a marriage with Sarah. Along the way, Raphael provides healing remedies, exorcises the demon, and restores Tobit's sight.

### Key Themes

1. **Healing and Restoration:** Raphael cures Tobit's blindness and liberates Sarah from demonic torment, showcasing his role as a divine healer.
2. **Divine Guidance:** Acting as Tobias's companion, Raphael provides wisdom and protection during their journey.
3. **Faith and Obedience:** The characters' trust in divine guidance exemplifies the importance of faith in spiritual practice.

### Canonical Significance

The *Book of Tobit* highlights Raphael's identity as one of the seven angels who stand before God (Tobit 12:15), emphasizing his proximity to the divine throne and his role as an intermediary.

## Symbolism and Esoteric Lessons

### 1. The Healing Fish

When Tobias catches a fish in the Tigris River, Raphael instructs him to use its heart, liver, and gall for healing and exorcism. This fish symbolizes divine provision and the healing power inherent in creation.

### 2. The Disguised Guide

Raphael's assumption of human form underscores the idea that divine assistance often arrives subtly, requiring faith and discernment.

### 3. The Journey

The physical journey undertaken by Tobias mirrors the spiritual journey of seeking divine alignment, with Raphael as a guide.

## Ritual for Divine Healing Inspired by Tobit

This ritual invokes Raphael's energy to heal physical, emotional, or spiritual ailments.

### Materials

- A green candle (symbolizing Raphael's healing light)
- A fish-shaped talisman or bowl of water (representing the healing fish)
- Frankincense incense

- A piece of green aventurine or malachite
- A copy of the *Book of Tobit* or printed excerpts

**Steps**

1. **Prepare the Space**
   Light the green candle and incense. Place the talisman or water bowl and the crystal on your altar. Say:
   *"Raphael, divine healer and guide, I invite your presence to this sacred space. Let your light restore me to wholeness."*
2. **Read from the *Book of Tobit***
   Recite Tobit 6:2-9, where Raphael instructs Tobias on the fish's healing properties. Visualize Raphael's emerald light filling the space.
3. **Hold the Crystal**
   Take the crystal in your hands, focusing on the area of your body or life that needs healing. Say:
   *"Raphael, with the power of divine wisdom, heal me as you healed Tobit and Sarah. Restore balance to my body, mind, and spirit."*
4. **Bless the Water or Talisman**
   Dip your fingers in the water or hold the fish talisman. Visualize Raphael's energy flowing through it. Say:
   *"By the sacred fish of healing, may Raphael's light cleanse and restore me."*
5. **Conclude with Gratitude**
   Extinguish the candle and thank Raphael. Say:
   *"Raphael, I thank you for your guidance and light. May your blessings remain with me."*

# Invocation for Divine Guidance

This invocation mirrors Raphael's role as Tobias's guide and protector.

*"Raphael, divine companion and guide,*

*As you walked with Tobias, walk with me.
Illuminate my path with wisdom and clarity,
And shield me from all harm and missteps.
With your light, I am whole and safe. Amen."*

## Magical Correspondences

- **Colors:** Green (healing), blue (protection)
- **Crystals:** Green aventurine (healing), clear quartz (clarity)
- **Herbs:** Sage (cleansing), mint (renewal)
- **Incense:** Frankincense (purification)
- **Symbols:** Fish, staff, emerald light

## Raphael's Teachings in the *Book of Tobit*

The *Book of Tobit* provides profound insights into Raphael's role as a healer and guide. Its narrative offers both inspiration and practical frameworks for engaging with his energy in magical and spiritual practices.

### Advanced Tips for Integrating Tobit's Lessons

1. **Daily Reflection:** Read passages from the *Book of Tobit* to draw continuous inspiration and guidance.
2. **Symbolic Rituals:** Create a permanent altar with symbols from the story, such as a fish, staff, or emerald light, to maintain a connection with Raphael.
3. **Journey Work:** Use visualization meditations to imagine Raphael guiding you on a spiritual journey, mirroring Tobias's path.

Through these practices, you can align with Raphael's healing and guiding energy, bringing the sacred wisdom of the *Book of Tobit* to life in your magical and spiritual endeavors.

# Mentions of Raphael in Other Biblical Texts: Unveiling the Archangel's Subtle Presence

## A Hidden Hand in the Sacred Narrative

Though explicit references to Raphael are limited outside the *Book of Tobit*, his presence and influence are inferred in other biblical texts through descriptions of angelic healing, guidance, and divine interventions. These subtle mentions, combined with interpretations from mystical traditions, form a richer tapestry of Raphael's celestial role.

# Historical and Spiritual Context

## Explicit Mentions and Implications

- **Tobit 12:15:** Raphael identifies himself as "one of the seven angels who stand ready and enter before the glory of the Lord," suggesting his high rank and proximity to the divine throne.
- **Daniel 8:15-17:** While Gabriel is explicitly named in Daniel's visions, Raphael's role as a healing and guiding presence aligns with the angelic functions described, making his involvement plausible in interpreting and restoring balance.
- **Revelation 8:2:** The seven angels standing before God, each given a trumpet, echo Raphael's declared role in Tobit, implying his participation in these celestial missions.

## Esoteric Interpretations

- **Healing Themes in Scripture:** Instances of angelic healing, such as the stirring of the waters at the Pool of

Bethesda (John 5:1-4), are often attributed to Raphael's influence.
- **Cosmic Balance:** Raphael's role in guiding and restoring order is seen as integral to maintaining harmony, especially in texts that describe angelic interventions in human affairs.

## Symbolism and Esoteric Lessons

### 1. The Seven Archangels

Raphael's identification as one of the seven archangels emphasizes his role in divine order. The number seven symbolizes completeness and divine perfection. In 1 Enoch 20, the Greek text lists the seven angels: Uriel, Raphael, Raguel, Michael, Sariel, Gabriel, and Remeiel.

### 2. Healing as Restoration

The healing acts attributed to angels, including Raphael, symbolize the restoration of divine alignment, where illness or disruption represents spiritual misalignment.

### 3. Raphael's Connection to Prophecy

Although not directly named, Raphael's guiding and restorative nature aligns with the angelic missions in prophetic texts, underscoring his function as a bridge between divine wisdom and human understanding.

## Ritual for Angelic Guidance and Insight

This ritual calls upon Raphael's guiding energy to illuminate your understanding of sacred texts and their deeper meanings.

## Materials

- A blue or green candle (symbolizing divine guidance and healing)
- A Bible or other sacred text
- Frankincense incense
- A feather or small wing charm (representing angelic presence)
- A journal for reflections

**Steps**

1. **Prepare Your Space**
   Light the candle and incense. Place the feather or wing charm next to the Bible. Say:
   *"Raphael, divine guide and healer, I invite your presence. Illuminate my heart and mind with your wisdom."*
2. **Read and Reflect**
   Open the Bible to passages such as Daniel 8:15-17 or Revelation 8:2. Read slowly, imagining Raphael standing beside you, helping you discern the deeper meanings. Say:
   *"Raphael, reveal the divine truths within these sacred words. Guide me to understand and integrate their wisdom."*
3. **Meditate on Raphael's Energy**
   Close your eyes and hold the feather. Visualize Raphael's emerald light enveloping you, bringing clarity and insight. Say:
   *"By your light, Raphael, may my understanding deepen, and my spirit align with divine truth."*
4. **Record Your Insights**
   Write down any thoughts, images, or feelings that arise during the ritual. Thank Raphael, saying:
   *"Raphael, I thank you for your guidance and light. May your wisdom remain with me always."*

# Invocation for Angelic Healing

This invocation draws on Raphael's broader biblical presence to invite healing and protection.

*"Raphael, guardian of divine order,
One of seven who stand before the throne,
I call upon your healing and guiding light.
Align me with the Creator's will,
Restore my balance and illuminate my path.
By your wisdom, I am healed and whole. Amen."*

# Magical Correspondences

- **Colors:** Green (healing), blue (guidance), gold (divine connection)
- **Crystals:** Green aventurine (healing), lapis lazuli (insight), clear quartz (clarity)
- **Herbs:** Sage (cleansing), rosemary (memory and insight)
- **Incense:** Frankincense (purification), sandalwood (spiritual connection)
- **Symbols:** Feather, Bible, emerald aura

# Raphael's Subtle but Significant Presence

Though Raphael's direct mentions in biblical texts are sparse, his essence resonates throughout scripture, where themes of healing, guidance, and divine order emerge. By recognizing his subtle yet powerful influence, practitioners can deepen their connection to Raphael and unlock the wisdom encoded in sacred narratives.

## Advanced Tips for Deepening Your Practice

1. **Daily Reading with Raphael:** Begin each day by reading a short biblical passage, inviting Raphael's presence to guide your understanding.
2. **Visualize the Seven Archangels:** During meditation, imagine Raphael and the six other archangels surrounding you, their energies harmonizing your spiritual growth.
3. **Integrate Raphael into Study Rituals:** Use the ritual above whenever you seek insight or clarity in your spiritual or magical studies.

By integrating these practices, you strengthen your alignment with Raphael's divine energy, allowing his guidance to enrich your understanding of sacred texts and their relevance to your magical path.

# Raphael in the Book of Enoch: Healing and Judgment in the Divine Plan

## A Celestial Arbiter of Balance

In the *Book of Enoch*, Archangel Raphael emerges as a figure of profound importance, entrusted with tasks of healing and judgment that restore divine harmony to creation. His role underscores the interconnectedness of cosmic order, human well-being, and spiritual alignment. For the magician, these revelations from Enochian texts offer not only historical insights but also practical frameworks for working with Raphael in transformative and restorative rituals.

# Historical and Spiritual Context

## The Book of Enoch: A Portal to Angelic Realms

The *Book of Enoch*, an ancient Jewish apocryphal text, provides one of the earliest detailed accounts of angelology. Divided into several sections, it narrates the fall of the Watchers—angelic beings who defied divine law—and the subsequent corruption of creation. Raphael's presence in these texts demonstrates his multifaceted role:

1. **Healer of the Earth:** Tasked with cleansing the Earth from the consequences of the Watchers' sins.
2. **Judge of Fallen Angels:** Raphael binds Azazel and other rebellious angels, ensuring divine justice.
3. **Protector of Humanity:** Acting as a mediator between divine mercy and cosmic judgment, Raphael safeguards humanity's spiritual and physical well-being.

## Key Passages

- **Binding of Azazel (1 Enoch 10:4-7):** Raphael is commanded to bind Azazel, a fallen angel responsible for corrupting humanity, and to bury him in darkness as a judgment.
- **Healing of the Earth (1 Enoch 10:9-11):** Raphael purifies the Earth from the contamination caused by the Nephilim, restoring balance and harmony.

## Esoteric Interpretations

- **Cosmic Restorer:** Raphael's actions symbolize the healing of both macrocosmic and microcosmic disruptions.
- **Mediator of Mercy and Judgment:** He exemplifies the balance between divine compassion and accountability.

# Symbolism and Esoteric Lessons

### 1. Binding as Purification

The act of binding Azazel represents the containment and neutralization of harmful energies that disrupt divine harmony. For practitioners, this can serve as a metaphor for overcoming internal and external negativity.

### 2. Healing of the Earth

Raphael's cleansing of the Earth reflects the interconnectedness of human actions, spiritual well-being, and ecological balance, offering lessons in stewardship and holistic healing.

### 3. Light Overcoming Darkness

By carrying out acts of judgment, Raphael reaffirms the triumph of divine light over corruption, symbolizing the eternal potential for renewal and transformation.

# Ritual for Purification and Balance

This ritual invokes Raphael's energy to cleanse and balance the practitioner's spiritual, physical, and environmental space.

## Materials

- A white candle (symbolizing divine light and purity)
- A green candle (symbolizing healing and renewal)
- A small jar of salt (representing purification)
- Frankincense incense
- A piece of green aventurine or clear quartz

**Steps**

1. **Prepare the Space**
   Light the white and green candles. Place the salt and crystal on your altar. Light the incense and say:
   *"Raphael, healer and restorer of balance, I call upon your light to cleanse and renew this space and my spirit."*
2. **Invocation of Raphael**
   Hold the crystal and visualize Raphael's emerald light enveloping you. Say:
   *"Raphael, binding force of divine order,*
   *Cleanser of the Earth and protector of humanity,*
   *I invite your presence to restore harmony within and around me."*
3. **Salt Purification**
   Sprinkle a small amount of salt around your space or in a bowl of water. Visualize Raphael's energy flowing through the salt, neutralizing negativity. Say:
   *"By the salt of purification and Raphael's light, all imbalance is cleansed and harmony restored."*
4. **Meditation on Healing the Earth**
   Sit quietly and visualize Raphael's emerald light descending into the Earth, healing its waters, lands, and atmosphere. Imagine this light flowing through you as a steward of creation.
5. **Seal the Ritual**
   Thank Raphael and extinguish the candles. Say:
   *"Raphael, divine healer, I thank you for your presence and guidance. May your light remain with me always."*

# Invocation for Binding Negativity

This invocation mirrors Raphael's act of binding Azazel, helping to overcome destructive forces or internal struggles.

*"Raphael, binder of discord,*

*By divine command, contain and dissolve all harm.*
*Let your light shield me and your wisdom guide me,*
*Restoring peace to my soul and balance to my path. Amen."*

Hold the green aventurine and visualize harmful energies being bound and neutralized in Raphael's light.

## Magical Correspondences

- **Colors:** Green (healing), white (purity), gold (divine authority)
- **Crystals:** Green aventurine (renewal), clear quartz (clarity), smoky quartz (neutralization)
- **Herbs:** Sage (cleansing), rosemary (protection), cedar (purification)
- **Incense:** Frankincense (spiritual purification), myrrh (grounding)
- **Symbols:** Emerald aura, salt, binding cords

## Raphael's Role in Healing and Judgment

The *Book of Enoch* provides profound insights into Raphael's dual mission of healing and judgment. By studying his actions and integrating their symbolic meanings into your practice, you can harness his transformative energy to purify, restore, and protect.

### Advanced Tips for Deepening Your Practice

1. **Meditation on Cosmic Balance:** Visualize Raphael's role as a mediator of mercy and judgment, integrating these energies within your spiritual practice.
2. **Regular Earth Healing Work:** Dedicate rituals to Raphael's Earth-healing mission, incorporating elements like plants, water, and natural crystals.

3. **Study of Enochian Texts:** Engage with the *Book of Enoch* regularly, focusing on Raphael's passages to deepen your understanding of his celestial role.

Through these practices, you align with Raphael's divine mission and contribute to the ongoing restoration of balance and harmony in the world and within yourself.

# Raphael in the Book of Jubilees: A Steward of Divine Order and Angelic Responsibilities

## A Record of Angelic Duties and Cosmic Balance

The *Book of Jubilees*, an ancient Jewish text often called "The Lesser Genesis," provides a rich framework for understanding the responsibilities of angels, including Archangel Raphael. This apocryphal text expands upon angelic roles in divine governance, revealing Raphael's duties as a healer, guide, and custodian of balance. For practitioners, the insights from the *Book of Jubilees* illuminate Raphael's connection to cosmic cycles, sacred timing, and humanity's covenant with creation.

# Historical and Spiritual Context

## The Book of Jubilees: An Overview

- **Origin and Content:** Written between the 2nd century BCE and the 1st century CE, the *Book of Jubilees* recounts biblical history from creation to the Exodus, emphasizing divine covenants and sacred timing.
- **Angelic Roles:** Jubilees details the angelic hierarchy, highlighting the roles of the "Angels of the Presence" and "Angels of Sanctification." Raphael's duties are inferred through his healing and guiding actions, aligning him with the Angels of the Presence who serve directly before God.

## Raphael's Responsibilities in Jubilees

- **Custodian of Sacred Timing:** Raphael's connection to the Earth's cycles and humanity's spiritual obligations links him to divine timing and the fulfillment of cosmic law.
- **Mediator of Covenants:** As a healer and guide, Raphael reinforces humanity's covenant with God by aiding in physical, spiritual, and ecological restoration.

## Esoteric Significance

- **Healing as Divine Stewardship:** Raphael's actions underscore the responsibility of maintaining harmony between divine law and earthly existence.
- **Sacred Time and Cycles:** Raphael's work resonates with the cycles of jubilees (50-year periods), symbolizing renewal and liberation.

# Symbolism and Esoteric Lessons

### 1. The Angelic Covenant

Raphael's role reflects the angels' responsibility to guide humanity in upholding divine law, particularly through healing and moral alignment.

### 2. Cosmic Renewal

In Jubilees, the cyclical nature of time mirrors Raphael's healing duties, where restoration is a continuous process aligned with divine will.

### 3. Guardianship of Sacred Spaces

Raphael's inferred duties include safeguarding sacred spaces and ensuring their purity, aligning with his role as a healer of creation.

# Ritual for Aligning with Sacred Cycles

This ritual connects you to Raphael's energy to harmonize with sacred timing and cosmic balance.

## Materials

- A green candle (symbolizing Raphael's healing energy)
- A small clock or timepiece (representing sacred timing)
- A piece of malachite or fluorite (symbolizing renewal)
- Frankincense incense
- A bowl of water with a sprig of rosemary (symbolizing purification and covenant)

## Steps

1. **Prepare Your Space**
   Light the green candle and incense. Place the clock, crystal, and bowl of water on your altar. Say:
   *"Raphael, custodian of sacred order, I call upon your light to align me with divine timing and cosmic balance."*
2. **Invoke Raphael's Presence**
   Hold the crystal in your hands and visualize Raphael's emerald light enveloping you. Say:
   *"Raphael, guardian of renewal and harmony, guide me to align with the sacred cycles of creation."*
3. **Focus on Sacred Timing**
   Gaze at the clock or timepiece, contemplating the passage of time as a divine rhythm. Dip the rosemary sprig into the water and sprinkle it around the space. Say:
   *"By Raphael's guidance, I align with the divine flow of time and the covenant of creation."*

4. **Meditate on Cosmic Renewal**
   Close your eyes and imagine the Earth bathed in Raphael's light, its cycles renewed and harmonized. Visualize yourself as a steward of these cycles.
5. **Seal the Ritual**
   Thank Raphael and extinguish the candle. Say: *"Raphael, healer and guide, I thank you for your presence and alignment. May your blessings sustain me in sacred harmony."*

## Invocation for Divine Alignment

This invocation draws on Raphael's inferred role in the *Book of Jubilees* to foster spiritual alignment with sacred cycles.

*"Raphael, steward of cosmic balance,*
*Guardian of divine timing and sacred renewal,*
*Align me with the rhythms of creation.*
*Guide my steps to honor the covenant of light,*
*And restore harmony to my path and the Earth.*
*In your name, I am whole. Amen."*

Dip your fingers in rosemary water and touch your forehead, heart, and palms as you recite the invocation.

## Magical Correspondences

- **Colors:** Green (healing), gold (divine timing), blue (cosmic truth)
- **Crystals:** Malachite (renewal), fluorite (clarity), moonstone (cyclical alignment)
- **Herbs:** Rosemary (purification), sage (cleansing), lavender (peace)
- **Incense:** Frankincense (spiritual connection), sandalwood (harmony)

- **Symbols:** Timepiece, emerald aura, sacred cycles

## Raphael's Role in Sacred Timing and Renewal

The *Book of Jubilees* offers a profound lens through which to view Raphael's responsibilities as a healer and mediator of divine order. By exploring these themes, practitioners can integrate Raphael's wisdom into their magical and spiritual practices.

### Advanced Tips for Deepening Your Practice

1. **Daily Rituals of Sacred Time:** Mark the beginning and end of each day with short prayers or invocations to Raphael, aligning with divine timing.
2. **Seasonal Celebrations:** Incorporate Raphael's energy into solstice or equinox rituals, honoring the Earth's cycles.
3. **Study of Jubilees' Themes:** Reflect on passages from the *Book of Jubilees* that emphasize angelic guidance and sacred timing to deepen your understanding of Raphael's cosmic role.

By working with Raphael in this context, you harmonize your spiritual practice with the rhythms of creation, fostering alignment with divine law and cosmic renewal.

## Raphael in the Testament of Solomon: Angelic Intervention and Mastery of Spiritual Forces

### A Guide to Overcoming Darkness

The *Testament of Solomon*, a pseudepigraphal text attributed to the legendary King Solomon, offers a unique perspective on angelic interactions. Archangel Raphael appears as a key figure in the text, assisting Solomon in his quest to command spirits and restore divine harmony. Raphael's role emphasizes healing, guidance, and the transcendence of human limitations through spiritual wisdom.

# Historical and Spiritual Context

## The Testament of Solomon: An Overview

- **Authorship and Significance:** Believed to have been composed between the 1st and 5th centuries CE, the *Testament of Solomon* is a mystical text that details King Solomon's ability to summon, command, and banish spirits through a divinely given ring.
- **Raphael's Role:** While the text focuses heavily on Solomon's interactions with spirits and demons, Raphael is invoked as an angelic intermediary, aiding in the purification of spaces and individuals from spiritual harm.

## Raphael's Contributions in the Text

- **Healing and Protection:** Raphael is associated with providing remedies for physical and spiritual ailments caused by malevolent spirits.
- **Guidance in Spiritual Mastery:** The archangel's wisdom assists Solomon in maintaining balance and aligning his practices with divine will.

## Mystical Significance

- **Mastery of Forces:** Raphael represents the divine authority that enables Solomon to command spiritual energies for the greater good.
- **Healing Through Alignment:** Raphael's interventions emphasize the importance of aligning human actions with divine principles to overcome adversity.

# Symbolism and Esoteric Lessons

### 1. The Healing Light of Raphael

In the *Testament of Solomon,* Raphael's energy is depicted as a purifying and restorative force, emphasizing his role as a healer of both physical and spiritual ailments.

### 2. The Ring of Power

The ring granted to Solomon symbolizes the integration of divine wisdom and earthly authority, with Raphael acting as a bridge between these realms.

### 3. Banishing Malevolence

Raphael's interventions highlight the triumph of divine light over darkness, teaching practitioners the importance of spiritual clarity and discipline in confronting negativity.

# Ritual for Spiritual Protection and Mastery

This ritual draws on Raphael's role in the *Testament of Solomon* to banish negative energies and cultivate spiritual authority.

## Materials

- A gold or silver ring (symbolizing divine authority)
- A white candle (purification) and a green candle (healing)
- A bowl of saltwater (cleansing)
- Frankincense incense
- A small sigil of Raphael (drawn or carved)

**Steps**

1. **Prepare the Space**
   Light the white and green candles and incense. Place the ring, bowl of saltwater, and sigil on your altar. Say:
   *"Raphael, divine healer and protector, I call upon your presence to cleanse and empower this space."*
2. **Invoke Raphael's Energy**
   Hold the ring in your hands and visualize it glowing with Raphael's emerald light. Say:
   *"By the light of Raphael, this ring becomes a symbol of divine authority, banishing all harm and restoring harmony."*
3. **Cleansing with Saltwater**
   Dip your fingers into the saltwater and sprinkle it around your space. Visualize Raphael's energy purifying the area. Say:
   *"By Raphael's wisdom and the waters of purity, all negativity is banished."*
4. **Meditation on Spiritual Authority**
   Place the ring on your finger and sit quietly. Imagine Raphael standing beside you, empowering you with clarity and strength to command spiritual forces. Say:
   *"With Raphael's guidance, I walk in divine light, free from harm and aligned with truth."*
5. **Seal the Ritual**
   Extinguish the candles and thank Raphael. Say:
   *"Raphael, I thank you for your protection and wisdom. May your blessings remain with me always."*

## Invocation for Mastery Over Challenges

This invocation channels Raphael's energy to help overcome spiritual and personal challenges.

*"Raphael, guardian of divine harmony,
Healer of wounds seen and unseen,
Grant me wisdom to command my path,*

*And strength to banish all that obstructs my light.
By your grace, I am whole, I am free, I am aligned."*

Hold the sigil of Raphael (see Appendix) to your heart as you recite the invocation, symbolizing the integration of his energy within you.

## Magical Correspondences

- **Colors:** Green (healing), white (purification), gold (divine authority)
- **Crystals:** Clear quartz (clarity), amethyst (spiritual strength), green aventurine (renewal)
- **Herbs:** Sage (cleansing), rosemary (protection), bay leaf (spiritual authority)
- **Incense:** Frankincense (purification), sandalwood (spiritual connection)
- **Symbols:** Raphael's sigil, Solomon's ring, emerald aura

## Raphael's Wisdom in the *Testament of Solomon*

The *Testament of Solomon* highlights Raphael's pivotal role in empowering spiritual mastery and protection. By working with his energy, practitioners can navigate spiritual challenges, maintain harmony, and align with divine purpose.

### Advanced Tips for Deepening Your Practice

1. **Create a Permanent Sigil for Protection:** Keep Raphael's sigil near your altar or workspace to maintain his protective energy.
2. **Incorporate the Ring into Daily Practice:** Use a ring or similar object as a talisman, periodically recharging it through rituals invoking Raphael.

3. **Study Angelic Command:** Reflect on passages from the *Testament of Solomon* that describe angelic interactions, using them as a guide for developing spiritual authority.

By integrating these teachings and practices, you deepen your connection to Raphael, enabling his wisdom and protection to guide you in achieving balance, healing, and spiritual mastery.

# Zohar and Kabbalistic Insights: Raphael's Role in Angelic Healing

## A Guide to Divine Harmony and Restoration

In the mystical tradition of the *Zohar* and Kabbalistic teachings, Archangel Raphael is revered as a divine healer whose energy harmonizes the physical and spiritual realms. These insights illuminate Raphael's connection to the *sefirot* (emanations of divine energy), emphasizing his role in restoring balance and guiding humanity toward unity with the Creator. For the practicing magician, this sacred knowledge offers profound frameworks for invoking Raphael's healing power and aligning with divine harmony.

# Historical and Spiritual Context

## The Zohar: A Mystical Cornerstone

- **Foundational Text:** The *Zohar* is the central text of Kabbalistic mysticism, attributed to Rabbi Shimon bar Yochai (2nd century CE) and written in Aramaic. It offers esoteric interpretations of the Torah, emphasizing divine emanations, cosmic balance, and spiritual ascent.

- **Raphael's Presence:** Though not always named explicitly, Raphael's qualities align with key Kabbalistic concepts, particularly within the *sefirot*.

## Raphael and the *Sefirot*

- **Tiferet (Beauty, Harmony):** Raphael's healing light corresponds to *Tiferet*, the central *sefirah* representing balance, compassion, and divine alignment.
- **Yesod (Foundation):** As a mediator between spiritual and physical realms, Raphael also resonates with *Yesod*, which bridges the divine flow to the material world.
- **Hod (Splendor):** Raphael's wisdom and clarity align with *Hod*, emphasizing intellectual healing and understanding.

## Healing Through Divine Flow

In Kabbalistic tradition, healing is viewed as restoring the flow of divine energy through the *sefirot*. Raphael facilitates this restoration, mending disruptions caused by spiritual, emotional, or physical imbalances.

# Symbolism and Esoteric Lessons

### 1. The Emerald Light of Raphael

In Kabbalistic thought, green represents life, renewal, and the flow of divine abundance. Raphael's emerald light symbolizes the healing energy that restores equilibrium across all planes.

### 2. The Tree of Life as a Healing Map

The Tree of Life, a central Kabbalistic symbol, provides a blueprint for Raphael's healing work. By moving through the *sefirot*, one can channel Raphael's energy to address specific areas of imbalance.

### 3. The Healing Name of God

Kabbalistic practice often involves the invocation of divine names. The *Zohar* emphasizes the use of sacred names to access angelic and divine energies. Raphael's connection to the name *YHVH* (יהוה) is particularly significant in healing rituals.

## Kabbalistic Healing Ritual with Raphael

This ritual uses the *sefirot* and sacred names to invoke Raphael's energy for holistic healing.

## Materials

- A diagram of the Tree of Life (for focus)
- A green candle (symbolizing Raphael's healing light)
- A piece of green aventurine or emerald (for renewal)
- Frankincense incense (to elevate the space)
- A small bowl of water (representing *Yesod* and the flow of life)

**Steps**

1. **Prepare the Space**
   Light the green candle and incense. Place the Tree of Life diagram, stone, and water bowl on your altar. Say: "Raphael, divine healer, I call upon your presence to restore balance and harmony."
2. **Focus on the Tree of Life**
   Meditate on the *sefirot*, beginning with *Malkhut* (Earthly realm) and ascending toward *Tiferet*. Visualize divine energy flowing through the Tree into your being.

3. **Invoke Raphael Through Sacred Names**
   Chant:
   *"YHVH, Elohim, El Shaddai,*
   *By your names, may Raphael's light descend.*
   *Heal and restore, renew and align,*
   *In your eternal harmony, I am whole."*
4. **Channel Raphael's Energy**
   Hold the crystal in your hands. Visualize Raphael's emerald light enveloping you, focusing on any areas of imbalance. Say:
   *"Raphael, healer of light, flow through me. Restore the paths of the Tree within and around me."*
5. **Use the Water for Cleansing**
   Dip your fingers in the water and touch your forehead, heart, and palms, symbolizing the alignment of thought, emotion, and action with divine healing. Say:
   *"Through Raphael's guidance, I am purified, balanced, and renewed."*
6. **Conclude the Ritual**
   Extinguish the candle and thank Raphael. Say:
   *"Raphael, I thank you for your light and wisdom. May your healing presence remain with me always."*

# Meditation for Aligning with *Tiferet*

This meditation aligns your energy with Raphael's healing flow through the central *sefirah* of *Tiferet*.

1. **Visualize the Tree of Life:** Picture yourself standing at the base of the Tree.
2. **Ascend to *Tiferet*:** Imagine golden-green light flowing from *Tiferet* into your heart, harmonizing your body, mind, and spirit.
3. **Chant the Name of God:** Whisper *YHVH* repeatedly, feeling its vibration resonate through you.

## Magical Correspondences

- **Colors:** Green (healing and renewal), gold (divine balance)
- **Crystals:** Green aventurine (healing), emerald (renewal), clear quartz (clarity)
- **Herbs:** Sage (cleansing), rosemary (memory and alignment), lavender (peace)
- **Incense:** Frankincense (spiritual elevation), sandalwood (harmony)
- **Symbols:** Tree of Life, emerald aura, sacred names

## Raphael's Kabbalistic Wisdom

The *Zohar* and Kabbalistic teachings provide profound insights into Raphael's healing energy and its connection to divine harmony. By working with the *sefirot* and invoking sacred names, practitioners can channel Raphael's energy to restore balance, elevate their spiritual practice, and deepen their connection to divine wisdom.

### Advanced Tips for Deepening Your Practice

1. **Daily Meditation on the Tree of Life:** Regularly visualize the Tree of Life, focusing on *Tiferet* as Raphael's seat of healing energy.
2. **Work with Sacred Names:** Study and integrate the sacred names associated with healing, using them in rituals and meditations.
3. **Combine with Planetary Timing:** Perform rituals invoking Raphael during Mercury's planetary hours to align with his celestial correspondence.

By integrating these practices, you cultivate a profound relationship with Raphael, unlocking his healing light and wisdom for both personal and universal transformation.

# Sefer Raziel HaMalakh: Raphael and Angelic Invocations

## A Gateway to Divine Mysteries

The *Sefer Raziel HaMalakh* (Book of the Angel Raziel) is a mystical text attributed to the angel Raziel, believed to have delivered divine secrets to Adam. Among these secrets are detailed instructions for invoking angelic beings, including Raphael. This text serves as a foundational source for magicians seeking to align with angelic energies and access divine wisdom. Raphael's presence in this text underscores his role as a healer and guide, making him an essential ally in esoteric and magical practices.

# Historical and Spiritual Context

## The Sefer Raziel HaMalakh

- **Origin and Content:** Believed to have originated in the Middle Ages, this text compiles Kabbalistic, astrological, and magical knowledge, emphasizing the power of divine names and angelic invocations.
- **Raphael's Role:** As one of the primary archangels, Raphael is frequently invoked for healing, protection, and guidance. His name appears in conjunction with sacred names of God and specific invocations to summon his presence.

## The Structure of Angelic Invocations

The *Sefer Raziel* outlines precise methods for angelic invocations, which include:

1. **Preparation:** Purification of the practitioner and sacred space.

2. **Sacred Names:** Chanting of divine names to open spiritual pathways.
3. **Symbolic Tools:** Use of sigils, talismans, and sacred objects to anchor angelic energies.
4. **Focused Intent:** A clear purpose for summoning the angel.

## Symbolism and Esoteric Lessons

### 1. Raphael's Sigil

The sigil of Raphael, often featured in the text, acts as a gateway to his energy. Its intricate lines represent his healing light and connection to divine harmony.

### 2. The Power of Sacred Names

The *Sefer Raziel* emphasizes the invocation of specific divine names, such as *YHVH* (יהוה) and *El Shaddai* (אל שדי), to align with Raphael's energy and invite his presence.

### 3. The Emerald Light

As in other mystical traditions, Raphael's emerald light symbolizes renewal, balance, and the flow of divine healing through the Tree of Life.

## Ritual for Invoking Raphael Using the Sefer Raziel

### Materials

- A green candle (symbolizing Raphael's healing energy)
- A small parchment with Raphael's sigil (drawn by hand)

- Frankincense incense
- A piece of green aventurine or clear quartz
- A bowl of water (symbolizing purification)
- The divine names: *YHVH*, *El Shaddai*, and *Adonai Tzva'ot*

**Steps**

1. **Purify Yourself and the Space**
   Wash your hands and sprinkle water around the space, symbolizing spiritual cleansing. Say:
   *"By the sacred waters of purification, may this space be prepared for divine presence."*
2. **Light the Candle and Incense**
   Light the green candle and incense, focusing on the rising smoke as a vehicle for your intentions. Say:
   *"Raphael, divine healer and guide, I invite your presence into this sacred space."*
3. **Activate Raphael's Sigil**
   Hold the parchment with Raphael's sigil in your hands. Visualize the sigil glowing with emerald light. Chant the divine names:
   *"YHVH, El Shaddai, Adonai Tzva'ot. By these sacred names, I call upon Raphael, healer of light and protector of harmony."*
4. **Invoke Raphael's Energy**
   Place the parchment on the altar and hold the crystal over it. Visualize Raphael's emerald light descending, filling the space with warmth and healing. Say:
   *"Raphael, bearer of divine healing, surround me with your light. Cleanse my spirit, align my path, and restore my balance."*
5. **Meditate on Raphael's Presence**
   Sit quietly, holding the crystal. Imagine Raphael standing before you, his emerald wings enveloping you in healing energy. Whisper:
   *"Raphael, healer of hearts, restore and renew me in divine grace."*
6. **Seal the Ritual**
   Extinguish the candle and thank Raphael. Say:

*"Raphael, I thank you for your presence and light. May your blessings remain with me always."*

## Invocation for Healing and Guidance

This invocation uses sacred names from the *Sefer Raziel* to call upon Raphael for healing and guidance.

*"YHVH, the Eternal Source,
El Shaddai, the Almighty One,
Adonai Tzva'ot, Lord of Hosts,
By your names, I call upon Raphael,
Guardian of healing and light.
Surround me with your emerald grace,
And guide me on the path of wholeness. Amen."*

Trace Raphael's sigil in the air with your finger as you speak, visualizing its lines glowing with light.

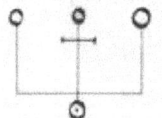

## Magical Correspondences

- **Colors:** Green (healing and renewal), gold (divine light)
- **Crystals:** Green aventurine (healing), emerald (renewal), selenite (clarity)
- **Herbs:** Rosemary (protection), lavender (peace), sage (cleansing)
- **Incense:** Frankincense (spiritual connection), myrrh (grounding)
- **Symbols:** Raphael's sigil, emerald aura, sacred names

# Raphael in the Sefer Raziel HaMalakh

The *Sefer Raziel HaMalakh* provides a detailed and structured approach to invoking Raphael, emphasizing the importance of preparation, sacred names, and focused intent. This text offers magicians a profound tool for accessing Raphael's healing and guiding energy, aligning with divine harmony and wisdom.

## Advanced Tips for Deepening Your Practice

1. **Create a Dedicated Raphael Sigil:** Use parchment or wood to craft a permanent sigil of Raphael, empowering it with rituals like the one above.
2. **Study the Sefer Raziel Regularly:** Reflect on its teachings to deepen your understanding of angelic hierarchies and their roles.
3. **Incorporate Planetary Energies:** Align your invocations with Mercury's planetary hours to enhance your connection with Raphael.

By integrating these practices, you build a strong, harmonious relationship with Raphael, enabling his light and wisdom to transform your magical and spiritual path.

# Raphael in the Key of Solomon and the Sixth and Seventh Books of Moses: Rituals and Sigils of Healing and Guidance

## Unlocking Ancient Magical Systems

The *Key of Solomon* and the *Sixth and Seventh Books of Moses* are two of the most influential grimoires in Western esotericism. These texts are rich with rituals, invocations, and sigils designed to summon angelic and divine powers. Archangel Raphael features prominently within these traditions as a figure of healing, guidance, and protection. By exploring these texts, magicians can deepen their connection with Raphael and integrate his energy into a structured magical practice.

# Historical and Spiritual Context

## The Key of Solomon

- **Origins and Influence:** Attributed to King Solomon, this grimoire is a cornerstone of ceremonial magic, likely composed in the 14th or 15th century. It outlines methods for invoking angelic and planetary forces to achieve spiritual and material goals.
- **Raphael's Role:** In the *Key of Solomon*, Raphael is invoked primarily for healing, protection, and spiritual enlightenment. He is often associated with Mercury, which governs communication, wisdom, and travel.

## The Sixth and Seventh Books of Moses

- **Biblical-Mystical Roots:** These grimoires, attributed to the legendary knowledge of Moses, combine Christian, Jewish, and folk magic elements. They include invocations, seals, and sigils for summoning angelic powers.
- **Raphael's Place:** Raphael is identified as a healer and guide, often invoked through specific seals and divine names to facilitate healing and protection.

## Magical Principles in Both Texts

- **Sacred Names and Symbols:** Both grimoires emphasize the power of sacred names, sigils, and rituals to connect with Raphael's energy.
- **Planetary and Elemental Alignments:** Raphael's association with Mercury and the element of air is central to these texts, reflecting his role in communication and healing.

# Symbolism and Esoteric Lessons

### 1. Sigils as Angelic Gateways

Sigils attributed to Raphael serve as conduits for his energy, amplifying intentions for healing, protection, and spiritual clarity.

### 2. Sacred Names of Power

The divine names invoked alongside Raphael's sigils—such as *YHVH* (יהוה), *Adonai* (אדני), and *El Shaddai* (אל שדי)—serve to focus and elevate the practitioner's spiritual energy.

### 3. Ritual Tools

The use of specific tools, such as a consecrated wand or staff, reflects Raphael's role as a guide. These tools symbolize the practitioner's alignment with divine wisdom.

# Raphael's Healing Ritual from the Key of Solomon

This ritual invokes Raphael for physical, emotional, or spiritual healing.

## Materials

- A green candle (symbolizing Raphael's healing light)
- Frankincense incense
- A parchment with Raphael's sigil (from the *Key of Solomon*)
- A consecrated wand or staff
- A small bowl of spring water

**Steps**

1. **Prepare Your Space**
   Cleanse the area with incense and sprinkle the spring water, saying:
   *"By the light of divine purity, may this space be prepared for the presence of Raphael."*
2. **Light the Candle and Incense**
   Light the green candle and incense. Focus on the flame as a connection to Raphael's healing energy. Say:
   *"Raphael, healer of the divine, I call upon your presence to restore balance and harmony."*
3. **Activate Raphael's Sigil**
   Hold the parchment with Raphael's sigil. Trace its lines with your wand or finger, visualizing it glowing with emerald light. Chant:
   *"YHVH, Elohim, Raphael. By these sacred names, I invoke the light of healing and renewal."*
4. **Invoke Raphael's Energy**
   Place the sigil on your altar and dip your fingers into the spring water. Touch your forehead, heart, and hands, saying:
   *"Raphael, flow through me with your healing grace. Restore my body, mind, and spirit to wholeness."*
5. **Meditate on Healing**
   Sit quietly, visualizing Raphael's wings enveloping you, their emerald glow filling you with vitality and peace.
6. **Seal the Ritual**
   Extinguish the candle and thank Raphael. Say:
   *"Raphael, I thank you for your light and guidance. May your blessings remain with me always."*

# Protection Ritual from the Sixth and Seventh Books of Moses

This ritual invokes Raphael for protection during travel or spiritual work.

## Materials

- A parchment with Raphael's sigil (from the *Sixth and Seventh Books of Moses*)
- A blue or white candle
- Sandalwood incense
- A feather (symbolizing Raphael's association with air)

**Steps**

1. **Set the Intent**
   Light the candle and incense, focusing on your intent for protection. Say:
   *"Raphael, guardian of light and protector of travelers, shield me with your divine presence."*
2. **Activate the Sigil**
   Hold the sigil in your hands, visualizing it glowing with light. Say:
   *"By the sacred names of Adonai and El Shaddai, I invoke Raphael to guard my path."*
3. **Create a Protective Aura**
   Wave the feather around yourself, imagining Raphael's wings surrounding you in a shield of light. Say:
   *"Raphael, by your wings, I am safe. By your light, I am guided."*
4. **Carry the Sigil**
   Keep the sigil with you as a talisman during your travels or spiritual endeavors.

## Magical Correspondences

- **Colors:** Green (healing), white (protection), blue (guidance)
- **Crystals:** Green aventurine (healing), clear quartz (clarity), amethyst (spiritual protection)
- **Herbs:** Sage (cleansing), rosemary (protection), lavender (calm)

- **Incense:** Frankincense (spiritual elevation), sandalwood (grounding)
- **Symbols:** Raphael's sigil, wand, feather

## Raphael's Wisdom in the Grimoires

The *Key of Solomon* and the *Sixth and Seventh Books of Moses* provide practical tools for working with Raphael's energy, offering rituals and sigils to facilitate healing, protection, and spiritual enlightenment.

## Advanced Tips for Deepening Your Practice

1. **Daily Use of Sigils:** Draw Raphael's sigil on parchment or jewelry to keep his energy present in your daily life.
2. **Combine with Planetary Magic:** Perform rituals during Mercury's planetary hours to enhance their efficacy.
3. **Study the Grimoires Thoroughly:** Reflect on the texts' descriptions of angelic hierarchies and divine names to refine your invocations.

By integrating these practices, you cultivate a deeper connection with Raphael, unlocking his transformative energy to guide and heal your life and spiritual path.

## Raphael in The Sworn Book of Honorius and the Grimoire of Armadel: Pathways to Angelic Wisdom and Healing

### Unlocking Raphael's Presence in Folk and Magical Texts

The *Sworn Book of Honorius* and the *Grimoire of Armadel* stand as significant texts within the Western esoteric tradition, offering profound insights into angelic invocation and magical practice. These grimoires provide structured rituals, sigils, and divine names for connecting with archangels, including Raphael. As a magician deeply connected with Raphael, these texts can serve as vital tools for invoking his healing energy, spiritual guidance, and protective presence.

## Historical and Spiritual Context

### The Sworn Book of Honorius

- **Origins and Influence:** Dating back to the 13th century, the *Sworn Book of Honorius* is attributed to Honorius of Thebes. This grimoire emphasizes attaining divine wisdom through angelic invocation, focusing on purification, alignment, and spiritual elevation.
- **Raphael's Role:** In the *Sworn Book*, Raphael is invoked as a mediator of divine grace, protector against spiritual harm, and healer of the soul. His role aligns with the magician's goal of achieving divine alignment.

### The Grimoire of Armadel

- **Mystical Knowledge:** A 17th-century grimoire, the *Grimoire of Armadel* focuses on angelic sigils and their application in spiritual development and practical magic.
- **Raphael's Presence:** Raphael's sigils are explicitly linked to healing, wisdom, and divine protection, reflecting his celestial responsibilities.

### Key Principles Across Both Grimoires

1. **Purity of Intent:** Both texts stress the importance of purity and alignment with divine will before summoning angelic energies.

2. **Sacred Names and Sigils:** Invocations often involve sacred names of God, combined with Raphael's sigils, to channel his energy effectively.
3. **Angelic Hierarchy:** The grimoires present Raphael as part of a larger celestial hierarchy, working in harmony with other archangels.

## Symbolism and Esoteric Lessons

### 1. The Healing Sigil of Raphael

In the *Grimoire of Armadel*, Raphael's sigil serves as a focal point for invoking his presence. The intricate lines of the sigil symbolize the flow of divine energy, harmonizing the practitioner with Raphael's healing light.

### 2. Sacred Names as Keys

The *Sworn Book of Honorius* emphasizes the use of sacred names such as *El Shaddai*, *Adonai*, and *YHVH* to connect with divine forces. These names, combined with Raphael's sigil, unlock his healing and guiding energies.

### 3. Ritual Tools

Tools such as consecrated wands, parchment, and candles are essential for creating a sacred space, amplifying the practitioner's connection to Raphael.

## Healing and Guidance Ritual from The Sworn Book of Honorius

### Materials

- A green and a white candle
- A parchment with Raphael's sigil (from the *Sworn Book of Honorius*)
- Frankincense incense
- A small bowl of consecrated water
- A wand or staff (symbolizing guidance)

**Steps**

1. **Purify the Space and Yourself**
   Sprinkle consecrated water around the room and on yourself, saying:
   *"By the waters of divine purity, may this space be prepared for the presence of Raphael."*
2. **Light the Candles and Incense**
   Light the green candle (healing) and white candle (purity). Focus on the flames as representations of divine energy. Say:
   *"Raphael, divine healer and guide, I call upon your presence to bring light and harmony."*
3. **Activate Raphael's Sigil**
   Hold the sigil over the green candle flame (without burning it), visualizing it glowing with emerald light. Chant the sacred names:
   *"El Shaddai, Adonai, YHVH. By these sacred names, I invoke Raphael's light and grace."*
4. **Invoke Raphael's Healing Energy**
   Place the sigil on your altar and dip the wand into the

bowl of consecrated water. Touch it to your forehead, heart, and palms, saying:
*"Raphael, flow through me with your healing grace. Restore my body, mind, and spirit to divine harmony."*

5. **Meditate on Raphael's Presence**
Sit quietly, holding the wand. Visualize Raphael standing before you, his emerald wings enveloping you in light. Whisper:
*"Raphael, guardian of divine harmony, heal and guide me."*

6. **Seal the Ritual**
Extinguish the candles and thank Raphael. Say:
*"Raphael, I thank you for your presence and light. May your blessings remain with me always."*

# Protection and Wisdom Ritual from the Grimoire of Armadel

## Materials

- A parchment with Raphael's sigil (from the *Grimoire of Armadel*, See Appendix)
- A blue candle (symbolizing wisdom and guidance)
- Sandalwood incense
- A feather (symbolizing Raphael's association with air)

**Steps**

1. **Set the Space**
Light the blue candle and incense, focusing on your intent for wisdom and protection. Say:
*"Raphael, divine protector and guide, I invite your presence into this sacred space."*

2. **Activate Raphael's Sigil**
Hold the parchment with the sigil in your hands. Visualize it glowing with divine light. Say:

> "By the sacred names of Adonai and El Shaddai, I invoke Raphael to guard my path."

3. **Create a Protective Aura**
   Use the feather to wave incense smoke around yourself, imagining Raphael's wings surrounding you with light. Say:
   > "Raphael, shield me with your wings, and guide me with your wisdom."
4. **Meditate on Clarity and Protection**
   Sit quietly, holding the sigil. Visualize Raphael's light illuminating your mind and shielding your spirit.

## Magical Correspondences

- **Colors:** Green (healing), blue (wisdom), white (purity)
- **Crystals:** Green aventurine (renewal), clear quartz (clarity), lapis lazuli (wisdom)
- **Herbs:** Sage (cleansing), rosemary (protection), lavender (peace)
- **Incense:** Frankincense (elevation), sandalwood (guidance)
- **Symbols:** Raphael's sigil, wand, feather

## Raphael's Wisdom in Folk and Magical Texts

The *Sworn Book of Honorius* and the *Grimoire of Armadel* offer profound frameworks for connecting with Raphael's energy. By combining sacred names, sigils, and ritual tools, these texts guide practitioners in channeling Raphael's healing, protection, and wisdom.

## Advanced Tips for Deepening Your Practice

1. **Craft a Dedicated Raphael Sigil:** Keep his sigil near your altar or in your workspace to maintain a connection to his energy.

2. **Combine with Planetary Timing:** Perform rituals invoking Raphael during Mercury's planetary hours for enhanced effectiveness.
3. **Study Angelic Names:** Reflect on the divine names and their meanings, integrating them into your rituals for deeper alignment with Raphael's essence.

By integrating these practices, you align with Raphael's divine energy, enabling his healing and guiding light to transform your magical and spiritual path.

# Raphael in the Greek Magical Papyri: Angelic Invocation in Ancient Traditions

## Ancient Wisdom Meets Angelic Presence

The *Greek Magical Papyri* (PGM), a collection of magical texts from Greco-Roman Egypt, provides a unique lens for understanding angelic invocation. These texts blend Egyptian, Greek, and Jewish traditions, forming a rich tapestry of magical practice. Within this framework, Raphael emerges as a figure associated with healing, guidance, and divine light. For the magician, the PGM offers powerful methods to integrate Raphael's energy into ritual work, connecting ancient practices with modern spiritual goals.

# Historical and Spiritual Context

## The Greek Magical Papyri: An Overview

- **Origins and Scope:** The PGM, dating from the 2nd century BCE to the 5th century CE, comprises spells, hymns, invocations, and rituals for purposes ranging from healing to protection.
- **Angelic Influence:** Jewish and Christian influences permeate many texts, introducing angelic figures, divine names, and invocations into the Greco-Egyptian magical tradition.

## Raphael in the PGM

- **Healing and Protection:** Raphael's reputation as a healer aligns with the PGM's emphasis on physical and spiritual restoration.
- **Mediator of Divine Light:** Raphael's connection to divine wisdom and cosmic harmony resonates with the PGM's focus on accessing higher spiritual realms.

## Key Features of Raphael's Presence

1. **Divine Names and Angelic Hierarchies:** The PGM often invokes angels alongside sacred names, such as *IAO* (a Greek transliteration of YHVH) and *Adonai*.
2. **Blended Symbolism:** Raphael's energy is adapted into the syncretic traditions of the PGM, combining Jewish angelology with Greco-Roman magical concepts.

# Symbolism and Esoteric Lessons

### 1. Raphael's Role as Healer

In the PGM, healing is viewed as a restoration of divine balance. Raphael's energy embodies this principle, offering renewal for body, mind, and spirit.

### 2. Invoking Light Through Sacred Names

The PGM emphasizes the power of divine names to open channels for angelic presence. Raphael's connection to light and healing is amplified through these invocations.

### 3. Magical Symbols and Tools

The PGM incorporates symbols, amulets, and ritual tools to anchor angelic energies. Raphael's presence is often invoked through specific gestures, chants, and sacred objects.

# Healing Ritual Inspired by the PGM

## Materials

- A gold or green candle (symbolizing divine light and healing)
- Frankincense incense
- A parchment or amulet with Raphael's name in Greek (*Ραφαήλ*)
- A bowl of spring water mixed with a pinch of salt (purification)
- A small mirror (symbolizing reflection and clarity)

**Steps**

1. **Prepare the Space**
   Light the candle and incense. Sprinkle the salt water around the space, saying:
   *"By the light of IAO, may this space be cleansed and made sacred for the presence of Raphael."*
2. **Activate Raphael's Name**
   Hold the parchment or amulet with Raphael's name and trace the letters with your finger or wand, visualizing them glowing with emerald light. Say:
   *"Raphael, healer of divine light, I invoke you by the sacred name of Adonai, to bring your presence into this space."*
3. **Invoke Raphael's Healing Energy**
   Place the mirror before the candle and gaze into it. Visualize Raphael's emerald light flowing through the flame and reflecting into you. Say:
   *"Raphael, healer of the divine, let your light flow through me. Restore my body, mind, and spirit to perfect harmony."*
4. **Purify with Sacred Water**
   Dip your fingers into the water and touch your forehead, heart, and hands. Whisper:
   *"By the waters of life and Raphael's grace, I am healed, renewed, and whole."*

5. **Seal the Ritual**
   Extinguish the candle and thank Raphael. Say:
   *"Raphael, I thank you for your light and healing. May your blessings remain with me always."*

## Invocation for Protection and Guidance

This invocation calls upon Raphael's protective energy as adapted from the PGM.

*"IAO, Adonai, Elohim,
By these sacred names, I call upon Raphael,
Guardian of light and divine healer.
Surround me with your wings of emerald light,
Guide my path and shield me from harm.
By your grace, I am safe, I am whole, I am aligned."*

Hold your arms outward, palms up, as if receiving Raphael's light, then bring your hands to your heart in gratitude.

## Magical Correspondences

- **Colors:** Green (healing), gold (divine light), blue (wisdom)
- **Crystals:** Emerald (renewal), green aventurine (healing), clear quartz (clarity)
- **Herbs:** Rosemary (protection), sage (cleansing), thyme (healing)
- **Incense:** Frankincense (spiritual elevation), myrrh (grounding)
- **Symbols:** Raphael's name in Greek, a mirror (reflection), salt water (purification)

# Raphael's Energy in the Greek Magical Papyri

The *Greek Magical Papyri* offers a unique perspective on working with Raphael, blending angelic invocation with ancient magical practices. By integrating Raphael's energy into your rituals, you can access his healing light, protection, and guidance in profound and transformative ways.

## Advanced Tips for Deepening Your Practice

1. **Study the PGM's Angelic Invocations:** Reflect on how the PGM incorporates angelic hierarchies and adapt these techniques to your own rituals.
2. **Use Greek Names and Sigils:** Incorporate Greek spellings and symbols into your work with Raphael to align with the PGM's tradition.
3. **Combine with Elemental Magic:** Use the PGM's elemental correspondences (air for Raphael) to deepen your connection to his energy.

Through these practices, you enhance your understanding of Raphael's energy and align with the ancient wisdom preserved in the *Greek Magical Papyri*. This integration offers a bridge between historical traditions and your modern magical path.

# Raphael and Comparative Mythology: Healing Archetypes Across Cultures

## An Amalgamation of Universal Healing

Archangel Raphael's attributes as a healer and guide resonate deeply with healing figures in comparative mythology. Parallels with Asclepius (Greek), Thoth (Egyptian), and Dhanvantari (Hindu) reveal Raphael's archetype as a universal symbol of restoration, wisdom, and divine intervention. Exploring these connections offers a broader understanding of healing practices and provides rich material for crafting rituals that integrate Raphael's energy with these traditions.

## Historical and Spiritual Context

### Raphael and Asclepius: The Divine Physician

- **Asclepius in Greek Mythology:** A god of healing and medicine, Asclepius was believed to possess the power to restore life. He is often depicted holding a rod entwined with a serpent, a symbol of healing and transformation.
- **Connections to Raphael:** Both figures are associated with divine healing, protection, and guidance. Raphael's role in the *Book of Tobit* parallels Asclepius's role as a compassionate healer who bridges mortal and divine realms.

### Raphael and Thoth: Keeper of Knowledge

- **Thoth in Egyptian Mythology:** Known as the god of wisdom, writing, and medicine, Thoth is a scribe of the gods and a master of sacred knowledge. He is often depicted with an ibis or baboon and carries tools of measurement and writing.
- **Connections to Raphael:** Like Thoth, Raphael is a mediator of divine wisdom and a guide for spiritual transformation. Both figures emphasize the integration of intellectual and spiritual healing.

### Raphael and Dhanvantari: The Divine Healer

- **Dhanvantari in Hindu Mythology:** Revered as the physician of the gods and an incarnation of Vishnu, Dhanvantari is associated with Ayurveda, the traditional Indian system of medicine. He is often depicted holding a pot of amrita (nectar of immortality).
- **Connections to Raphael:** Both figures represent holistic healing and divine restoration. Raphael's

emerald light echoes Dhanvantari's nectar of immortality, symbolizing renewal and vitality.

## Symbolism and Esoteric Lessons

### 1. Healing as Transformation

The serpent of Asclepius, the writing of Thoth, and the amrita of Dhanvantari all symbolize transformation through healing, aligning with Raphael's role as a divine restorer.

### 2. The Bridge Between Realms

Each figure serves as an intermediary between the divine and human realms, guiding practitioners toward balance, wisdom, and spiritual elevation.

### 3. Holistic Healing

The focus on physical, mental, and spiritual health in these traditions underscores Raphael's comprehensive approach to restoration.

## Ritual of Universal Healing

This ritual integrates the energies of Raphael, Asclepius, Thoth, and Dhanvantari for holistic healing.

## Materials

- A green candle (Raphael), white candle (Thoth), blue candle (Dhanvantari), and gold candle (Asclepius)
- A small bowl of water (purification)
- A feather (Thoth's wisdom)
- A serpent-shaped charm (Asclepius's transformation)
- A small container of honey or herbal tea (Dhanvantari's nectar)

**Steps**

1. **Prepare the Space**
   Arrange the candles in a circle, with the bowl of water in the center. Light the candles, starting with green, and say:
   *"I call upon Raphael, healer of divine light, to guide this circle of healing."*
   Continue lighting each candle, invoking the corresponding figure.
2. **Invoke Universal Healing**
   Hold the feather and dip it into the water. Wave it over the candles, saying:
   *"By Thoth's wisdom, Raphael's light, Dhanvantari's nectar, and Asclepius's transformation, may healing flow into this space."*
3. **Meditate on Divine Light**
   Sit quietly, visualizing each figure's energy blending into a radiant sphere of healing light. Whisper:
   *"I am restored, I am whole, I am aligned."*
4. **Drink the Nectar**
   Sip the honey or tea, symbolizing divine restoration. Say:
   *"With this nectar, I embody divine renewal and vitality."*
5. **Seal the Ritual**
   Extinguish the candles in reverse order, thanking each figure. Say:
   *"Raphael and healers divine, I thank you for your light and wisdom. May your blessings remain with me."*

# Invocation for Divine Healing

This invocation calls upon the combined energies of Raphael, Asclepius, Thoth, and Dhanvantari.

*"Raphael, divine healer of light,*
*Asclepius, guardian of transformation,*
*Thoth, keeper of wisdom and balance,*

*Dhanvantari, bearer of the nectar of life,*
*Together, restore me to harmony and grace.*
*Through your guidance, I am whole."*

Hold the serpent charm in one hand and the feather in the other, symbolizing the integration of wisdom and transformation.

## Magical Correspondences

- **Colors:** Green (Raphael's healing), gold (Asclepius's transformation), white (Thoth's wisdom), blue (Dhanvantari's renewal)
- **Crystals:** Emerald (Raphael), serpentine (Asclepius), lapis lazuli (Thoth), aquamarine (Dhanvantari)
- **Herbs:** Sage (cleansing), rosemary (healing), turmeric (renewal)
- **Incense:** Frankincense (spiritual elevation), sandalwood (balance), myrrh (grounding)
- **Symbols:** Serpent (transformation), feather (wisdom), amrita (renewal)

## Raphael Among Healing Archetypes

The parallels between Raphael, Asclepius, Thoth, and Dhanvantari illustrate the universal principles of healing, wisdom, and divine restoration. By weaving these traditions into your magical practice, you can access a profound synergy of energies for holistic transformation.

## Advanced Tips for Deepening Your Practice

1. **Integrate Mythological Studies:** Explore the myths and stories of Asclepius, Thoth, and Dhanvantari to enrich your understanding of their archetypes.

2. **Combine Practices:** Align rituals with specific healing needs by emphasizing the attributes of one figure over others.
3. **Seasonal and Lunar Timing:** Perform these rituals during significant celestial events, such as solstices or full moons, to amplify their power.

By embracing the shared wisdom of these figures, you deepen your relationship with Raphael and harmonize your practice with universal principles of healing and transformation.

# Raphael's Healing Role Across Cultures: A Universal Archetype of Restoration

## A Cross-Cultural Perspective on Divine Healing

Archangel Raphael's identity as a healer transcends religious boundaries, echoing through diverse cultural interpretations and mystical traditions. His role as a guide, protector, and restorer of balance aligns with archetypes found in global mythologies, from Christianity and Judaism to indigenous and Eastern spiritual practices. This exploration reveals the universality of Raphael's energy and offers practical methods to incorporate his cross-cultural resonance into your magical work.

# Historical and Spiritual Context

## Raphael in Abrahamic Traditions

- **Judaism:** In Jewish tradition, Raphael's name, *Rafa-El* ("God heals"), signifies his divine mission to restore health and harmony. The *Book of Tobit* explicitly portrays Raphael as a guide and healer, demonstrating his dual roles in physical and spiritual restoration.

- **Christianity:** Within Christian contexts, Raphael's role as a patron of healing extends to emotional and spiritual well-being, often depicted in Christian art guiding Tobias or interacting with humanity.
- **Islam:** Known as Israfil in Islamic tradition, Raphael's role is focused on cosmic renewal and spiritual awakening, aligning him with themes of divine restoration.

## Raphael in Indigenous and Shamanic Traditions

- **North American Indigenous Traditions:** Raphael's healing light finds parallels in the practices of shamanic healing, where spiritual guides and spirits of the air are invoked to restore balance to individuals and communities.
- **Andean Cosmology:** In the Andes, Raphael's energy resonates with Pachamama's life-sustaining essence, emphasizing harmony with nature and divine alignment.

## Raphael in Eastern Mysticism

- **Hinduism and Ayurveda:** Raphael's healing qualities parallel Dhanvantari, the divine physician and guardian of life's sacred nectar, symbolizing health and longevity.
- **Buddhism:** Though not directly named, Raphael's light mirrors the concept of compassionate healing embodied by bodhisattvas like Avalokiteshvara, emphasizing selflessness and spiritual renewal.

# Symbolism and Esoteric Lessons

### 1. The Universal Symbol of Light

Across cultures, light symbolizes healing, clarity, and transformation. Raphael's emerald light embodies these qualities, bridging the physical and spiritual realms.

## 2. Healing as Harmony

In cross-cultural contexts, healing is not merely physical restoration but the alignment of body, mind, and spirit with universal balance, a principle central to Raphael's energy.

## 3. The Air Element

Raphael's association with the element of air connects him to the breath of life, communication, and the flow of divine wisdom across traditions.

# Cross-Cultural Healing Ritual with Raphael

## Materials

- A green candle (Raphael's healing light)
- A feather (air element and indigenous wisdom)
- A small bowl of herbal tea or spring water (renewal)
- Incense (frankincense or sage for cleansing)

**Steps**

1. **Prepare Your Space**
   Light the candle and incense. Sprinkle the area with water, invoking Raphael's presence. Say:
   *"Raphael, universal healer, I call upon your light to fill this space."*
2. **Invoke Cross-Cultural Energies**
   Hold the feather and visualize the energies of various traditions blending with Raphael's light. Say:
   *"Raphael, I invoke your wisdom, guided by the sacred breath of life, the nectar of Dhanvantari, and the compassion of Avalokiteshvara."*

3. **Meditate on Harmony**
   Sit quietly, holding the feather. Imagine Raphael's emerald light merging with the elemental forces of air, water, and earth, filling you with vitality. Whisper:
   *"In your light, I am whole. In your guidance, I am healed."*
4. **Drink the Water or Tea**
   Sip the water or tea, symbolizing the integration of divine healing. Say:
   *"With this sacred drink, I embody the healing of the universe."*
5. **Seal the Ritual**
   Extinguish the candle and thank Raphael and the universal energies invoked. Say:
   *"Raphael, I thank you and all guiding forces of light. May your blessings remain with me."*

# Invocation for Cross-Cultural Healing

This invocation blends cultural elements to deepen your connection to Raphael.

*"Raphael, guardian of light and harmony,*
*Bearer of divine healing across all realms,*
*Guide me with the breath of life,*
*Heal me with the wisdom of all traditions.*
*Through your light, I am whole,*
*Through your guidance, I am renewed."*

Hold your hands palms upward, symbolizing openness to receiving universal healing energy.

# Magical Correspondences

- **Colors:** Green (healing), blue (spiritual renewal), gold (divine light)

- **Crystals:** Emerald (Raphael), turquoise (indigenous wisdom), lapis lazuli (Eastern mysticism)
- **Herbs:** Sage (cleansing), rosemary (protection), holy basil (renewal)
- **Incense:** Frankincense (spiritual connection), sandalwood (balance), myrrh (grounding)
- **Symbols:** Feather (air and spirit), amrita (nectar of life), emerald aura

## Raphael's Universal Healing Role

Raphael's healing role resonates across cultures, making him a universal symbol of restoration, balance, and spiritual guidance. By integrating cross-cultural elements into your practice, you can deepen your connection to Raphael and broaden your spiritual horizons.

### Advanced Tips for Deepening Your Practice

1. **Study Cross-Cultural Healing Figures:** Explore the myths and practices of Dhanvantari, Avalokiteshvara, and indigenous shamans to enhance your understanding of Raphael's archetype.
2. **Combine with Seasonal Energies:** Perform rituals aligned with solstices, equinoxes, or other natural cycles to amplify their transformative power.
3. **Create a Healing Mandala:** Incorporate symbols from multiple traditions into a mandala to serve as a focus for meditation and healing work.

Through these practices, you embody Raphael's light as a universal healer, aligning yourself with the divine harmony that transcends boundaries and traditions.

# Exploring Raphael in *Archangels and Ascended Masters* by Doreen Virtue: Modern Insights into Ancient Healing

## Raphael Through a Contemporary Lens

Doreen Virtue's *Archangels and Ascended Masters* offers a modern and accessible approach to understanding Archangel Raphael. This work integrates traditional depictions of Raphael with contemporary spiritual practices, providing tools for healing, guidance, and connection to his energy. By exploring this text, magicians can deepen their relationship with Raphael while blending ancient wisdom with modern applications.

# Historical and Spiritual Context

## Doreen Virtue's Approach to Angelic Guidance

- **A Practical Framework:** Virtue's text emphasizes direct, personal relationships with archangels, focusing on their attributes and how they can assist in daily life.
- **Raphael's Role:** Raphael is highlighted as the archangel of healing, associated with physical, emotional, and spiritual restoration. His role as a guide and protector of travelers also features prominently.
- **The Energy of Emerald Light:** Virtue consistently emphasizes Raphael's connection to emerald green energy, symbolizing growth, renewal, and the vibrational frequency of healing.

## Raphael in the Modern Spiritual Movement

- **Relevance to Holistic Practices:** Raphael is often invoked in contemporary healing modalities like Reiki, chakra alignment, and meditation.

- **Focus on Accessibility:** Virtue provides affirmations, invocations, and practical techniques to make Raphael's energy accessible to practitioners at all levels.

## Symbolism and Esoteric Lessons

### 1. The Healing Light of Raphael

Virtue describes Raphael's healing presence as a warm, emerald green light that envelops individuals, promoting balance and vitality.

### 2. Raphael as a Protector

In Virtue's work, Raphael is portrayed as a guide for travelers, safeguarding physical journeys and life paths. This protective quality is symbolized through visualization techniques and invocations.

### 3. Integrating Raphael into Daily Life

Virtue emphasizes Raphael's willingness to assist in everyday matters, from easing physical pain to providing clarity and emotional support.

## Healing Ritual Inspired by Archangels and Ascended Masters

### Materials

- A green candle (symbolizing Raphael's light)
- Frankincense or eucalyptus incense (for purification)
- A piece of green aventurine or malachite
- A glass of water (to hold Raphael's healing energy)

Steps

1. **Prepare Your Space**
   Light the green candle and incense. Create a quiet, meditative atmosphere. Say:
   *"Raphael, divine healer, I call upon your emerald light to fill this space with your healing grace."*
2. **Activate the Crystal**
   Hold the green aventurine or malachite in your hand. Visualize it glowing with emerald light, infused with Raphael's energy. Whisper:
   *"Raphael, infuse this crystal with your healing energy. Let it be a vessel of restoration and balance."*
3. **Invoke Raphael's Healing Presence**
   Close your eyes and place the crystal over the area needing healing (or your heart if the healing is emotional or spiritual). Say:
   *"Raphael, healer of the divine, flow through me now. Restore my body, mind, and spirit to harmony."*
4. **Drink the Healing Water**
   Hold the glass of water and visualize Raphael's light entering it. Say:
   *"By Raphael's grace, may this water carry healing to every cell of my being."*
   Drink the water slowly, feeling its soothing energy.
5. **Seal the Ritual**
   Extinguish the candle and thank Raphael. Say:
   *"Raphael, I thank you for your light and love. May your healing presence remain with me always."*

# Invocation for Daily Guidance

Virtue emphasizes Raphael's availability for everyday support. This invocation can be used as part of your morning or evening practice.

*"Raphael, angel of healing and guidance,*

*I welcome your presence into my day.*
*Illuminate my path with your emerald light,*
*Protect me on my journey, and restore my strength.*
*With your grace, I am whole, I am safe, I am guided."*

Place your hands over your heart and visualize a glowing green light radiating outward, symbolizing Raphael's protective and healing energy surrounding you.

## Magical Correspondences

- **Colors:** Green (healing), white (purity), blue (guidance)
- **Crystals:** Green aventurine (healing), malachite (renewal), clear quartz (clarity)
- **Herbs:** Eucalyptus (restoration), rosemary (protection), sage (cleansing)
- **Incense:** Frankincense (spiritual elevation), sandalwood (balance)
- **Symbols:** Emerald light, healing hands, crystal-infused water

## Raphael's Modern Healing Energy

*Archangels and Ascended Masters* highlights Raphael's accessibility and versatility in contemporary spiritual practice. Virtue's emphasis on direct connection, visualization, and practical techniques enables practitioners to easily integrate Raphael's healing energy into their daily lives.

## Advanced Tips for Deepening Your Practice

1. **Combine with Chakra Work:** Align Raphael's emerald light with the heart chakra during meditative practices for emotional and physical healing.

2. **Incorporate Affirmations:** Use affirmations from Virtue's work to reinforce your connection to Raphael's energy and enhance your focus.
3. **Create a Raphael Journal:** Document your experiences working with Raphael, noting signs, synchronicities, and outcomes to deepen your understanding of his presence.

By integrating Raphael's teachings and energy as described in *Archangels and Ascended Masters*, you can build a transformative relationship with this healing archangel, merging ancient wisdom with modern spirituality.

# Raphael in *The Angelical Language* by Aaron Leitch: Mastering Angelic Communication

## Bridging the Gap Between the Divine and the Practitioner

Aaron Leitch's *The Angelical Language* offers an in-depth exploration of angelic communication, particularly focusing on the Enochian system as transmitted by John Dee and Edward Kelley. While the text primarily revolves around Enochian magic, it provides significant insights into invoking and working with archangels like Raphael. The system's focus on celestial hierarchies, divine names, and angelic sigils provides a structured framework for connecting with Raphael's energy in a profound and systematic way.

## Historical and Spiritual Context

### Enochian Magic and Angelic Hierarchies

- **Origins of Enochian Magic:** Developed in the late 16th century by John Dee and Edward Kelley, Enochian magic is a system of angelic invocation based on the received language of angels. It emphasizes

direct communication with celestial beings for divine wisdom and guidance.
- **The Role of Archangels in the Enochian System:** Raphael, as a healer and guide, is an essential figure within the celestial hierarchy. His energy aligns with the healing and communicative aspects of the Enochian keys and sigils.

## Raphael in Leitch's Work

- **Raphael's Alignment with Air and Mercury:** Leitch emphasizes Raphael's elemental and planetary associations, reinforcing his role in communication, guidance, and healing.

**The Angelical Language as a Medium:** Leitch's exploration of the Enochian language highlights its vibrational alignment with angelic energies, making it an effective tool for summoning Raphael's presence. For instance, The First Enochian Call, also known as the First Key, is the opening invocation in the system of Enochian magic as dictated by the angelic entities to John Dee and Edward Kelley. This Call is a declaration of the divine order and power of creation, invoking the forces of the divine spirit that underpins the universe. While it is not explicitly tied to a specific element, practitioners often associate the First Call with air because of its connection to the celestial hierarchy and the breath of divine speech.

Here is the text of the First Enochian Call, along with its translation and suggested applications in working with the elemental forces of air.

Ol sonf vorsg, goho Iad balta,

el yoloch casarman vpaahi,

od dooain chis-ge-gon, noar micaolz aaiom,

bagle pap norz chis othil gigipah vnmade zacar,

ca od zamran; odo cicle qaa, zorge, lap zirdo noco mad, hoath Iaida.

## Phonetic Transcription

Ohl soh-nuf vor-sag, go-hoh ee-ahd balt,

lons ka-od go-hoh-lor, goh-hus ah-mee-ran!

Mad zoh-deer kom-sel-ah ahf nor moh-lap.

Zoh-dee-en doh oh ah-ee ta pee-ap,

pee-ah-mol od voh-ahn.

Zah-kah-reh ka od zahm-ran;

oh-doh see-kleh kah;

zor-geh, lahp zeer-doh noh-ko mad, hoh-ath ee-ah-ee-dah.

## Pronunciation Notes

- **Vowels:**
    - 'A' as in 'father' (ah)
    - 'E' as in 'grey' (eh)
    - 'I' as in 'machine' (ee)
    - 'O' as in 'go' (oh)
    - 'U' as in 'flute' (oo)
- **Consonants:**
    - 'C' is pronounced as 'k'
    - 'G' is always hard, as in 'go'
    - 'Q' is pronounced as 'kw'

For a more in-depth understanding of Enochian pronunciation, you may refer to the "Guide to the Pronunciation of the Enochian Keys" available at Hermetic.com.

## Audio Resources

To hear the First Enochian Call pronounced correctly, you can listen to recordings by practitioners and scholars. One such resource is available on YouTube, where the call is recited with attention to traditional pronunciation.

Listening to these recordings while following along with the phonetic transcription can enhance your understanding and ability to pronounce the Enochian words accurately.

## English Translation

"I reign over you, says the God of Justice, in power exalted above the firmaments of wrath, in whose hands the sun is a sword, and the moon a thrusting fire, who measures your garments in the midst of my vestures, and trussed you together as the palms of my hands; whose seats I garnished with the fire of gathering, and beautified your garments with admiration. To whom I made a law to govern the holy ones, and delivered you a rod with the ark of knowledge. Moreover, you lifted up your voices and swore obedience and faith to him that lives and triumphs, whose beginning is not, nor end can be, which shines as a flame in the midst of your palace, and reigns amongst you as the balance of righteousness and truth."

## Application in Air Elemental Magic

Although the First Call is universal, it can be adapted to focus on the element of air when calling upon the energies of Raphael or working with the Watchtower of Air. Here's how:

1. **Preparation**:
    - Perform the Lesser Banishing Ritual of the Pentagram (LBRP) to clear the space.

- Set up your altar with air-aligned correspondences: yellow candles, feathers, incense, and symbols of Raphael.

2. **Invocation**:
   - Face east, the direction associated with air and Raphael.
   - Recite the First Enochian Call aloud, visualizing streams of golden or yellow light radiating outward like the breath of creation.
3. **Focused Visualization**:
   - As you recite the Call, imagine the air around you becoming charged with divine power. Feel the energies of wisdom, clarity, and healing entering your space, harmonizing with Raphael's presence.
4. **Anchor the Energy**:
   - While continuing to visualize, speak an invocation to Raphael:
     - *"Raphael, ruler of air, divine healer and guide, I call upon your light to witness this sacred space and guide my actions in alignment with the divine will."*

## Tips for Effective Use

- The Enochian phonetics are essential for capturing the vibrational energy of the Call. Practice pronouncing the Enochian words accurately to resonate with their original intent.
- Pair the Call with corresponding air elemental rituals, such as drawing the invoking pentagram of air while facing east.
- Enhance the experience by using frankincense or other air-aligned incenses to create a sacred atmosphere.

The First Enochian Call is a powerful tool for invoking the divine forces of creation. When aligned with the element of air, it can connect you to the celestial hierarchies associated with wisdom, clarity, and healing. Incorporating Raphael's presence into this Call deepens your connection to angelic guidance, allowing you to harness these energies for personal and spiritual transformation.

## Symbolism and Esoteric Lessons

### 1. Raphael's Sigil

Leitch emphasizes the importance of sigils in creating a direct link to angelic forces. Raphael's sigil can be drawn and activated during rituals to focus his healing energy.

### 2. Divine Names as Vibrational Keys

The sacred names associated with Raphael, such as *IAO* (a Greek form of YHVH) and *Adonai,* resonate with the vibrational frequency of the Enochian calls, facilitating a powerful connection to his energy.

### 3. The Elemental Power of Air

In Enochian magic, air represents intellect, communication, and clarity, qualities that resonate with Raphael's role as a healer and guide.

## Enochian Healing Ritual with Raphael

### Materials

- A green candle (symbolizing Raphael's healing light)
- Frankincense incense (spiritual elevation)
- A parchment with Raphael's sigil (drawn in Enochian script)
- A consecrated wand or feather (symbolizing air and guidance)
- The First and Third Enochian Calls (as translated by Leitch)

### Steps

1. **Prepare the Space**
   Light the green candle and incense. Place Raphael's sigil at the center of your altar. Say:
   *"By the divine power of IAO, may this space be cleansed and prepared for angelic presence."*
2. **Activate Raphael's Sigil**
   Hold the parchment with Raphael's sigil and trace it with your wand or feather, visualizing it glowing with emerald light. Chant:
   *"Raphael, healer of divine light, I call upon your presence through this sacred sigil."*
3. **Recite the Enochian Call**
   Read the First Enochian Call aloud, focusing on the vibrational power of the words. Visualize Raphael's energy descending into your space. Say:
   *"By the sacred language of angels, I invoke the healing light of Raphael."*
4. **Invoke Raphael's Healing Energy**
   Place the wand or feather over your heart and visualize Raphael's emerald light enveloping you. Whisper:
   *"Raphael, flow through me. Heal my body, mind, and spirit with your divine grace."*
5. **Seal the Ritual**
   Extinguish the candle and thank Raphael. Say:
   *"Raphael, I thank you for your presence and light. May your blessings remain with me always."*

# Daily Invocation for Guidance

This invocation uses Enochian elements to call upon Raphael for daily guidance.

*"Raphael, bearer of divine wisdom,
Through the sacred language of the heavens,
Guide my thoughts and heal my spirit.
Illuminate my path with your emerald light,
And align my soul with divine harmony."*

Hold your arms outward, palms up, visualizing Raphael's wings enfolding you.

## Magical Correspondences

- **Colors:** Green (healing), gold (divine light), white (purity)
- **Crystals:** Emerald (renewal), green aventurine (healing), lapis lazuli (spiritual insight)
- **Herbs:** Frankincense (elevation), sage (cleansing), lavender (peace)
- **Incense:** Frankincense (spiritual connection), sandalwood (balance)
- **Symbols:** Raphael's sigil, Enochian script, feather

## Raphael in *The Angelical Language*

Leitch's *The Angelical Language* provides a comprehensive framework for integrating Enochian principles into your work with Raphael. By combining sacred names, sigils, and vibrational calls, you can access Raphael's healing energy with clarity and precision.

### Advanced Tips for Deepening Your Practice

1. **Master the Enochian Calls:** Study the Enochian keys thoroughly to enhance your connection to angelic energies.
2. **Create a Raphael-Specific Sigil:** Adapt Raphael's sigil into Enochian script for personalized rituals.
3. **Combine with Planetary Magic:** Align your rituals with Mercury's planetary hours to amplify their effectiveness.

By weaving the insights of *The Angelical Language* into your magical practice, you align with Raphael's transformative energy, bridging ancient angelic wisdom with modern spiritual tools.

# Raphael in Reiki and Chakra Alignment: A Harmonious Union of Angelic Healing and Energy Work

## Merging Ancient and Modern Healing Modalities

Reiki and chakra alignment offer profound tools for integrating Archangel Raphael's healing energy into contemporary spiritual practice. As the archangel of healing, Raphael's presence aligns naturally with the energetic principles of Reiki and the chakra system, particularly the heart and third-eye chakras. Exploring these connections provides a pathway to enhanced physical, emotional, and spiritual well-being.

# Historical and Spiritual Context

## Reiki: A Universal Energy System

- **Origins of Reiki:** Developed by Mikao Usui in early 20th-century Japan, Reiki is a system of energy healing that channels universal life force energy (Ki) to restore balance and harmony.
- **Raphael's Role in Reiki Practice:** As a conduit of divine healing energy, Raphael is often called upon in Reiki sessions to amplify the practitioner's connection to higher frequencies of light and healing.

## The Chakra System and Raphael

- **The Heart Chakra (Anahata):** Raphael's emerald green light resonates with the heart chakra, symbolizing love, compassion, and renewal.

- **The Third-Eye Chakra (Ajna):** Associated with intuition and divine insight, the third-eye chakra aligns with Raphael's role as a guide and illuminator.

## Modern Interpretations

- **Holistic Healing:** Contemporary Reiki practitioners often incorporate angelic presences, such as Raphael, to bridge the gap between spiritual and physical healing.
- **Chakra Alignment:** Raphael's energy is used to clear blockages in the chakra system, facilitating the flow of life force energy.

# Symbolism and Esoteric Lessons

### 1. Raphael's Emerald Light and the Heart Chakra

The heart chakra's green energy aligns with Raphael's healing light, symbolizing emotional balance and the capacity to give and receive love.

### 2. Third-Eye Clarity Through Angelic Guidance

The third-eye chakra represents intuition and spiritual insight. Calling on Raphael enhances one's ability to perceive divine guidance.

### 3. Reiki and Angelic Energy

Reiki acts as a channel for universal energy, while Raphael provides a divine focus, deepening the healing experience.

# Reiki Healing Session with Raphael

## Materials

- A green candle (representing Raphael's healing light)
- Essential oil such as eucalyptus or rose (heart chakra activation)
- A piece of green aventurine or clear quartz
- Incense or a smudge stick (e.g., sage or frankincense)

**Steps**

1. **Prepare the Space**
   Light the green candle and incense to cleanse and elevate the space. Say:
   *"Raphael, healer of light, I invite your presence into this sacred space to guide this healing session."*
2. **Invoke Raphael's Energy**
   Hold the crystal in your hands, visualizing it glowing with emerald light. Whisper:
   *"Raphael, flow through me with your healing grace. Let your light align and restore my energy."*
3. **Activate the Chakras**
   Place your hands over your heart chakra and then your third-eye chakra. Focus on the warmth of Raphael's energy flowing through your hands into these centers. Say:
   *"By Raphael's grace, my heart is open, my intuition clear, and my spirit renewed."*
4. **Reiki Healing Flow**
   Perform Reiki hand positions on yourself or a recipient, focusing on each chakra. Visualize Raphael's light clearing blockages and restoring balance.
5. **Seal the Session**
   Extinguish the candle and thank Raphael. Say:
   *"Raphael, I thank you for your light and love. May your healing presence remain with me always."*

# Chakra Alignment Meditation with Raphael

**Steps**

1. **Center Yourself**
   Sit in a comfortable position with your spine straight. Close your eyes and take deep breaths.
2. **Visualize Raphael's Light**
   Imagine a beam of emerald light descending from above, entering your heart chakra, and radiating outward.
3. **Affirmations for Each Chakra**
   Repeat affirmations for each chakra while visualizing Raphael's light moving through them:
   - Root Chakra: *"I am grounded in Raphael's protection."*
   - Sacral Chakra: *"I create with divine harmony."*
   - Solar Plexus Chakra: *"I am empowered by Raphael's grace."*
   - Heart Chakra: *"I give and receive love freely."*
   - Throat Chakra: *"I speak my truth with clarity."*
   - Third-Eye Chakra: *"I see with Raphael's guidance."*
   - Crown Chakra: *"I am connected to divine wisdom."*
4. **Conclude with Gratitude**
   Place your hands over your heart and whisper: *"Raphael, I thank you for aligning my energy and guiding my spirit."*

# Magical Correspondences

- **Colors:** Green (healing), blue (intuition), white (spiritual purity)
- **Crystals:** Green aventurine (heart chakra), amethyst (third-eye chakra), rose quartz (emotional healing)

- **Herbs:** Sage (cleansing), rosemary (protection), lavender (peace)
- **Incense:** Frankincense (spiritual elevation), rose (love and compassion)
- **Symbols:** Emerald light, Reiki hands, angelic wings

# Integrating Raphael with Reiki and Chakra Work

Raphael's presence enriches Reiki and chakra practices, creating a bridge between angelic healing and energy work. By aligning with Raphael's emerald light, practitioners can amplify the flow of universal energy, restoring balance and vitality to the body, mind, and spirit.

## Advanced Tips for Deepening Your Practice

1. **Combine Reiki with Angelic Invocations:** Chant Raphael's name or recite invocations during Reiki sessions to enhance their effectiveness.
2. **Create a Chakra Crystal Grid:** Use Raphael's symbols and healing crystals in a grid to maintain alignment and balance between sessions.
3. **Journal Your Experiences:** Document your interactions with Raphael during Reiki and chakra practices to track growth and deepen your understanding of his energy.

Through these practices, you can harmonize ancient angelic wisdom with modern energy healing, creating a transformative path to wholeness and divine connection.

To fully embrace the transformative power of Archangel Raphael, preparation is essential. Building a meaningful connection with Raphael requires attunement to his energy, an understanding of the tools and symbols that align with his essence, and the creation of a sacred space to facilitate communication and ritual work. This next section will guide you through the foundational steps of working with Raphael, from recognizing his presence and establishing intuitive communication to curating the tools and environment that amplify his healing and guiding energies. By laying these spiritual and practical foundations, you open yourself to a deeper relationship with Raphael, ensuring your practices are enriched with clarity, focus, and divine alignment.

# { 4 }

# Foundations of Divine Connection: Preparing to Work with Raphael

Preparing to work with Archangel Raphael is a sacred process that combines intention, intuition, and ritual practice. This section explores the essential steps to cultivate a profound connection with Raphael, from attuning to his healing energy to recognizing the signs of his presence. You will learn to select and consecrate tools that resonate with Raphael's essence—emerald green hues, sacred crystals, herbs, and symbols—and create a dedicated space where his energy can flourish. Through these preparations, you establish a strong foundation for invoking Raphael's guidance, healing, and protection, ensuring each encounter is filled with divine alignment and purpose. This preparation marks the beginning of a transformative journey into angelic magic and spiritual growth.

## Attuning to Raphael's Energy: The Foundation of a Sacred Connection

### Understanding Raphael's Energy

Attuning to Archangel Raphael's energy is the initial step toward establishing a profound spiritual relationship. His presence is marked by a warm, emerald green light that radiates healing, guidance, and protection. Raphael's energy resonates with the heart chakra, symbolizing love and compassion, and the air element, reflecting clarity, communication, and inspiration. By aligning with his frequency, you open yourself to divine healing and spiritual illumination.

# Historical and Spiritual Context

## Raphael in Sacred Texts

- **The Book of Tobit:** Raphael's role in guiding and healing Tobias demonstrates his compassionate and restorative nature. The journey symbolizes the process of attunement—trust, openness, and gradual spiritual alignment.
- **Mystical and Esoteric Traditions:** Kabbalistic texts associate Raphael with the Sephirah Tiferet (beauty), embodying balance and harmony in creation. His presence integrates physical and spiritual healing.

## Modern Interpretations

- Raphael's energy is often described as gentle yet powerful, offering subtle signs such as feelings of warmth, sudden clarity, or visions of green light during meditation.

# Daily Attunement Ritual with Raphael

## Materials

- A green candle (symbolizing Raphael's healing energy)
- Frankincense incense (spiritual elevation)
- A piece of green aventurine or malachite
- A feather or small fan (air element)

**Steps**

1. **Prepare the Space**
   Light the green candle and incense. Place the crystal and feather on an altar or sacred space. Say:
   *"Raphael, divine healer and guide, I invite your presence into this sacred space."*

2. **Visualize Emerald Light**
   Sit comfortably and close your eyes. Imagine an emerald green light descending from above, enveloping you. Feel its warmth and healing energy.
3. **Invoke Raphael's Energy**
   Hold the crystal in your hand and the feather in the other. Whisper:
   *"Raphael, archangel of light, align my energy with your divine frequency. Heal, guide, and illuminate my path."*
4. **Focus on the Breath**
   Take deep breaths, imagining each inhale drawing in Raphael's light and each exhale releasing tension and negativity. Let the feather or fan gently waft the incense toward you, symbolizing Raphael's presence.
5. **Meditate on Alignment**
   Spend 10–15 minutes in silent meditation, focusing on your heart chakra. Feel the emerald light radiating outward, connecting you with Raphael.
6. **Seal the Ritual**
   Extinguish the candle and thank Raphael. Say:
   *"Raphael, I thank you for your light and presence. May I walk in your healing grace."*

## Affirmations for Attunement

- "I align my heart with Raphael's divine light."
- "I am open to healing and guidance from Raphael."
- "Through Raphael's presence, I am whole and illuminated."

## Magical Correspondences

- **Colors:** Emerald green (healing), white (purity), gold (divine light)
- **Crystals:** Green aventurine (healing), malachite (renewal), clear quartz (clarity)

- **Herbs:** Sage (cleansing), rosemary (protection), lavender (peace)
- **Incense:** Frankincense (spiritual elevation), sandalwood (balance)
- **Symbols:** Feather (air and spirit), emerald aura, Raphael's sigil

## Symbolic and Esoteric Significance

### 1. Emerald Green Light

Emerald green represents growth, vitality, and renewal. Visualizing this light helps align your energy with Raphael's healing and guiding essence.

### 2. The Air Element

The feather or fan symbolizes the air element, representing Raphael's role as a messenger and his connection to clarity and communication.

### 3. The Heart Chakra

The heart chakra's resonance with Raphael reflects his emphasis on love, compassion, and emotional healing.

## Advanced Techniques for Attunement

### Chanting Raphael's Name

Repeat Raphael's name or its Hebrew equivalent (*Rafa-El*) during meditation to attune to his vibrational frequency.

## Dream Connection

Before sleep, place the green crystal under your pillow and ask Raphael to visit you in dreams. Record any visions or feelings upon waking.

## Moonlight Charging

Charge your tools (crystals, feather) under the full moon, dedicating them to Raphael's energy for enhanced connection.

# Attuning to Raphael

Attuning to Raphael's energy is a transformative experience, fostering a deep sense of healing and guidance. Through visualization, ritual, and meditation, you align with his emerald light, opening pathways to divine wisdom and restoration.

## Advanced Tips for Deepening Your Connection

1. **Consistency:** Regularly perform attunement rituals to strengthen your bond with Raphael.
2. **Symbol Integration:** Incorporate Raphael's symbols, such as his sigil or emerald light, into your daily life.
3. **Journaling:** Document your experiences and insights during rituals to track your spiritual growth and connection with Raphael.

Through these practices, you create a harmonious relationship with Raphael, allowing his energy to guide and heal you on all levels of being.

# Recognizing Raphael's Presence: Signs and Synchronicities from the Divine Healer

## The Subtle Language of Angels

Archangel Raphael communicates through signs, synchronicities, and intuitive nudges, offering guidance and healing to those who attune to his presence. Recognizing these messages requires heightened awareness, trust, and a willingness to embrace his subtle yet profound forms of interaction. From sensations of warmth to visual cues like flashes of emerald light, Raphael's signs serve as affirmations of his healing presence and guidance.

# Historical and Spiritual Context

## Angelic Signs in Sacred Texts

- **The Book of Tobit:** Raphael's interaction with Tobias is filled with practical yet miraculous guidance, showcasing how angelic assistance can manifest through ordinary events with extraordinary outcomes. Raphael's ability to heal and guide Tobias reflects his willingness to engage directly with human needs.
- **Kabbalistic Mysticism:** In the Zohar, angels are described as messengers of divine will, communicating through dreams, symbols, and synchronicities to guide seekers toward spiritual alignment.

## Modern Interpretations of Angelic Communication

- Raphael's signs are often associated with healing and clarity, manifesting as sensations, symbols, or intuitive insights that align with his roles as a guide and healer.
- In contemporary angelic magic, practitioners recognize Raphael's presence through emerald-green flashes of

light, sudden emotional calm, or intuitive knowledge about healing and self-care.

## Symbolism and Esoteric Lessons

### 1. Signs of Raphael's Presence

- **Visual Cues:** Flashes of emerald green light or dreams involving healing or guidance.
- **Physical Sensations:** A feeling of warmth or tingling, especially in the heart or third-eye chakra.
- **Emotional Shifts:** Sudden clarity, peace, or relief during times of stress or illness.
- **Symbolic Messages:** Recurring symbols like feathers, the image of a staff, or encounters with fish (referencing the Book of Tobit).

### 2. Synchronicities as Raphael's Signature

- Repeated encounters with the color green, particularly emerald shades, in unexpected contexts.
- Hearing or reading references to healing, guidance, or journeys in close succession.
- The sudden appearance of symbols associated with Raphael, such as his name, sigil, or planetary and elemental correspondences.

## Daily Awareness Practice for Recognizing Raphael's Signs

### Materials

- A journal or notebook
- A green candle or emerald crystal (optional, to enhance focus)

**Steps**

1. **Set an Intention**
   Begin the day by setting an intention to notice signs of Raphael's presence. Say:
   *"Raphael, divine healer and guide, I open my heart and mind to your signs and guidance this day."*
2. **Practice Mindful Awareness**
   Pay close attention to your surroundings throughout the day, noticing any recurring symbols, colors, or intuitive nudges. Carry an emerald crystal or green item to remind you of your intention.
3. **Record Observations**
   At the end of the day, journal any notable signs, synchronicities, or intuitive insights. Reflect on how these experiences might connect to Raphael's energy.
4. **Express Gratitude**
   Light the green candle and thank Raphael for his presence. Say:
   *"Raphael, I thank you for your light and guidance. May your presence continue to illuminate my path."*

## Invoking Raphael to Heighten Awareness

**Steps**

1. **Prepare the Space**
   Light a green candle and burn frankincense incense. Create a quiet, meditative environment.
2. **Invoke Raphael's Presence**
   Close your eyes and place your hands over your heart. Say:
   *"Raphael, healer of light and guardian of wisdom, I invite your presence into my life. Help me recognize your signs and trust your guidance."*
3. **Meditate on Openness**
   Visualize a beam of emerald light entering your heart

chakra, expanding outward. Imagine this light sharpening your perception of Raphael's messages.
4. **Seal the Practice**
Blow out the candle, symbolizing trust that Raphael's presence will remain with you.

## Magical Correspondences

- **Colors:** Emerald green (healing), white (purity)
- **Crystals:** Green aventurine (openness), clear quartz (clarity), rose quartz (emotional awareness)
- **Herbs:** Lavender (calm), rosemary (focus), sage (cleansing)
- **Incense:** Frankincense (spiritual elevation), sandalwood (balance)
- **Symbols:** Feathers, staff, fish

## Trusting Raphael's Presence

Recognizing Raphael's signs and synchronicities deepens your connection to his healing and guiding energy. Through mindfulness, intention, and gratitude, you align with Raphael's subtle language, opening yourself to divine guidance.

### Advanced Tips for Deepening Your Practice

1. **Dream Journaling:** Before bed, invite Raphael to communicate through dreams. Record any vivid dreams or symbols upon waking.
2. **Nature Walks:** Spend time in nature, paying attention to recurring patterns or symbols that resonate with Raphael's energy.

3. **Synchronicity Mapping:** Track repeated symbols, colors, or themes over time to uncover deeper patterns in Raphael's guidance.

By cultivating an awareness of Raphael's signs, you build a dynamic and intuitive relationship with this archangel, allowing his presence to guide and heal you in profound ways.

# Developing Intuitive Communication with Raphael: Opening the Channels to Divine Wisdom

## The Art of Listening to Angels

Intuitive communication with Archangel Raphael involves cultivating a heightened awareness of his guidance and messages. This form of communion transcends verbal language, relying on emotional impressions, visual symbols, and subtle shifts in energy. By honing your intuition through meditation, ritual, and dedicated practice, you can deepen your ability to sense, hear, and interpret Raphael's presence and wisdom.

# Historical and Spiritual Context

## Angelic Communication in Sacred Texts

- **The Book of Tobit:** Raphael's guidance to Tobias exemplifies how angels interact with humans, providing practical advice cloaked in divine wisdom. This narrative serves as a model for how intuitive communication with Raphael can blend spiritual insight with actionable steps.
- **Mystical Traditions:** Kabbalistic teachings describe angels as channels of divine thought, acting as intermediaries between humanity and the Creator.

Developing intuitive communication mirrors this spiritual relationship.

## Modern Interpretations

- In contemporary angelic magic, Raphael's messages are often experienced as flashes of inspiration, emotional clarity, or dreams. Practitioners interpret these signals by tuning into their inner senses and remaining open to divine influence.

## Symbolism and Esoteric Lessons

### 1. The Emerald Light as a Bridge

Raphael's emerald green light serves as a conduit for communication, symbolizing clarity, healing, and divine connection.

### 2. The Heart and Third-Eye Chakras

Raphael's energy aligns with the heart chakra (love and compassion) and the third-eye chakra (intuition and insight), making these energy centers key focal points for intuitive work.

### 3. Symbols of Raphael's Presence

Recurring symbols such as feathers, staff, or emerald hues often accompany Raphael's messages, providing tangible anchors for his guidance.

# Daily Practice for Intuitive Communication

## Materials

- A green candle (Raphael's light)
- A notebook or journal (to record insights)
- A piece of clear quartz or green aventurine (to enhance clarity)

**Steps**

1. **Create a Sacred Space**
   Light the green candle and hold the crystal in your hand. Close your eyes and take deep breaths to center yourself. Say:
   *"Raphael, divine healer and guide, I open my heart and mind to your wisdom."*
2. **Focus on the Heart and Third-Eye Chakras**
   Place your hands over your heart, then your third-eye chakra. Visualize Raphael's emerald light connecting these centers, forming a bridge of clarity and intuition.
3. **Ask for Guidance**
   Whisper or think of a specific question or area of your life where you seek Raphael's insight. Say:
   *"Raphael, illuminate my path with your light. I am open to your guidance."*
4. **Listen and Observe**
   Spend 10–15 minutes in quiet meditation, noticing any impressions, emotions, or images that arise. Trust the subtle messages, even if they seem abstract.
5. **Record Your Experience**
   After the meditation, write down any thoughts, feelings, or symbols that came to you. Reflect on how these might relate to your question or life situation.

# Invocation for Intuitive Alignment

This invocation helps you align with Raphael's energy for clear communication.

*"Raphael, messenger of divine wisdom,*
*I open my heart to your light,*
*I open my mind to your truth.*
*Through your emerald radiance, may I see,*
*Through your healing breath, may I hear.*
*Guide me with your loving grace,*
*That I may walk the path of clarity and peace."*

Hold your arms open, palms upward, symbolizing receptivity to Raphael's guidance.

# Magical Correspondences

- **Colors:** Emerald green (healing and clarity), blue (spiritual insight), white (purity)
- **Crystals:** Clear quartz (amplification), green aventurine (openness), amethyst (spiritual clarity)
- **Herbs:** Lavender (peace), rosemary (focus), mint (mental clarity)
- **Incense:** Frankincense (spiritual elevation), sandalwood (intuition)
- **Symbols:** Feathers, emerald light, Raphael's sigil

# Advanced Techniques for Deepening Communication

## Dream Work

Before bed, invite Raphael to send messages through dreams. Place a green crystal under your pillow and say: *"Raphael, guide of the divine, visit me in my dreams.*

*Illuminate my path with your wisdom."*
Record your dreams upon waking to uncover Raphael's messages.

## Automatic Writing

Use a journal to practice automatic writing. Begin with a short invocation to Raphael and allow your hand to move freely, trusting that his guidance will flow through your subconscious mind.

## Nature Meditation

Spend time in nature, focusing on elements of air and greenery. Visualize Raphael's presence in the natural world and ask for guidance in your current journey.

# Opening the Channels to Raphael's Guidance

Developing intuitive communication with Raphael is a transformative journey that bridges the physical and spiritual worlds. Through meditation, invocation, and a commitment to self-awareness, you can attune to his messages and integrate his guidance into your life.

## Advanced Tips for Deepening Your Practice

1. **Consistency is Key:** Establish a daily practice of connecting with Raphael to strengthen your intuitive abilities.
2. **Trust the Process:** Intuition grows through trust. Embrace the messages you receive, even if they seem unclear at first.
3. **Combine Practices:** Blend meditation, journaling, and dream work to create a multifaceted approach to communication.

By cultivating these techniques, you create a dynamic and ongoing relationship with Raphael, allowing his wisdom to illuminate your spiritual path and enhance your life's purpose.

## Harnessing Raphael's Tools: Colors, Crystals, and Sacred Herbs

### The Energetic Blueprint of Angelic Magic

In angelic magic, tools such as colors, crystals, and herbs serve as physical representations of celestial energies. When working with Archangel Raphael, specific items like emerald green hues, malachite crystals, and sacred herbs such as frankincense help to amplify his healing and guiding presence. These tools align the practitioner's energy with Raphael's, creating a harmonious channel for communication, healing, and spiritual growth.

## Historical and Spiritual Context

### The Symbolism of Emerald Green

- **Sacred Light of Healing:** Emerald green is often associated with Raphael's energy, symbolizing growth, renewal, and divine healing. In the Book of Tobit, Raphael's guidance brings restoration, a theme resonating with the regenerative power of this color.
- **Kabbalistic Connection:** In the Sephirotic Tree of Life, green relates to Tiferet, the sphere of beauty and balance, which aligns with Raphael's role as a healer and harmonizer.

### Crystals in Healing Traditions

- **Malachite:** Known for its transformative and protective qualities, malachite resonates with Raphael's healing

energy, particularly for emotional and physical ailments.
- **Emerald:** A stone of unconditional love and vitality, emerald embodies Raphael's restorative essence.
- **Green Aventurine:** Often called the "stone of opportunity," this crystal works well for enhancing Raphael's guidance in personal and spiritual journeys.

## Sacred Herbs and Aromatics

- **Frankincense:** Revered in religious traditions for its purifying properties, frankincense elevates spiritual vibrations, making it ideal for invoking Raphael's presence.
- **Rosemary:** A herb of clarity and focus, it complements Raphael's guidance for mental and emotional healing.
- **Lavender:** Known for its calming effects, lavender aids in aligning with Raphael's compassionate and soothing energy.

# Practical Applications: Tools in Rituals

### 1. Using Colors to Connect with Raphael

Color is a powerful frequency that can influence energy and intention. Incorporating emerald green into your environment and rituals enhances your connection to Raphael.

**Steps**

1. **Decorate Your Space:** Use emerald green candles, altar cloths, or gemstones to create a dedicated area for Raphael.
2. **Visualization Exercise:** During meditation, imagine yourself surrounded by an emerald green light, symbolizing Raphael's presence. Say:

*"Raphael, healer of light, I align myself with your emerald radiance. Heal and guide me with your divine grace."*

## 2. Crystals as Conduits for Raphael's Energy

Crystals resonate with specific frequencies that amplify angelic magic. When consecrated and aligned with Raphael, they serve as powerful tools for healing and guidance.

**Steps**

1. **Crystal Cleansing:** Cleanse your chosen crystal (malachite, emerald, or green aventurine) using moonlight, sage, or saltwater to remove residual energies.
2. **Charging the Crystal:** Hold the crystal in your hands, visualizing it glowing with emerald green light. Say: *"By Raphael's grace, I consecrate this crystal as a vessel of healing and divine wisdom."*
3. **Using the Crystal:** Place the crystal on your heart chakra during meditation or carry it with you as a talisman for healing and protection.

## 3. Incorporating Sacred Herbs

Herbs like frankincense, rosemary, and lavender can be used to purify spaces, enhance rituals, and deepen your connection to Raphael.

**Steps**

1. **Burning Incense:** Place frankincense on a charcoal disc in a fireproof bowl. As the smoke rises, focus on inviting Raphael's energy into your space. Say:

> "Raphael, divine healer and guide, may this sacred smoke carry my invocation to the heavens."

2. **Herbal Anointing Oil:** Blend essential oils of frankincense, rosemary, and lavender with a carrier oil. Use this oil to anoint candles, crystals, or yourself before rituals.

## Symbolism and Esoteric Lessons

### The Energetic Significance of Tools

- **Emerald Green:** Represents Raphael's light, bridging the physical and spiritual realms for healing and clarity.
- **Malachite and Crystals:** Act as amplifiers of Raphael's energy, focusing intentions and aligning chakras.
- **Sacred Herbs:** Their vibrational properties enhance spiritual clarity, purification, and healing.

### Integration into Daily Life

These tools can be incorporated into everyday practices, such as wearing green clothing, carrying a consecrated crystal, or burning frankincense during prayer, to maintain a constant connection with Raphael's energy.

## Magical Correspondences

- **Colors:** Emerald green (healing), gold (illumination), white (purity)
- **Crystals:** Malachite (transformation), emerald (vitality), green aventurine (opportunity)
- **Herbs:** Frankincense (elevation), rosemary (clarity), lavender (peace)

- **Incense:** Frankincense (divine connection), sandalwood (balance)
- **Symbols:** Emerald light, Raphael's sigil, feathers

## Empowering Your Work with Raphael

Using colors, crystals, and sacred herbs allows you to align your energy with Raphael's frequency, creating a dynamic and harmonious connection. These tools act as bridges between the physical and spiritual realms, enhancing the potency of your rituals and meditations.

### Advanced Tips for Deepening Your Practice

1. **Create a Raphael Grid:** Arrange crystals in a sacred geometric pattern, placing a candle or Raphael's sigil at the center to amplify healing and guidance.
2. **Combine Elements:** Use emerald light visualization alongside crystals and herbs during rituals for a multi-layered approach to connection.
3. **Seasonal Alignments:** Incorporate Raphael's tools during the spring equinox, a time of growth and renewal, to harmonize with his restorative energy.

By integrating these tools into your magical practice, you establish a tangible and transformative relationship with Raphael, enhancing your ability to receive his healing and guidance.

## Illuminating the Path: Candles, Oils, and Sigils for Raphael's Invocation

### The Essential Tools of Angelic Magic

Candles, oils, and sigils are fundamental tools in angelic magic, serving as physical anchors for spiritual energies. When invoking Archangel Raphael, these items amplify your intention, creating a sacred bridge between the material and celestial realms. Each component—whether it's the light of a candle, the aroma of consecrated oil, or the intricate design of a sigil—vibrates in harmony with Raphael's essence, inviting his healing and guiding presence into your practice.

## Historical and Spiritual Context

### Candles in Spiritual Traditions

- **Symbol of Light and Guidance:** Candles are universal symbols of illumination, representing divine wisdom and presence. In Christian traditions, lighting candles is an act of prayer and devotion, aligning with Raphael's role as a divine guide.
- **Color Correspondence:** Green candles resonate with Raphael's energy, symbolizing healing, growth, and renewal. Gold or white candles can also be used to invoke purity and divine illumination.

### Oils in Sacred Practices

- **Anointing as a Ritual Act:** Oils have been used in sacred rituals across cultures for purification, consecration, and healing. The use of specific oils like frankincense or lavender aligns with Raphael's healing frequency.
- **Biblical Reference:** Anointing with oil is a practice rooted in scripture, often symbolizing divine favor and sanctification (e.g., James 5:14).

### Sigils in Magical Practices

- **Sacred Geometry:** Sigils are symbolic representations of spiritual entities, designed to focus intention and energy. Raphael's sigil, when inscribed and activated, acts as a beacon for his presence.

- **Historical Roots:** Sigils have a rich history in mysticism and the occult, featured prominently in grimoires like the *Key of Solomon*.

## Symbolism and Esoteric Lessons

### 1. The Flame as a Connection to Raphael

The candle flame represents divine presence and the transformative power of Raphael's healing light, symbolizing clarity, purification, and renewal.

### 2. Oils as Vessels of Sacred Intention

Oils infused with herbs or essential essences carry the vibrational properties of their ingredients, enhancing your alignment with Raphael's energy.

### 3. Sigils as Keys to Divine Interaction

Sigils encapsulate Raphael's essence into a tangible form, serving as a focal point for meditation, invocation, and magic.

## Practical Applications: Rituals and Techniques

### 1. Candle Invocation Ritual for Raphael

**Materials**

- A green candle (primary) and white or gold candles (optional)
- Matches or a lighter
- Raphael's sigil (drawn or printed)

**Steps**

1. **Prepare the Space**
   Place the candle and Raphael's sigil on your altar. Light the candle, visualizing its flame connecting to Raphael's emerald light. Say:
   *"Raphael, guardian of light and healing, I ignite this flame as a beacon for your presence."*
2. **Focus on the Flame**
   Stare into the flame, imagining it growing brighter as Raphael's energy fills the space. Whisper:
   *"By this light, I welcome your guidance and healing."*
3. **Meditate with the Sigil**
   Hold or gaze at Raphael's sigil, allowing its patterns to draw your focus inward. Say:
   *"Raphael, through this sacred symbol, I attune to your divine essence."*
4. **Seal the Ritual**
   Extinguish the candle gently, symbolizing trust in Raphael's continuing presence. Say:
   *"Raphael, I thank you for your light and blessings. Remain with me in grace."*

## 2. Crafting and Using Anointing Oil

**Materials**

- Carrier oil (e.g., jojoba or almond oil)
- Essential oils (frankincense, lavender, and rosemary)
- A small vial or bottle
- A green ribbon or label (to signify Raphael)

**Steps**

1. **Blend the Oils**
   Combine the carrier oil with 3 drops each of frankincense, lavender, and rosemary oils. While blending, say:
   *"By the grace of Raphael, I infuse this oil with healing light."*

2. **Consecrate the Oil**
   Hold the vial in both hands, visualizing it glowing with emerald light. Whisper:
   *"Raphael, bless this oil as a vessel of your divine essence."*
3. **Use the Oil**
   Anoint your wrists, third-eye chakra, or candles with the oil before rituals to enhance your connection to Raphael.

## 3. Activating Raphael's Sigil

**Materials**

- Raphael's sigil (drawn on parchment or a stone)
- Green candle
- Frankincense incense

**Steps**

1. **Light the Candle and Incense**
   Place the sigil in front of the candle. Light the candle and incense, inviting Raphael's presence. Say:
   *"Raphael, I activate this sigil as a key to your divine light."*
2. **Trace the Sigil**
   Use your finger or a wand to trace over the sigil, visualizing it glowing with emerald light. Whisper:
   *"By your name, Raphael, may this sigil carry your essence and grace."*
3. **Meditate with the Sigil**
   Hold the sigil during meditation or place it on your altar as a permanent connection to Raphael.

## Magical Correspondences

- **Candles:** Green (healing and growth), white (purity), gold (illumination)
- **Oils:** Frankincense (elevation), lavender (calm), rosemary (clarity)
- **Sigils:** Raphael's sigil (focus and connection)
- **Incense:** Frankincense (divine communication)
- **Symbols:** Feathers, staff, emerald light

## Anchoring Raphael's Presence

Candles, oils, and sigils provide tangible and potent means of invoking Raphael's energy, creating a sacred framework for your magical practice. Through these tools, you establish a profound and lasting connection to Raphael's guidance, healing, and protection.

### Advanced Tips for Deepening Your Practice

1. **Layered Tools:** Combine candles, oils, and sigils in a single ritual to amplify your connection with Raphael.
2. **Seasonal Rituals:** Perform these rituals during the spring equinox or on Mercury's planetary day (Wednesday) to align with Raphael's natural rhythms.
3. **Personalize Sigils:** Infuse Raphael's sigil with your unique energy by adding personal symbols or intentions during its creation.

By integrating these tools into your magical practice, you create a bridge between the physical and spiritual realms, allowing Raphael's light to guide and transform your life.

# Symbols and Talismans of Raphael: Anchoring Divine Energy in the Physical Realm

## The Power of Sacred Representation

Symbols and talismans act as physical embodiments of Archangel Raphael's essence, creating a tangible connection to his healing and guiding energy. These tools serve as focal points for invocation, meditation, and protection, bridging the gap between the celestial and the earthly. Whether crafted with intricate designs or simple intentions, symbols and talismans representing Raphael carry his divine signature, amplifying your spiritual practice.

## Historical and Spiritual Context

### Symbolism in Sacred Texts

- **The Book of Tobit:** Raphael's presence is marked by the staff and fish, representing guidance and healing. These symbols provide a foundational blueprint for understanding how Raphael interacts with the material world.
- **Mystical Traditions:** Kabbalistic teachings associate Raphael with Tiferet (beauty and harmony) and the Hebrew letter ר (Resh), both of which symbolize balance and divine alignment.

### The Use of Talismans in Angelic Magic

- Talismans have long been used in magical traditions to harness specific angelic energies. In texts like the *Key of Solomon*, angelic sigils and seals act as portals to divine assistance.
- Raphael's sigil, often inscribed on talismans, is a key to invoking his energy for healing, protection, and guidance.

## Modern Interpretations

- Practitioners of angelic magic create personalized symbols for Raphael, combining traditional sigils with contemporary designs to align with their unique intentions.

## Symbolism and Esoteric Lessons

### 1. The Staff as a Symbol of Guidance

The staff represents Raphael's role as a divine guide, leading the faithful through challenges with wisdom and clarity. It also signifies the spiritual journey and the support provided by divine forces.

### 2. The Fish as a Symbol of Healing

Rooted in the Book of Tobit, the fish embodies healing and nourishment. It symbolizes the purifying aspects of water and Raphael's ability to cleanse and restore.

### 3. Raphael's Sigil as a Gateway

The sigil of Raphael encapsulates his divine essence into a geometric form, creating a focal point for spiritual work. Its intricate design represents the interconnectedness of physical and spiritual healing.

## Practical Applications: Rituals and Techniques

### 1. Creating a Talisman for Raphael

**Materials**

- A piece of malachite, emerald, or other green stone (or parchment for drawing)
- Raphael's sigil (inscribed or drawn)

- A green ribbon or thread
- Anointing oil (frankincense or rosemary)

**Steps**

1. **Cleanse the Material**
   Purify the stone or parchment using moonlight, sage, or saltwater. Say:
   *"By the light of divine purity, I cleanse this vessel for Raphael's essence."*
2. **Inscribe the Sigil**
   Use a tool or pen to inscribe Raphael's sigil onto the stone or parchment. As you draw, focus on your intention. Whisper:
   *"Raphael, divine healer, I craft this talisman as a channel for your guidance and light."*
3. **Consecrate the Talisman**
   Anoint the talisman with the oil while visualizing it glowing with emerald green light. Say:
   *"By Raphael's grace, I consecrate this talisman as a vessel of healing and protection."*
4. **Activate the Talisman**
   Hold the talisman in your hands, focusing on your connection to Raphael. Say:
   *"Raphael, may your energy flow through this talisman. Guide me, heal me, and protect me."*

## 2. Using Symbols in Rituals

**Steps**

1. **Incorporate Symbols into an Altar**
   Place representations of Raphael's symbols, such as a staff, fish, or his sigil, on your altar to enhance its energy.
2. **Meditate with the Symbols**
   Hold or gaze at the symbol during meditation, focusing on its connection to Raphael. Visualize the symbol glowing with his emerald light.

3. **Include Symbols in Sigil Magic**
   Use Raphael's sigil as the centerpiece of a healing grid or protection spell, amplifying your intention with his divine energy.

## Magical Correspondences

- **Symbols:** Staff (guidance), fish (healing), Raphael's sigil (connection)
- **Colors:** Emerald green (healing), gold (illumination)
- **Crystals:** Malachite (transformation), green aventurine (growth), clear quartz (clarity)
- **Herbs:** Frankincense (elevation), rosemary (focus), lavender (peace)
- **Incense:** Frankincense (divine connection), sandalwood (balance)

## Advanced Techniques for Working with Raphael's Symbols

### Personalizing Raphael's Sigil

Inscribe your own name or initials into Raphael's sigil to create a personalized connection. Meditate on how your energy merges with his divine essence.

### Creating a Portable Talisman

Wrap your talisman in green silk or place it in a pouch with herbs like rosemary or lavender. Carry it with you for ongoing protection and healing.

### Seasonal Alignments

Use Raphael's symbols during seasonal transitions, such as the spring equinox, to align with his energies of growth and renewal.

## Integrating Symbols and Talismans

Symbols and talismans representing Raphael act as conduits for his divine energy, providing tangible anchors for healing, guidance, and protection. By incorporating these tools into your practice, you establish a sacred connection with Raphael that enhances every aspect of your spiritual journey.

### Advanced Tips for Deepening Your Work

1. **Symbolic Layers:** Combine multiple symbols, such as Raphael's sigil and the fish, in a single talisman to amplify its power.
2. **Daily Use:** Meditate with your talisman daily, reinforcing your connection to Raphael and deepening its influence in your life.
3. **Elemental Integration:** Align your talisman with the element of air by passing it through incense smoke, strengthening its connection to Raphael's domain.

Through these practices, you create a dynamic and enduring relationship with Raphael, allowing his symbols and talismans to guide and support you in both magical and mundane endeavors.

## Creating Sacred Space: Setting Up an Altar for Raphael

### The Altar as a Portal to Raphael's Presence

An altar dedicated to Archangel Raphael serves as both a spiritual anchor and a channel for his healing and guiding energy. This sacred space is designed to resonate with Raphael's attributes, creating an environment where his presence can be felt and his wisdom accessed. It reflects your commitment to working with him, offering a physical manifestation of your spiritual intentions.

# Historical and Spiritual Context

## Altars in Sacred Tradition

- **Biblical Altars:** Altars have long been used as places of divine encounter. In the Old Testament, altars were constructed to honor God's presence and receive blessings. This practice is mirrored in creating a space to honor Raphael.
- **Mystical Interpretations:** Kabbalistic teachings emphasize the importance of sacred geometry and balance in altar design, aligning the physical space with spiritual energies.
- **Contemporary Practices:** Modern angelic magic integrates traditional altar practices with personalized touches to enhance resonance with specific archangels.

## Raphael's Sacred Symbols

- **The Staff and Fish:** Central to Raphael's story in the *Book of Tobit*, these symbols represent his roles as a guide and healer.
- **Emerald Green:** This color embodies Raphael's healing light and growth energy.
- **Air Element:** Raphael's association with the element of air reflects his role as a messenger and communicator.

# Symbolism and Esoteric Lessons

### 1. The Altar as a Microcosm

The altar represents the universe in miniature, with each object symbolizing an aspect of Raphael's essence or your connection to him.

### 2. The Power of Intention

Every element placed on the altar holds the energy of your intention. Thoughtful arrangement ensures harmony and alignment with Raphael's energy.

### 3. The Balance of Elements

Incorporating Raphael's element of air, along with complementary elements like earth (crystals), fire (candles), and water (purity), creates a balanced energetic field.

## Practical Applications: Setting Up the Altar

### 1. Choosing the Location

- **Quiet and Undisturbed:** Select a space where you can regularly perform rituals and connect with Raphael without interruptions.
- **Facing East:** Align the altar with the direction of the rising sun, symbolizing light, healing, and Raphael's guiding nature.

### 2. Preparing the Base

- **Emerald Green Cloth:** Cover the altar with a green cloth, representing Raphael's healing energy.
- **Sacred Geometry:** Arrange the space in a balanced pattern, using Raphael's sigil or sacred geometric shapes as a guide.

### 3. Essential Items for the Altar

#### Symbols and Representations

- **Raphael's Sigil:** Center the sigil on the altar as a focal point for invocation.
- **Staff or Feather:** Representing guidance and the air element, these items honor Raphael's role as a guide.

- **Fish Symbol or Offering:** Acknowledge Raphael's healing and transformative power, as seen in the Book of Tobit.

**Crystals**

- **Malachite:** Transformation and healing.
- **Green Aventurine:** Growth and alignment.
- **Clear Quartz:** Amplification of energy.

**Candles**

- **Green Candle:** Primary symbol of Raphael's light and presence.
- **White or Gold Candles:** Supporting purity and divine connection.

**Sacred Herbs and Oils**

- **Frankincense Incense:** Elevates the altar's vibration, inviting Raphael's energy.
- **Anointing Oil:** Blend of rosemary, frankincense, and lavender for consecration.

**Water and Air**

- **A Bowl of Water:** Symbolizing purification and emotional healing.
- **Incense or Feather:** Representing Raphael's alignment with the air element.

## 4. Consecrating the Altar

**Steps**

1. **Cleanse the Space**
   Use sage, rosemary, or frankincense incense to purify the area. As the smoke rises, say:
   *"I cleanse this space for the light and grace of Raphael. May it be a sanctuary of healing and guidance."*

2. **Arrange the Items**
   Thoughtfully place each object, focusing on its symbolic significance. For example:
   - Place Raphael's sigil at the center.
   - Surround it with candles, crystals, and symbols.
3. **Light the Candle and Incense**
   As you light them, visualize emerald light filling the space. Say:
   *"Raphael, healer of the divine, I dedicate this altar to your presence. Guide me, heal me, and protect me."*
4. **Bless the Altar**
   Sprinkle water or anoint the items with oil. Say:
   *"By this water and oil, I consecrate this altar in your name, Raphael. May it shine with your grace."*

## Magical Correspondences

- **Colors:** Emerald green (healing), white (purity), gold (illumination)
- **Crystals:** Malachite (transformation), green aventurine (growth), clear quartz (clarity)
- **Herbs:** Frankincense (elevation), rosemary (clarity), lavender (peace)
- **Incense:** Frankincense (divine connection), sandalwood (balance)
- **Symbols:** Staff, fish, Raphael's sigil

## A Sacred Gateway to Raphael

An altar dedicated to Raphael becomes a dynamic space for invocation, meditation, and ritual. Each element is infused with intention, creating a powerful connection to his healing and guiding energy.

## Advanced Tips for Enhancing Your Altar

1. **Seasonal Adjustments:** Refresh the altar during seasonal transitions to align with Raphael's energy of growth and renewal.
2. **Personal Offerings:** Add personal items, such as a handwritten prayer or a photograph, to deepen your connection.
3. **Daily Devotion:** Light the green candle and meditate at the altar daily to maintain and strengthen your bond with Raphael.

Through this sacred space, you create a sanctuary where Raphael's presence can heal, guide, and inspire your spiritual journey.

## Invoking Raphael's Presence: Prayers, Chants, and Sacred Sounds

### The Resonance of Divine Communication

Invoking Archangel Raphael through prayers, chants, and sounds establishes a profound spiritual connection. These vocal and auditory practices act as vibrational keys, opening a gateway for his healing and guiding presence. Rooted in sacred traditions, these methods harness the power of sound to align your energy with Raphael's, creating a harmonious field for healing, guidance, and protection.

## Historical and Spiritual Context

### Prayers and Invocations in Sacred Texts

- **Biblical Prayers:** Throughout the Bible, prayers are used to invoke divine assistance. Raphael, as a healer and guide in the *Book of Tobit*, responds to direct calls for aid, illustrating the efficacy of prayer in inviting his presence.

- **Chants in Mystical Traditions:** Kabbalistic practices emphasize the vibrational power of sacred names. Chanting Raphael's name in Hebrew (רפאל) resonates with his healing energy and aligns the practitioner with divine will.

## Sacred Sounds and Angelic Magic

- **The Role of Sound:** In mystical and esoteric traditions, sound is seen as a medium for creation and transformation. Invoking Raphael through sacred sounds bridges the gap between the physical and celestial realms.
- **The Element of Air:** As an archangel associated with air, Raphael's energy naturally harmonizes with breath and sound, making vocal invocations particularly effective.

## Symbolism and Esoteric Lessons

### 1. The Healing Power of Raphael's Name

Chanting Raphael's name invokes his essence, with each syllable acting as a vibrational conduit for his energy. The Hebrew pronunciation (*Rafa-El*) translates to "God heals," emphasizing his divine role.

### 2. The Use of Chants and Mantras

Chants create a repetitive rhythm that deepens focus and enhances the practitioner's connection to Raphael. These sacred sounds act as spiritual beacons, drawing his energy closer.

### 3. Prayers as Intentional Communication

Prayers combine words and intent, creating a heartfelt call to Raphael. Each word carries the practitioner's sincerity, amplifying the invocation's effectiveness.

# Practical Applications: Methods of Invocation

## 1. Using Prayers to Invite Raphael's Presence

**Steps**

1. **Prepare the Space**
   Light a green candle and burn frankincense incense to purify and elevate the energy of the space.
2. **Focus on Raphael's Image or Sigil**
   Place an image or sigil of Raphael on your altar. Gaze at it, visualizing emerald light radiating outward.
3. **Say the Prayer**
   Recite the following:
   "Archangel Raphael, divine healer and guide,
   I call upon your presence in this sacred space.
   Surround me with your emerald light,
   And fill my heart with your divine grace.
   By your mercy, heal and protect me,
   Illuminate my path with your guiding light. Amen."
4. **Seal the Invocation**
   Bow your head in gratitude, affirming your trust in Raphael's presence.

## 2. Chanting Raphael's Name in Hebrew

**Steps**

1. **Begin with Breathwork**
   Take deep breaths, focusing on the flow of air, aligning with Raphael's element.
2. **Chant the Name**
   Repeat Raphael's name in Hebrew: *Rafa-El (רפאל)*.
   Stretch the syllables to create a melodic rhythm. For example:
   *Raa-faa-eeeellll.*
   Visualize each chant resonating as emerald light expanding outward.

3. **Continue for 10–15 Minutes**
   Allow the chant to deepen your focus and elevate the energy of the space.

## 3. Invoking Through Sacred Sounds

**Steps**

1. **Select a Sound Instrument**
   Use a singing bowl, chime, or wind instrument that resonates with you. Instruments that produce soft, airy tones are particularly effective for invoking Raphael.
2. **Play the Instrument with Intention**
   As you produce sound, visualize the vibrations carrying your call to Raphael. Imagine emerald light swirling around the space with each tone.
3. **Incorporate the Chant or Prayer**
   Combine the sound with vocal invocation, repeating Raphael's name or reciting a prayer to amplify the energy.

# Magical Correspondences

- **Colors:** Emerald green (healing), gold (illumination)
- **Crystals:** Clear quartz (clarity), green aventurine (growth)
- **Herbs:** Frankincense (elevation), rosemary (focus)
- **Instruments:** Singing bowls, wind chimes, flutes

# Advanced Techniques for Enhanced Invocation

## Creating a Sound-Infused Ritual

Combine all elements—prayers, chants, and sacred sounds—for a layered invocation. Begin with a prayer, transition into chanting Raphael's name, and conclude by playing a singing bowl or chime.

## Dream Invocation

Before bed, chant Raphael's name softly, allowing the sound to resonate through your body. Invite him to communicate through dreams, enhancing your connection.

## Daily Breath Practice

Incorporate Raphael's energy into your breathwork. With each inhale, imagine drawing in emerald light, and with each exhale, release all negativity.

# Resonating with Raphael's Divine Frequency

Invoking Raphael through prayers, chants, and sounds creates a dynamic and sacred interaction, drawing his energy closer for healing, guidance, and protection. These practices allow you to integrate his presence into your daily life and rituals, deepening your spiritual connection.

## Advanced Tips for Deepening Your Practice

1. **Develop Personalized Chants:** Combine Raphael's name with affirmations or mantras that align with your intentions.
2. **Incorporate Elemental Energy:** Perform these invocations outdoors, allowing the natural element of air to amplify your practice.
3. **Experiment with Sacred Languages:** Explore invocations in Hebrew, Latin, or other sacred languages to enhance resonance.

By mastering these techniques, you create a sacred and harmonious relationship with Raphael, allowing his divine wisdom and healing light to illuminate every facet of your magical practice.

# Preparing the Physical and Energetic Environment for Raphael's Presence

## The Foundation of Sacred Preparation

Before invoking Archangel Raphael, it is essential to create an environment that resonates with his divine frequency. A well-prepared physical and energetic space acts as a bridge to connect with Raphael's healing, guiding, and protective energies. This preparation reflects both your respect for his presence and your readiness to receive his blessings.

## Historical and Spiritual Context

### Sacred Spaces in Spiritual Traditions

- **Biblical Roots:** Altars and sacred spaces are central to the Abrahamic traditions. In the *Book of Tobit*, Raphael's guidance unfolds in a context of prayerful preparation and intentional action, reflecting the importance of a prepared environment.
- **Mystical Traditions:** Kabbalistic teachings emphasize the alignment of physical and spiritual energies, making preparation a foundational step in angelic invocation.
- **Esoteric Practices:** Energetic cleansing and alignment of space are common in angelic and magical traditions to create a resonant frequency for divine connection.

## Symbolism and Esoteric Lessons

### 1. Aligning with Raphael's Element of Air

Raphael's association with air emphasizes the importance of clarity, movement, and balance. Preparing the environment with open airflow or air-aligned tools (such as incense) enhances this connection.

## 2. The Purity of Emerald Light

Emerald green represents Raphael's healing light. Infusing this color into your environment creates a visual and energetic resonance with his essence.

## 3. Balancing Physical and Spiritual Energy

A harmonious environment reflects the balance of the physical (clean, organized space) and spiritual (cleansed, high-vibration energy).

# Practical Applications: Steps to Prepare Your Environment

## 1. Physical Preparation

**Steps**

1. **Clean the Space**
   Physically clean the area where you will work with Raphael. Dust, vacuum, and organize, as clutter can disrupt energetic flow.
   - **Symbolic Meaning:** Cleaning signifies clearing old energy to welcome divine presence.
2. **Arrange Sacred Items**
   Place items associated with Raphael on your altar or within your space:
   - **Green Cloth:** Represents Raphael's emerald light.
   - **Crystals:** Malachite, green aventurine, or clear quartz.
   - **Candles:** Green and white to symbolize healing and purity.
   - **Incense Holder:** For burning sacred herbs like frankincense or rosemary.
3. **Create a Central Focal Point**
   Use Raphael's sigil, an image, or a feather to create a

central focus. This object will anchor the space as a point of connection.

## 2. Energetic Cleansing

**Steps**

1. **Smudging with Herbs**
   Burn sage, rosemary, or frankincense to cleanse the space energetically. Begin at the entrance, moving clockwise around the room. Say:
   *"I cleanse this space of all negativity, preparing it for the presence of Archangel Raphael."*
2. **Sound Cleansing**
   Use a singing bowl, chime, or bell to clear stagnant energy. Walk around the space, ringing the bell or playing the bowl, focusing on each corner.
3. **Visualize Emerald Light**
   Close your eyes and imagine Raphael's emerald green light descending into the space, filling every corner with healing and clarity. Say:
   *"Raphael, healer of the divine, may your light purify and sanctify this space."*

## 3. Aligning the Space to Raphael's Energy

**Steps**

1. **Invoke the Element of Air**
   Light a stick of frankincense or sandalwood incense. As the smoke rises, say:
   *"By the element of air, I align this space with the energy of Raphael, divine healer and guide."*
2. **Activate Sacred Items**
   Hold each item on your altar (crystals, candles, sigil) and infuse it with intention. Visualize each object glowing with emerald light.
3. **Bless the Space**
   Sprinkle a few drops of consecrated water or oil around the room while saying:

*"May this space be blessed by Raphael's healing light and guiding presence."*

## Magical Correspondences

- **Colors:** Emerald green (healing), white (purity)
- **Crystals:** Malachite (transformation), green aventurine (growth), clear quartz (clarity)
- **Herbs:** Frankincense (elevation), rosemary (clarity), sage (cleansing)
- **Incense:** Frankincense, sandalwood
- **Symbols:** Raphael's sigil, feathers, emerald light

## Advanced Techniques for Deepening Space Preparation

### 1. Seasonal and Lunar Alignments

Prepare your space during the waxing moon for growth or the full moon for illumination. Seasonal alignments, such as the spring equinox, resonate with Raphael's energies of renewal and healing.

### 2. Layered Energetic Practices

Combine smudging, sound cleansing, and visualization for a multi-layered approach to clearing and aligning your space.

### 3. Personalized Offerings

Place personal items or offerings, such as a written prayer or fresh flowers, on the altar to strengthen your connection to Raphael.

## A Sanctuary for Divine Connection

Preparing the physical and energetic environment is an essential step in building a strong and sacred connection with Archangel Raphael. By creating a space that resonates with his energy, you invite his healing, guidance, and protection into your practice and your life.

## Advanced Tips for Enhanced Preparation

1. **Daily Space Maintenance:** Regularly cleanse and refresh the space to maintain its energetic resonance with Raphael.
2. **Morning and Evening Blessings:** Begin and end your day with a brief invocation at the altar to keep the space attuned to Raphael's energy.
3. **Portable Sacred Space:** If a permanent altar isn't possible, create a portable kit with candles, crystals, and a small sigil to set up temporary spaces as needed.

Through these practices, your environment becomes a sacred sanctuary, fully aligned with Raphael's divine light and energy. This space will serve as a foundation for deepening your relationship with Raphael and enhancing every aspect of your magical practice.

Having established a profound connection with Archangel Raphael through attunement, sacred tools, and the creation of a dedicated space, we are now poised to engage directly with his transformative energies. Now we will delve into a rich array of rituals and magical practices designed to harness Raphael's healing, protective, and transformational powers. From physical healing ceremonies employing prayers and energy work to protective rituals for safe journeys, and even transformative practices aimed at personal renewal and breaking unhealthy habits, this next phase offers practical applications to deepen your relationship with Raphael. These rituals will provide you with step-by-step guidance to integrate his divine presence into your magical workings, fostering healing, protection, and spiritual growth in your daily life.

# { 5 }

# Harnessing Raphael's Power: Rituals for Healing, Protection, and Transformation

The rituals and magical practices dedicated to Archangel Raphael embody the essence of his divine mission: to heal, protect, and guide transformation. In this section, we will explore how to channel Raphael's celestial energy to address physical, emotional, and spiritual needs. From rituals for physical and emotional healing to protective practices that ensure safety during travel, these ceremonies align with Raphael's unique attributes as a healer and guardian. Additionally, transformational rituals will guide you through breaking unhealthy habits and embracing personal renewal.

Each practice is crafted to deepen your connection with Raphael, utilizing sacred tools, prayers, and invocations to enhance your magical practice. Through these rituals, you will tap into Raphael's profound wisdom and healing light, creating a pathway to growth, protection, and spiritual alignment. Prepare to transform your intentions into reality with the guidance of one of the most powerful archangels in the celestial hierarchy.

## Healing the Body: Physical Healing Rituals with Raphael

### The Healer of Body and Soul

Archangel Raphael, whose name means "God heals," is renowned for his divine mission to bring physical healing to those in need. Drawing on the vibrational power of prayers, candle rituals, and energy work, these practices align your intentions with Raphael's celestial energy. By invoking his presence, you can channel his healing light to restore vitality, balance, and well-being.

## Historical and Spiritual Context

### Raphael as a Healing Guide in the Book of Tobit

In the *Book of Tobit*, Raphael performs miraculous acts of healing, including restoring Tobit's sight and using the medicinal properties of a fish to drive away spiritual afflictions. These stories underscore his role as a divine healer with profound knowledge of both physical remedies and spiritual interventions.

### Mystical Traditions and Energy Healing

- **Kabbalistic Insights:** Raphael's alignment with Tiferet (beauty, balance, and harmony) in the Tree of Life highlights his ability to bring wholeness to the physical body through divine balance.
- **Esoteric Practices:** Raphael is often invoked in magical and healing traditions to channel energy into the body, harmonizing physical and spiritual forces.

## Symbolism and Esoteric Lessons

### 1. The Emerald Light of Healing

Raphael's emerald green light is symbolic of renewal, growth, and vitality. This color vibrates at a frequency that resonates with the heart chakra, the energetic center of healing and love.

### 2. The Element of Air

As the archangel of air, Raphael's energy aligns with breath, movement, and circulation—key elements in physical vitality and healing practices.

## 3. The Role of Intention and Focus

Healing rituals are most effective when performed with clarity of intention and deep focus. Each step in the ritual is an intentional act, drawing Raphael's energy closer.

# Practical Applications: Healing Rituals with Raphael

## 1. Physical Healing Prayer Ritual

**Materials**

- Green candle (symbolizing healing)
- Raphael's sigil (drawn or printed)
- Frankincense incense
- A bowl of water (symbolizing cleansing)

**Steps**

1. **Prepare the Space**
   Cleanse the area with frankincense incense. Visualize the smoke carrying away all negativity. Say:
   *"By this sacred smoke, I purify this space for the healing light of Raphael."*
2. **Light the Candle**
   Place the green candle on your altar and light it. Focus on the flame as a representation of Raphael's healing energy.
3. **Invoke Raphael**
   Hold Raphael's sigil in your hands. Say:
   *"Raphael, healer of the divine,*
   *I call upon your emerald light.*
   *Surround me with your grace and restore my body to health.*
   *By the mercy of God, I am healed and whole."*
4. **Use the Water for Cleansing**
   Dip your hands into the bowl of water, then place your hands over the area of your body in need of healing.

Visualize emerald light flowing from Raphael into your body. Say:
*"With this sacred water, may your healing energy flow through me,
Restoring balance, vitality, and peace."*

5. **Close the Ritual**
Extinguish the candle and thank Raphael. Say:
*"Raphael, I am grateful for your light and healing.
Remain with me as I walk the path of health and renewal."*

## 2. Candle Ritual for Physical Healing

**Materials**

- Seven green candles (representing seven days of healing)
- Anointing oil (frankincense or rosemary)
- Raphael's sigil or a feather (symbol of air and healing)

**Steps**

1. **Prepare the Candles**
Anoint each candle with the oil while focusing on your intention. As you anoint, say:
*"I charge this candle with Raphael's healing light."*
2. **Light the First Candle**
On the first day, light one candle and place it near Raphael's sigil. Say:
*"Raphael, surround me with your healing presence.
Let this light burn away illness and restore vitality."*
3. **Repeat for Seven Days**
Each day, light a new candle while repeating the invocation. Focus on the area of your body that needs healing.
4. **Conclude the Ritual**
On the seventh day, gather the candle stubs and bury them in the earth as an offering of gratitude.

### 3. Energy Work with Raphael's Healing Light

**Steps**

1. **Meditative Preparation**
   Sit in a comfortable position, close your eyes, and take deep breaths. Visualize yourself surrounded by emerald green light.
2. **Invoke Raphael**
   Place your hands over your heart and say:
   *"Raphael, divine healer, let your emerald light flow through me.*
   *Align my body, mind, and spirit in perfect health."*
3. **Channel Healing Energy**
   Move your hands slowly over the areas in need of healing, imagining them bathed in green light. Visualize any blockages dissolving and vitality being restored.
4. **Express Gratitude**
   End the session by thanking Raphael. Say:
   *"I honor your presence and trust in your healing.*
   *May your light continue to guide me to wholeness."*

## Magical Correspondences

- **Colors:** Emerald green (healing), white (purity)
- **Crystals:** Malachite (physical healing), green aventurine (growth), clear quartz (amplification)
- **Herbs:** Frankincense (elevation), rosemary (clarity), lavender (calm)
- **Incense:** Frankincense, sandalwood
- **Symbols:** Raphael's sigil, feathers, emerald light

## Embodying Raphael's Healing Energy

Physical healing rituals with Raphael are deeply transformative, blending intention, focus, and divine assistance to restore balance and vitality. These practices not only invite Raphael's presence but also empower you to actively participate in your healing process.

### Advanced Tips for Deepening Your Practice

1. **Daily Healing Devotions:** Light a green candle each morning and recite a prayer to Raphael for ongoing healing support.
2. **Seasonal Healing Work:** Perform these rituals during the spring equinox or other periods of renewal to align with Raphael's energy.
3. **Personalized Symbols:** Add personal items to the rituals, such as a photograph or a written intention, to enhance their potency.

By incorporating these rituals into your practice, you align yourself with Raphael's divine mission of healing, creating a sacred space for transformation and renewal.

## Healing the Mind and Heart: Emotional and Mental Healing Rituals with Raphael

### The Balm for the Weary Soul

Archangel Raphael's role as a healer extends beyond the physical realm into the depths of emotional and mental well-being. His energy brings solace to the anxious, clarity to the confused, and comfort to those carrying the burdens of stress or emotional pain. Through guided meditations and stress-release rituals, Raphael can assist in restoring inner peace and emotional harmony, allowing you to step into a state of renewed strength and clarity.

## Historical and Spiritual Context

### Raphael in the Book of Tobit: A Guide for Inner Peace

The *Book of Tobit* portrays Raphael as a steadfast guide, offering reassurance and protection during times of uncertainty. This reflects his ability to bring emotional stability and mental clarity, guiding individuals through moments of turmoil toward divine resolution.

### Mystical Interpretations of Raphael's Emotional Healing

- **Kabbalistic Insights:** In the Tree of Life, Raphael's connection to Tiferet (beauty and harmony) highlights his role in balancing emotions and cultivating inner peace.
- **Esoteric Symbolism:** Raphael's emerald light is associated with the heart chakra, the energetic center for emotional healing and love, making him a powerful ally in emotional and mental restoration.

## Symbolism and Esoteric Lessons

### 1. The Emerald Green Light of Raphael

This radiant light symbolizes renewal, forgiveness, and emotional equilibrium. Visualizing emerald light during rituals can dissolve stress and uplift the spirit.

### 2. The Element of Air and Breathwork

As the archangel of air, Raphael's energy is intertwined with breath, representing life force and the calming power of mindful breathing during stress-release practices.

### 3. Emotional Healing as Divine Alignment

Raphael's guidance emphasizes that emotional healing is a sacred process of aligning with divine love and compassion, fostering self-acceptance and inner peace.

## Practical Applications: Emotional and Mental Healing Rituals

### 1. Guided Meditation for Emotional Healing

**Steps**

1. **Prepare the Space**
   Create a serene environment with dim lighting, a green candle, and soft instrumental music. Burn frankincense or lavender incense to calm the atmosphere.
2. **Begin with Grounding**
   Sit comfortably, close your eyes, and take deep breaths. Visualize roots extending from your body into the earth, grounding you in stability.
3. **Invoke Raphael**
   Whisper or say aloud:
   *"Raphael, angel of healing and harmony,
   Surround me with your emerald light.
   Guide me to release the pain in my heart,
   And replace it with divine peace."*
4. **Visualize the Healing Light**
   Imagine a sphere of emerald light descending from above, enveloping your heart and mind. As the light grows brighter, visualize it dissolving stress, sadness, or fear.
5. **Focus on Emotional Renewal**
   Allow images or emotions to surface, acknowledging them without judgment. Let the emerald light soothe and transform these feelings into clarity and peace.
6. **Conclude with Gratitude**
   Whisper:

*"Thank you, Raphael, for your healing and grace.
I release all that no longer serves me and embrace your light."*


## 2. Stress Release Ritual with Breathwork

**Steps**

1. **Set the Intention**
   Light a green candle and place a feather or Raphael's sigil on your altar. Say:
   *"Raphael, healer of breath and spirit,
   Help me release the burdens I carry.
   May each breath bring peace and renewal."*
2. **Perform the Four-Part Breath**
   Inhale deeply for four counts, hold for four counts, exhale for four counts, and pause for four counts. Visualize each breath infusing your body with emerald light and releasing stress.
3. **Incorporate Affirmations**
   After several rounds of breathwork, repeat:
   *"With every breath, I find peace.
   With every exhale, I release tension.
   I am held in Raphael's healing light."*
4. **Close the Ritual**
   Blow out the candle, symbolizing the release of stress. Whisper:
   *"Raphael, I thank you for your healing presence.
   May your peace remain with me always."*


# Magical Correspondences

- **Colors:** Emerald green (heart healing), lavender (calm), white (clarity)
- **Crystals:** Rose quartz (emotional healing), green aventurine (growth), amethyst (mental clarity)

- **Herbs:** Lavender (calm), chamomile (relaxation), frankincense (spiritual elevation)
- **Incense:** Sandalwood, frankincense, lavender
- **Symbols:** Raphael's sigil, feathers, emerald light

## Advanced Techniques for Deepening Emotional Healing

### 1. Journaling with Raphael's Guidance

After rituals or meditations, journal your thoughts and emotions, addressing them directly to Raphael. Reflect on any insights or feelings of release that arise.

### 2. Dream Healing

Before sleep, invite Raphael to visit you in your dreams. Place a green crystal under your pillow and chant his name softly to prepare your mind for divine communication.

### 3. Group Healing Circles

Organize a group healing ritual, invoking Raphael's presence collectively. Combine chants, meditations, and shared intentions to amplify his energy.

## Aligning with Raphael's Compassion

Through guided meditations and stress-release rituals, Raphael offers a pathway to emotional and mental renewal. These practices create a sacred space for self-reflection, healing, and alignment with divine love and compassion.

## Advanced Tips for Enhancing Your Practice

1. **Daily Affirmations:** Incorporate affirmations inspired by Raphael into your morning or evening routine to sustain emotional balance.
2. **Seasonal Emotional Cleansing:** Perform these rituals during transitional periods, such as the spring equinox, to align with Raphael's energies of renewal.
3. **Layered Practices:** Combine emotional healing rituals with physical healing or spiritual cleansing for a holistic approach.

By embracing these practices, you will deepen your connection with Raphael, transforming emotional burdens into sources of strength and wisdom, guided by his healing light.

## Cleansing the Spirit: Spiritual Healing Rituals with Raphael

### The Purifier of Spirit and Soul

Archangel Raphael, as the healer of body, mind, and spirit, excels in cleansing rituals that renew the soul and elevate spiritual awareness. Spiritual healing with Raphael involves the use of holy water, incense, and sacred invocations to remove spiritual blockages, dispel negativity, and realign with divine energy. These practices offer profound restoration, leaving you spiritually renewed and attuned to higher realms.

### Historical and Spiritual Context

### Raphael as a Cleansing Guide in Sacred Texts

- **The Book of Tobit:** Raphael banishes the demon Asmodeus through a sacred ritual involving a fish,

highlighting his role in spiritual purification and divine protection.
- **Esoteric Traditions:** In mystical practices, Raphael's energy is invoked to cleanse spaces and individuals, ensuring alignment with divine grace.

## Mystical Interpretations of Spiritual Cleansing

- **Kabbalistic Symbolism:** Raphael's connection to Tiferet represents balance and harmony, which are key to spiritual renewal.
- **Element of Air:** As the angel of air, Raphael's energy is tied to the purifying properties of incense and breath, aligning the practitioner with the divine flow of life.

## Symbolism and Esoteric Lessons

### 1. Holy Water as a Conduit of Divine Energy

Holy water, blessed and imbued with intention, symbolizes purification, renewal, and the washing away of spiritual impurities. In Christian traditions, it is a powerful tool for sanctifying spaces and individuals.

### 2. Incense as a Symbol of Ascension

The rising smoke of incense represents prayers and intentions ascending to the heavens. When paired with Raphael's invocation, it becomes a medium for channeling his healing energy.

### 3. Invocations as Direct Communication

Sacred invocations bridge the gap between the physical and celestial realms, allowing you to connect with Raphael's presence and request his divine assistance.

# Practical Applications: Spiritual Healing and Cleansing Rituals

## 1. Ritual of Spiritual Renewal

**Materials**

- A bowl of holy water
- Frankincense or sandalwood incense
- Green and white candles
- Raphael's sigil or a feather

**Steps**

1. **Prepare the Space**
   Light the candles and incense. Place Raphael's sigil on your altar. Begin by saying:
   *"Raphael, healer of the divine, I call upon your presence in this sacred space. Let your emerald light purify and renew."*
2. **Bless the Holy Water**
   Hold the bowl of water and say:
   *"By the grace of the divine and the light of Raphael, may this water be a vessel of healing and renewal."*
   Visualize emerald light descending into the water, infusing it with Raphael's energy.
3. **Cleanse with the Holy Water**
   Dip your fingers into the water and anoint your forehead, heart, and hands. Say:
   *"With this sacred water, I release all that no longer serves me. I am cleansed and renewed in Raphael's healing light."*
4. **Use the Incense for Energetic Cleansing**
   Waft the incense smoke around your body or the space, visualizing it carrying away all negativity. Say:
   *"By this sacred smoke, may Raphael's light banish all shadows and restore divine harmony."*

5. **Conclude with Gratitude**
   Bow your head and say:
   *"Raphael, I thank you for your healing and grace. May your light guide me always."*

## 2. Ritual for Cleansing Negative Energies

**Steps**

1. **Set the Intention**
   Light a single green candle. Hold Raphael's sigil and say:
   *"Raphael, divine healer, I ask for your presence to cleanse and renew this space and spirit."*
2. **Create a Sacred Circle**
   Walk clockwise around your space, sprinkling holy water and wafting incense. As you move, repeat:
   *"By the light of Raphael, this space is cleansed. By the breath of Raphael, this space is healed."*
3. **Perform a Silent Meditation**
   Sit quietly, allowing the candle's flame and incense's aroma to fill the space. Visualize Raphael's emerald light enveloping you and the area.
4. **Seal the Space**
   Blow out the candle and sprinkle the remaining holy water at the room's entrance. Say:
   *"This space is blessed, protected, and filled with divine grace."*

# Magical Correspondences

- **Colors:** Emerald green (healing), white (purity)
- **Crystals:** Clear quartz (clarity), green aventurine (renewal), selenite (cleansing)
- **Herbs:** Frankincense (purification), sage (cleansing), sandalwood (spiritual elevation)
- **Incense:** Frankincense, sandalwood
- **Symbols:** Raphael's sigil, feathers, emerald light

# Advanced Techniques for Spiritual Cleansing

### 1. Combining Elements

Integrate water, incense, and light in a single ritual to create a multi-layered cleansing experience that addresses all energetic levels.

### 2. Seasonal Cleansing

Perform spiritual cleansing rituals during equinoxes or full moons to align with Raphael's energies of balance and renewal.

### 3. Personal Cleansing Amulet

Bless a small bottle of holy water with Raphael's invocation. Carry it as an amulet for on-the-go cleansing and spiritual alignment.

# Embracing Spiritual Renewal

Spiritual healing and cleansing rituals with Raphael open a pathway to divine clarity and emotional release. Through holy water, incense, and sacred invocations, you invite Raphael's energy into your life, creating a sanctuary for healing and peace.

## Advanced Tips for Enhancing Your Practice

1. **Daily Blessing Rituals:** Use a simple anointing ritual with holy water each morning to maintain spiritual alignment.
2. **Group Cleansing Ceremonies:** Collaborate with others to invoke Raphael's energy in a collective cleansing ritual, amplifying its effects.

3. **Dream Cleansing:** Perform these rituals before sleep, inviting Raphael to continue the cleansing process through your dreams.

By integrating these practices into your spiritual routine, you deepen your relationship with Raphael, fostering an enduring connection to his healing and cleansing energy.

## Guardian of Journeys: Protective Rituals for Safe Travel with Raphael

### The Archangel of the Way

Archangel Raphael, the divine guide in the *Book of Tobit*, is renowned for his role as a protector of travelers and journeys. Whether embarking on a physical trip or navigating a metaphorical journey, invoking Raphael ensures safety, clarity, and divine protection along the way. Rituals for safe travel draw upon his energy to create a spiritual shield, ensuring smooth passage and guarding against unforeseen challenges.

## Historical and Spiritual Context

### Raphael in the Book of Tobit: Protector and Guide

In the *Book of Tobit*, Raphael accompanies Tobias on a perilous journey, offering guidance, protection, and healing along the way. His role as a guardian highlights his ability to safeguard travelers from physical, emotional, and spiritual harm.

### Mystical Traditions and Raphael's Protective Energy

- **Kabbalistic Insights:** As the archangel of air, Raphael governs the freedom of movement, aligning with the element's association with travel and communication.

- **Esoteric Symbolism:** Raphael's staff represents guidance and direction, while his presence signifies divine oversight during journeys.

## Symbolism and Esoteric Lessons

### 1. The Emerald Light of Protection

Raphael's emerald green light is a protective aura, enveloping travelers in divine energy that shields them from harm.

### 2. The Element of Air

Raphael's association with air makes him an ideal guardian for journeys, as air symbolizes movement, freedom, and the breath of life that sustains travelers.

### 3. The Role of Intention in Travel Protection

Intention is the foundation of protective rituals. By consciously invoking Raphael and aligning with his energy, you create a spiritual safeguard that accompanies you throughout your journey.

## Practical Applications: Rituals for Safe Travel

### 1. Travel Protection Ritual

**Materials**

- A small green candle
- Raphael's sigil or a feather
- A travel-sized bottle of holy water or consecrated oil
- Frankincense incense

**Steps**

1. **Prepare the Ritual Space**
   Light the candle and incense. Place Raphael's sigil or a

feather on your altar as a focal point. Begin by saying:
*"Raphael, guardian of travelers, I call upon your light to protect me on my journey."*

2. **Bless the Holy Water or Oil**
   Hold the bottle in your hands and visualize emerald light infusing it with Raphael's energy. Say:
   *"By the grace of Raphael, may this water (or oil) shield me from harm and guide me safely to my destination."*

3. **Anoint Yourself and Your Luggage**
   Use the holy water or oil to anoint your forehead, heart, and feet. Say:
   *"With this blessing, I am protected in body, mind, and spirit."*
   Lightly anoint your luggage or vehicle, saying:
   *"May all that travels with me be guarded by Raphael's light."*

4. **Recite the Invocation**
   Hold Raphael's sigil or feather and say:
   *"Raphael, divine guide and healer,*
   *Surround me with your wings of light.*
   *Let no harm come near me, no obstacle impede my way.*
   *By your grace, may I journey safely and return in peace."*

5. **Extinguish the Candle**
   As you extinguish the candle, visualize Raphael's light remaining with you. Whisper:
   *"Raphael, I thank you for your presence. Guide me always."*

## 2. Feather Talisman for Travel Protection

**Steps**

1. **Choose a Feather**
   Select a feather, symbolic of Raphael's protective wings. Preferably green or white, but any feather can be consecrated for this purpose.

2. **Consecrate the Feather**
   Light a green candle and pass the feather through the flame (briefly and safely). Say:

> *"Raphael, by your light, I consecrate this feather as my guardian on this journey."*

3. **Carry the Feather**
   Keep the feather in your travel bag or vehicle as a talisman of Raphael's protection.

## 3. Portable Sigil Ritual for Travel

**Steps**

1. **Create a Travel Sigil**
   Draw Raphael's sigil on a small piece of paper or carve it into a green candle.
2. **Activate the Sigil**
   Hold the sigil and say:
   *"By this sacred symbol, I invoke Raphael's guidance and protection on my journey."*
3. **Carry the Sigil**
   Place the sigil in your wallet, passport case, or vehicle to maintain a connection to Raphael's energy.

# Magical Correspondences

- **Colors:** Emerald green (protection), white (purity)
- **Crystals:** Malachite (protection during travel), clear quartz (clarity), green aventurine (luck and success)
- **Herbs:** Frankincense (elevation), rosemary (clarity), sage (protection)
- **Incense:** Frankincense, sandalwood
- **Symbols:** Raphael's sigil, feathers, emerald light

# Advanced Techniques for Enhanced Travel Protection

## 1. Daily Blessing Before Travel

Recite a quick invocation to Raphael before beginning your journey. Light a green candle if possible and say:
*"Raphael, guide and protect me as I travel. May your light shine the path ahead."*

## 2. Layered Protection

Combine physical and spiritual protection by using both talismans and invocations. For instance, anoint your vehicle with consecrated oil while carrying a feather talisman.

## 3. Seasonal and Lunar Alignments

Align your travel rituals with the waxing moon or spring equinox, times associated with growth, renewal, and safe passage.

# Traveling with Raphael's Grace

Invoking Raphael for safe travel transforms your journey into a sacred experience, infused with divine guidance and protection. Through rituals, talismans, and invocations, you establish a connection to Raphael that shields you from harm and ensures peace throughout your travels.

## Advanced Tips for Deepening Your Practice

1. **Create a Traveler's Kit:** Assemble a small bag containing Raphael's sigil, a feather, a green candle, and a bottle of holy water for on-the-go rituals.
2. **Invoke Raphael for Others:** Perform these rituals for loved ones who are embarking on journeys, extending Raphael's protective light to them.
3. **Reflect and Give Thanks:** After a journey, take a moment to light a candle and thank Raphael for his guidance and protection.

With these practices, every journey becomes an opportunity to deepen your connection with Raphael, traveling with the assurance of his celestial care.

# The Emerald Shield: Creating Wards and Shields with Raphael's Energy

## Raphael, Protector of Light

Archangel Raphael, the divine healer and guardian, is also a master of protection. Through the creation of energetic wards and shields, Raphael's emerald light serves as a barrier against negative forces, ensuring safety and stability for individuals and spaces. These protective rituals harness his healing and transformative energy, providing both physical and spiritual safeguarding.

# Historical and Spiritual Context

## Raphael's Role in Protection

In the *Book of Tobit*, Raphael's guidance and protection are central to the safe passage of Tobias and the healing of his father. This narrative reflects Raphael's ability to shield and guide individuals through perilous situations, both physical and spiritual.

# Mystical Interpretations of Shields and Wards

- **Kabbalistic Insights:** In the Tree of Life, Raphael's connection to Tiferet (beauty, balance, and harmony) signifies his role in creating equilibrium and divine alignment, key elements in protective magic.
- **Esoteric Traditions:** Raphael's association with air and emerald light symbolizes clarity, purification, and the dispersal of harmful energies, making him a powerful ally in warding practices.

# Symbolism and Esoteric Lessons

### 1. The Emerald Light as a Shield

Raphael's emerald energy is symbolic of growth, renewal, and protection. This radiant light not only heals but also creates a boundary that repels negativity and harm.

### 2. The Element of Air in Protective Magic

Air, governed by Raphael, represents movement, communication, and the breath of life. It serves as a medium for creating and sustaining energetic shields, reflecting the flow of divine protection.

### 3. Intention as the Core of Protection

Protective wards and shields are most effective when imbued with clear, focused intention. Raphael's energy amplifies this intention, transforming it into a powerful barrier.

# Practical Applications: Wards and Shields with Raphael's Energy

### 1. Ritual for Creating a Personal Protective Shield

**Materials**

- Green candle
- Raphael's sigil or a feather
- A small piece of malachite or clear quartz
- Frankincense incense

**Steps**

1. **Prepare the Space**
   Light the green candle and incense. Place Raphael's

sigil and the crystal on your altar. Say:
*"Raphael, protector and healer, I call upon your emerald light to shield me from all harm."*

2. **Visualize the Shield**
Close your eyes and imagine a radiant sphere of emerald light forming around you. See it expanding with each breath, creating a protective barrier that is impenetrable yet permeable to love and positivity.

3. **Invoke Raphael's Energy**
Hold the crystal in your hand and say:
*"By the grace of Raphael, I am encircled by divine light. No harm may pass, no shadow may enter.
I stand within your sacred protection."*

4. **Seal the Shield**
Wave the feather or Raphael's sigil around your body, reinforcing the light. Say:
*"This shield is blessed by Raphael's presence, strong and enduring."*

5. **Carry the Crystal**
Keep the crystal in your pocket or wear it as a talisman to maintain the shield throughout the day.

## 2. Creating Protective Wards for a Space

**Steps**

1. **Cleanse the Area**
Burn frankincense and walk clockwise through the space, visualizing the smoke clearing away all negativity. Say:
*"Raphael, by your light, may this space be cleansed and protected."*

2. **Mark the Four Corners**
Place Raphael's sigil or a green candle in each corner of the room. Light the candles or visualize emerald light anchoring Raphael's energy in each location.

3. **Draw the Energetic Boundary**
Using a feather or your hand, trace an imaginary line connecting the four corners, visualizing an unbroken circle of emerald light. Say:

*"By the presence of Raphael, this space is sealed in divine protection.
No harm may enter, and all within are safe."*
4. **Seal with Intention**
Place a central object, such as a crystal or Raphael's sigil, in the room. Whisper:
*"This ward is strong and true, sustained by Raphael's light and love."*

## 3. Portable Ward for Travel or Temporary Spaces

**Steps**

1. **Create a Sigil Card**
Draw Raphael's sigil on a small piece of paper. Charge it by holding it between your hands and visualizing it glowing with emerald light.
2. **Bless the Sigil Card**
Say:
*"Raphael, protector and healer, bless this sigil with your light.
May it shield me wherever I go."*
3. **Carry the Sigil**
Keep the sigil card in your bag or pocket. Before entering a new space, hold the card and visualize Raphael's light spreading through the area.

# Magical Correspondences

- **Colors:** Emerald green (protection), white (purity)
- **Crystals:** Malachite (warding), clear quartz (amplification), black tourmaline (grounding)
- **Herbs:** Frankincense (purification), rosemary (protection), sage (cleansing)
- **Incense:** Frankincense, sandalwood
- **Symbols:** Raphael's sigil, feathers, emerald light

# Advanced Techniques for Strengthening Wards and Shields

### 1. Layered Shields

Create multiple layers of protection by combining personal shields, space wards, and talismans. Each layer amplifies the overall strength of the barrier.

### 2. Seasonal Reinforcement

Reinforce your wards during significant celestial events, such as equinoxes or full moons, when spiritual energies are heightened.

### 3. Dynamic Shields

Visualize your shield as a responsive barrier, expanding and contracting as needed to adapt to different situations.

## Empowering Your Space and Spirit

Creating wards and shields with Raphael's energy establishes a sacred sanctuary for you and your environment. These practices not only protect but also foster a sense of peace, allowing you to navigate life with confidence and grace.

## Advanced Tips for Deepening Your Practice

1. **Daily Shielding Rituals:** Begin each day by visualizing Raphael's light encircling you, reinforcing your personal shield.
2. **Custom Protective Tools:** Personalize your wards with symbols or objects that hold special meaning for you, enhancing their potency.

3. **Share Raphael's Protection:** Perform these rituals for loved ones, extending Raphael's shielding energy to those in need.

By mastering these techniques, you create an enduring connection with Raphael, ensuring that his protective light remains a steadfast presence in your life.

## Transforming the Self: Breaking Unhealthy Habits and Addictions with Raphael

### Raphael as the Divine Catalyst for Change

Archangel Raphael, the angel of healing and transformation, offers his emerald light to those seeking to overcome unhealthy habits and addictions. His guidance extends beyond physical healing to address the emotional, mental, and spiritual roots of destructive patterns. Working with Raphael allows for the release of harmful attachments, providing strength and clarity to embrace renewal.

## Historical and Spiritual Context

### Raphael's Role in Transformation

In the *Book of Tobit,* Raphael's guidance is transformative for Tobias and his family, delivering them from despair and aligning them with divine grace. This narrative reflects Raphael's ability to assist in profound personal change and liberation from spiritual or emotional bondage.

### Addiction as a Spiritual Imbalance

From a mystical perspective, addictions and harmful habits represent a misalignment with divine harmony. Raphael, as the angel of air and healing, works to restore this balance, clearing energetic blockages and fostering a renewed connection to the self and the divine.

## Symbolism and Esoteric Lessons

### 1. Emerald Light as a Beacon of Renewal

Raphael's emerald green light symbolizes growth, detoxification, and renewal. This light clears the energy body, dispelling negativity and fortifying resolve.

### 2. Air as the Element of Release

The element of air, governed by Raphael, represents breath, communication, and movement—essential tools for releasing attachments and inviting change.

### 3. Ritual as a Sacred Commitment

Rituals for breaking habits create a sacred space for intention-setting, aligning the practitioner with divine assistance and amplifying willpower.

## Practical Applications: Rituals for Breaking Unhealthy Habits and Addictions

### 1. Ritual of Release and Renewal

**Materials**

- Green candle
- Raphael's sigil
- A small bowl of water or a feather
- A piece of paper and a pen
- Frankincense incense

**Steps**

1. **Prepare the Space**
   Light the candle and incense, placing Raphael's sigil on

your altar. Say:
*"Raphael, healer and guide, I call upon your light to assist me in releasing what no longer serves me."*

2. **Write Your Intention**
On the paper, write down the habit or addiction you wish to release. Be specific and honest. Hold the paper and say:
*"This burden I carry, I am ready to release. With Raphael's light, I am renewed."*

3. **Immerse the Intention in Water**
Place the paper in the bowl of water (or hold it above the feather if using air symbolism). Visualize the emerald light dissolving the habit's hold on you. Say:
*"With this act, I release this habit into the divine flow. Raphael, cleanse and heal my spirit."*

4. **Burn or Bury the Paper**
After the ritual, burn the paper safely or bury it in the earth to symbolize release. Say:
*"As this is transformed, so am I. I am free."*

5. **Close the Ritual**
Extinguish the candle and give thanks:
*"Raphael, I thank you for your healing presence and guidance. May I walk forward in light and freedom."*

## 2. Breathwork for Emotional and Energetic Release

**Steps**

1. **Set the Intention**
Sit in a quiet place, holding a feather or a green crystal. Say:
*"Raphael, with each breath, I release the ties that bind me. Guide me toward renewal."*

2. **Perform Focused Breathing**
Inhale deeply for four counts, hold for four counts, exhale for six counts. Visualize the emerald light filling your body with each inhale and expelling negativity with each exhale.

3. **Repeat Affirmations**
      After several breaths, repeat:
      *"I am free. I am whole. I am guided by Raphael's light."*
   4. **Conclude with Gratitude**
      Bow your head and whisper:
      *"Thank you, Raphael, for your grace and healing. I am transformed."*

### 3. Empowering a Personal Talisman

**Steps**

   1. **Choose a Crystal or Symbol**
      Select a green crystal like malachite or a small token representing freedom.
   2. **Consecrate the Talisman**
      Light a candle and hold the object in your hands. Say:
      *"Raphael, bless this talisman with your healing light. Let it remind me of my strength and freedom."*
   3. **Carry the Talisman**
      Keep the talisman with you as a reminder of your commitment to change and Raphael's supportive energy.

## Magical Correspondences

- **Colors:** Emerald green (renewal), white (purity)
- **Crystals:** Malachite (release), clear quartz (clarity), amethyst (calm and sobriety)
- **Herbs:** Frankincense (purification), rosemary (focus), sage (cleansing)
- **Incense:** Frankincense, sandalwood
- **Symbols:** Raphael's sigil, feathers, emerald light

## Advanced Techniques for Transformational Healing

### 1. Layered Rituals

Combine physical, emotional, and spiritual healing practices into a single ritual for holistic transformation.

**2. Moon Phase Alignment**

Perform rituals during the waning moon to align with its energy of release and letting go.

**3. Affirmation Journaling**

After rituals, maintain a journal of affirmations and reflections to reinforce your commitment and track progress.

# Liberation through Raphael's Light

Breaking unhealthy habits and addictions with Raphael's guidance creates a pathway to spiritual renewal and personal freedom. His emerald light and protective energy provide the strength and clarity needed for lasting transformation.

## Advanced Tips for Deepening Your Practice

1. **Daily Affirmations:** Start each day by invoking Raphael's light and affirming your commitment to change.
2. **Ritual Repetition:** Repeat these rituals regularly, reinforcing their power and your intention over time.
3. **Seek Raphael's Guidance in Dreams:** Invite Raphael into your dreams to provide additional clarity and support on your journey.

By engaging in these practices, you establish a profound connection with Raphael, empowering yourself to embrace transformation and step into a life of greater harmony and freedom.

# Awakening the Soul: Rituals for Personal Renewal and Spiritual Growth with Raphael

## Raphael as the Catalyst for Transformation

Archangel Raphael, the divine healer and guide, is not only a protector and restorer but also a profound catalyst for personal renewal and spiritual growth. His presence fosters clarity, inspiration, and the courage to step into a higher version of yourself. Rituals for renewal and growth with Raphael align your intentions with divine will, enabling you to shed old layers and embrace spiritual evolution.

## Historical and Spiritual Context

### Raphael's Role in Renewal

In the *Book of Tobit*, Raphael's guidance leads to physical healing, familial restoration, and spiritual renewal. This narrative symbolizes Raphael's ability to inspire transformation on every level of existence.

### Symbolism in Mystical Traditions

- **Kabbalistic Insights:** Raphael's connection to Tiferet (beauty, balance, and harmony) emphasizes his role in fostering inner balance, which is essential for spiritual growth.
- **Emerald Light of Renewal:** His emerald aura is associated with healing, rebirth, and the nurturing energy of nature, symbolizing the continuous cycle of growth and renewal.

## Symbolism and Esoteric Lessons

### 1. The Element of Air as a Medium of Inspiration

Raphael governs the element of air, representing breath, clarity, and the expansive nature of spiritual awakening. Invoking air during rituals allows for a flow of divine wisdom and inspiration.

## 2. Transformation as a Cyclical Process

Rituals for renewal mirror the natural cycles of death and rebirth, enabling the practitioner to release the old and welcome the new.

## 3. Ritual as a Declaration of Intention

Each ritual becomes a sacred contract between the practitioner and the divine, affirming the desire for transformation and the willingness to align with higher energies.

# Practical Applications: Rituals for Renewal and Growth

### 1. Ritual for Personal Renewal

**Materials**

- A green and white candle
- Raphael's sigil
- A feather or small bowl of water
- A piece of malachite or clear quartz
- Journal and pen

**Steps**

1. **Prepare the Space**
   Light the candles and place Raphael's sigil, the feather, or the water on your altar. Begin by saying:
   *"Raphael, divine healer and guide, I call upon your presence to renew my spirit and awaken my soul."*
2. **Set Your Intention**
   In your journal, write down a single sentence

encapsulating your intention for renewal. Example: *"I release the past and embrace my divine potential."*

3. **Activate the Element of Air**
   Hold the feather and gently wave it in the air or gaze into the water. Say:
   *"By the breath of Raphael, may the winds of change carry away all that no longer serves me."*
4. **Visualize the Emerald Light**
   Close your eyes and visualize Raphael's emerald light descending upon you, enveloping your body. Imagine this light dissolving negativity and filling you with renewed vitality.
5. **Invoke Raphael's Guidance**
   Hold the malachite or quartz and say:
   *"Raphael, with your healing light, renew my strength, inspire my spirit, and guide me toward my highest self."*
6. **Conclude the Ritual**
   Extinguish the candles and give thanks:
   *"Raphael, I am grateful for your light and guidance. May I walk forward renewed and aligned with divine grace."*

## 2. Meditation for Spiritual Growth

**Steps**

1. **Set a Quiet Space**
   Light a green candle and sit comfortably, holding a feather or Raphael's sigil.
2. **Focus on Your Breath**
   Inhale deeply, visualizing emerald light filling your lungs, and exhale, releasing tension. Repeat for several breaths.
3. **Invite Raphael's Presence**
   Say:
   *"Raphael, guide of the soul, I invite your light to inspire and transform me."*
4. **Reflect on Growth**
   Meditate on areas of your life that need growth and renewal, asking Raphael for insights.

5. **Conclude with Gratitude**
   Whisper:
   *"Raphael, I thank you for your presence and the wisdom you share."*

## 3. Ritual for Embracing New Beginnings

**Steps**

1. **Symbolize the Old and New**
   Write two lists: one of what you wish to release and one of what you wish to embrace.
2. **Perform the Release**
   Burn the list of old patterns, saying:
   *"Raphael, with your light, I release these burdens and embrace renewal."*
3. **Bless the New Intentions**
   Hold the list of new intentions and visualize them being infused with emerald light. Say:
   *"With Raphael's guidance, I step into these new beginnings with clarity and strength."*

# Magical Correspondences

- **Colors:** Emerald green (renewal), white (purity), gold (divine wisdom)
- **Crystals:** Malachite (renewal), clear quartz (clarity), citrine (inspiration)
- **Herbs:** Frankincense (elevation), rosemary (focus), sage (cleansing)
- **Incense:** Frankincense, sandalwood
- **Symbols:** Raphael's sigil, feathers, emerald light

# Advanced Techniques for Spiritual Growth

### 1. Cyclical Renewal

Perform renewal rituals during significant seasonal changes (equinoxes, solstices) to align with natural cycles of growth.

## 2. Dream Work

Before sleep, invoke Raphael to provide guidance through dreams. Keep a journal to record insights upon waking.

## 3. Group Renewal Ceremonies

Collaborate with others to invoke Raphael's energy in collective rituals, amplifying the transformational power.

# Rebirth Through Raphael's Light

Rituals for renewal and spiritual growth with Raphael create a sacred pathway to self-discovery and transformation. Through his emerald light and divine guidance, you can release limitations and embrace your highest potential.

## Advanced Tips for Deepening Your Practice

1. **Daily Affirmations:** Begin each day by affirming your commitment to growth with Raphael's guidance.
2. **Sacred Journaling:** Record reflections and inspirations after rituals to deepen your understanding and track your journey.
3. **Enhanced Visualization:** Incorporate imagery of wings, emerald light, or Raphael's presence during meditations for greater connection.

By engaging with these practices, you integrate Raphael's transformative energy into your life, fostering continuous growth and alignment with divine purpose.

Having established a deep connection with Archangel Raphael and explored his transformative energies through foundational rituals and practices, we now journey into the sophisticated dimensions of advanced angelic magic. This next chapter will delve into ceremonial techniques for invoking and evoking Raphael's presence, unlocking profound guidance and assistance. We'll explore the rich web of angelic correspondences, aligning Raphael's energies with planetary and elemental magic to amplify your work. Finally, we'll expand the scope of angelic collaboration by harmonizing Raphael's healing light with the strength of Michael, the wisdom of Gabriel, and the illumination of Uriel, enabling comprehensive and powerful results. Prepare to deepen your mastery and elevate your practice as we venture into the esoteric heart of angelic magic.

# { 6 }

# The Pinnacle of Divine Connection: Advanced Angelic Magic with Raphael

As we ascend into the realm of advanced angelic magic, we step into a practice that harmonizes the celestial and the earthly, drawing from the deepest reservoirs of spiritual wisdom. This section explores the techniques and correspondences that empower a magician to invoke Archangel Raphael in ceremonial contexts, seeking not only his healing presence but his direct guidance and transformative assistance.

We will unravel Raphael's connection to planetary and elemental energies, understanding how these correspondences can amplify your magical workings. Additionally, we will journey into collaborative angelic practices, combining Raphael's light with the protective strength of Michael, the communicative grace of Gabriel, and the illuminating power of Uriel. These practices offer a profound opportunity to experience the synergy of angelic forces working in harmony for healing, protection, and enlightenment. Prepare to harness the full spectrum of divine potential as you deepen your practice and expand your connection to the angelic realms.

## The Art of Calling: Techniques for Invoking Raphael in Ceremonial Magic

### Invocation as Sacred Dialogue

Invoking Archangel Raphael in ceremonial magic transforms your ritual into a divine conversation. Unlike evocation, which calls an entity to appear externally, invocation is an internal process, inviting Raphael's energy to harmonize with your own. As the angel of healing, guidance, and renewal, Raphael's invocation is ideal for empowering rituals focused on healing, transformation, and divine clarity.

## Historical and Spiritual Context

### Invocation in Sacred Texts

The *Book of Tobit* provides a biblical foundation for invoking Raphael's presence. His role as a guide and healer highlights his readiness to respond to those who seek him with intention and reverence. This aligns with mystical traditions that regard Raphael as an ever-present ally to those in need of his light.

### Mystical Interpretations of Invocation

- **Kabbalistic Practices:** In Kabbalah, invoking Raphael connects the practitioner to Tiferet, the sefirah of balance, beauty, and harmony, symbolizing Raphael's role in mediating divine energy.
- **Hermetic Magic:** Hermetic texts emphasize the power of precise correspondences, such as colors, planetary energies, and sacred symbols, to enhance invocations.

## Symbolism and Esoteric Lessons

### 1. The Power of Names

Raphael's Hebrew name, רפאל (*Rafael*), meaning "God heals," is a sacred key. Speaking his name aloud during invocation vibrationally aligns your intentions with divine healing.

### 2. Elemental Energy as a Conduit

As the ruler of the element of air, Raphael's presence can be felt in the subtle movements of breath and wind. Incorporating air symbols like feathers or incense strengthens the invocation.

### 3. Ritual as a Gateway

A ceremonial invocation creates a liminal space where earthly and celestial energies converge, allowing Raphael's guidance to flow freely into your work.

## Practical Applications: Invoking Raphael in Ceremonial Magic

### 1. Setting the Stage for Invocation

**Materials**

- A green and white candle
- Raphael's sigil
- Frankincense incense
- A feather or malachite crystal
- Sacred space prepared for the ritual

**Steps**

1. **Prepare the Space**
   Cleanse the ritual area with incense or sage, saying: *"By the light of Raphael, I cleanse this space for divine work."*
2. **Activate the Altar**
   Light the candles and place Raphael's sigil and the feather or crystal on the altar.
3. **Ground and Center**
   Sit or stand quietly, focusing on your breath. Inhale deeply, visualizing emerald light filling your body, and exhale, releasing distractions.

## 2. The Invocation Ritual

**Steps**

1. **Recite the Opening Prayer**
   Begin by addressing Raphael:
   *"Raphael, healer of body, mind, and spirit,
   I call upon your light to guide me in this sacred work.
   By the breath of life and the divine name, El Shaddai,
   may your presence fill this space."*
2. **Present the Offering**
   Waft the feather or crystal over the incense smoke, saying:
   *"By this sacred smoke, I honor your presence.
   By this offering, I align my heart with your healing light."*
3. **Visualize Raphael's Presence**
   Close your eyes and imagine a radiant figure enveloped in emerald light. Feel his energy surrounding and merging with you. Whisper:
   *"Raphael, your light is my shield, your breath my inspiration."*
4. **Speak Your Intention**
   Clearly state your purpose for invoking Raphael, whether for healing, guidance, or clarity. For example:
   *"Raphael, I seek your guidance in healing my heart and aligning my spirit with divine will."*
5. **Recite the Invocation Chant**
   Chant Raphael's name rhythmically, matching your breath to the cadence:
   *"Rafael, Rafael, healer divine,
   Light of the heavens, your wisdom is mine."*
6. **Open Yourself to Guidance**
   Sit quietly, allowing thoughts, sensations, or insights to emerge. Keep a journal nearby to record any impressions.
7. **Conclude the Ritual**
   Thank Raphael for his presence:
   *"Raphael, I thank you for your light and wisdom.*

*May your healing touch remain with me always."*
Extinguish the candles.

## Magical Correspondences

- **Colors:** Emerald green (healing), white (purity)
- **Crystals:** Malachite (renewal), clear quartz (amplification)
- **Herbs:** Frankincense (clarity), sage (purification)
- **Symbols:** Raphael's sigil, feathers, emerald light

## Advanced Techniques for Invocation

### 1. Incorporate Sacred Names

Use divine names such as *El Shaddai* or *Yahweh Rapha* during invocation to enhance the connection to Raphael's energy.

### 2. Synchronize with Planetary Energies

Perform the invocation on a Wednesday, the day governed by Mercury, to align with Raphael's planetary correspondence.

### 3. Combine with Breathwork

Deep, rhythmic breathing amplifies the element of air, creating a stronger conduit for Raphael's presence.

## Deepening Your Connection

Invoking Raphael in ceremonial magic is a profound act of partnership, opening the gateway to divine healing and wisdom. Each invocation strengthens your alignment with his energy, empowering you to bring balance and renewal to your life and magical practice.

## Advanced Tips for Mastery

1. **Daily Invocations:** Integrate brief invocations into your daily practice to maintain a continuous connection with Raphael.
2. **Refine Your Focus:** Tailor each invocation to a specific purpose, such as healing, guidance, or protection.
3. **Collaborative Invocations:** Experiment with invoking Raphael alongside other archangels for multidimensional support.

Through dedication and intention, you can cultivate an enduring relationship with Raphael, transforming your spiritual path into a luminous journey of healing and growth.

# Calling Forth Divine Presence: Evocation of Raphael for Direct Guidance and Assistance

## The Power of Evocation: Bridging Realms

Evocation, in contrast to invocation, invites the external manifestation of a celestial being, creating a space where their presence can be experienced tangibly. Through Raphael's evocation, the practitioner establishes a sacred dialogue, seeking direct guidance, healing, and assistance. This advanced magical practice requires precision, reverence, and preparation to align with the angel's radiant energy.

## Historical and Spiritual Context

### Evocation in Sacred Traditions

The act of summoning celestial beings is well-documented in mystical texts, including the *Key of Solomon* and Kabbalistic practices. These works emphasize using divine names, sacred symbols, and aligned intention to ensure a successful and harmonious evocation.

- **Raphael in the Book of Tobit:** Raphael's guidance to Tobias serves as an archetypal model for evocation, demonstrating how direct interaction with Raphael fosters clarity, healing, and divine protection.

## Mystical Teachings on Angelic Presence

Kabbalistic teachings connect Raphael to Tiferet, the sefirah of beauty and balance. Evoking Raphael creates a bridge between the upper realms of divine light and the practitioner's earthly plane, allowing for the transmission of healing wisdom.

## Symbolism and Esoteric Insights

### 1. Raphael's Sigil as a Gateway

The sigil of Raphael, when inscribed or visualized, serves as a key to align your space with his energy. It acts as a celestial signature, opening the pathways for his presence.

### 2. Sacred Geometry in Evocation

Constructing a sacred circle or triangle incorporates divine geometry, ensuring that the ritual space resonates with Raphael's frequencies.

### 3. Elemental Alignment with Air

Raphael's connection to air amplifies evocation through the use of incense, feathers, or breathwork. These tools create a medium for Raphael's energy to manifest in your space.

## Practical Applications: Evoking Raphael for Guidance

### 1. Preparing for Evocation

**Materials**

- A green and gold candle
- Raphael's sigil, drawn on parchment or printed
- Frankincense or sandalwood incense
- A small bowl of purified water
- Malachite or clear quartz crystal

**Steps**

1. **Cleanse the Space**
   Use incense to purify your environment, saying:
   *"By the sacred light of Raphael, I cleanse this space for divine presence."*
2. **Set the Sacred Circle**
   Create a circle with salt or light anointing oil, focusing on Raphael's sigil in the center.
3. **Prepare Yourself**
   Center yourself with three deep breaths, visualizing emerald light surrounding your body.

## 2. The Evocation Ritual

**Steps**

1. **Light the Candles and Incense**
   Say:
   *"Raphael, guardian of light and healing,
   I call upon your presence to guide and assist me."*
2. **Trace Raphael's Sigil**
   Using your finger or a wand, trace Raphael's sigil in the air above the parchment or hold it before the candle flame. Visualize the sigil glowing with emerald energy. Say:
   *"By this sacred symbol, may Raphael's light descend into this space."*
3. **Offer the Elements**
   Place the bowl of water and the crystal beside the sigil. Waft the incense over them, saying:
   *"With water and air, I honor your presence.
   Raphael, healer and guide, reveal your wisdom to me."*

4. **Speak the Evocation**
   Recite:
   *"Raphael, angel of mercy and light,*
   *I summon your presence to this sacred circle.*
   *Bring your guidance, your healing breath,*
   *And your divine wisdom to aid me now.*
   *By the name of El Shaddai, I welcome you."*
5. **Wait for Manifestation**
   Sit in stillness, keeping your senses open. Raphael's presence may manifest as a subtle shift in energy, a warm sensation, or intuitive insights. Use your journal to record impressions.
6. **Ask Your Questions or State Your Intent**
   Speak directly to Raphael, expressing your needs or asking for guidance. Example:
   *"Raphael, show me the path to healing in this matter."*
7. **Thank Raphael and Conclude**
   Express gratitude:
   *"Raphael, I thank you for your presence and guidance.*
   *May your light remain with me as I walk forward."*
   Extinguish the candles and incense.

## Magical Correspondences

- **Colors:** Emerald green (healing), gold (divine connection)
- **Crystals:** Malachite (renewal), clear quartz (amplification)
- **Herbs:** Frankincense (clarity), lavender (calm)
- **Symbols:** Raphael's sigil, feathers, sacred circles

## Advanced Techniques for Evocation

### 1. Layered Energy Work

Combine Raphael's evocation with chakra alignment practices, focusing on the heart and third-eye chakras to deepen the connection.

## 2. Astral Evocation

In advanced practices, evoke Raphael on the astral plane during meditation or dream work for enhanced guidance.

## 3. Planetary Timing

Perform evocations on a Wednesday, during the hour of Mercury, to align with Raphael's planetary energy.

# The Gift of Direct Guidance

Evoking Raphael allows for an intimate connection with his wisdom and healing power. This practice not only enhances your magical work but also fosters spiritual growth and alignment with divine grace.

# Advanced Tips for Mastery

1. **Refinement Through Repetition:** Regularly evoke Raphael to build a strong and natural connection.
2. **Collaborative Work:** Combine Raphael's evocation with other archangels for specific goals, such as invoking Michael for protection or Gabriel for clarity.
3. **Symbolic Integration:** Use Raphael's sigil or an infused talisman as a focal point for maintaining his presence in daily life.

With dedication and practice, evoking Raphael will become a transformative cornerstone of your magical and spiritual journey.

# The Celestial Architect: Raphael's Connection to Planetary Magic and Astrology

## The Cosmic Healer

Archangel Raphael's association with Mercury, the swift planet of intellect, communication, and healing, reveals his profound connection to planetary magic and astrology. Mercury's dynamic and mutable energy resonates with Raphael's abilities to facilitate change, guide journeys, and heal through wisdom. Understanding this connection deepens your work with Raphael, allowing you to integrate planetary forces into your rituals and spiritual practices.

## Historical and Spiritual Context

### Raphael and Mercury: The Divine Correspondence

- **Mercury's Symbolism:** In classical astrology, Mercury governs intellect, communication, travel, and health—qualities reflected in Raphael's guidance of Tobias in the *Book of Tobit*. Just as Mercury symbolizes the movement of thought and matter, Raphael moves between divine and earthly realms, bringing clarity and healing.
- **Hermetic Influences:** Raphael's link to Mercury aligns with Hermetic principles, particularly the concept of "As above, so below." Working with Raphael through Mercury creates a bridge between the celestial and earthly planes, enabling profound transformation.

### Astrological Insights into Raphael's Energy

- **Zodiac Signs:** Mercury rules Gemini and Virgo, signs associated with adaptability, intellect, and healing. These traits mirror Raphael's role as a guide and restorer.

- **Planetary Day and Hour:** Mercury governs Wednesday, the ideal day for rituals involving Raphael. Working during the planetary hour of Mercury amplifies this connection.

## Symbolism and Esoteric Lessons

### 1. The Emerald Light and Celestial Guidance

Raphael's emerald aura reflects Mercury's quicksilver energy, symbolizing adaptability and renewal. This light serves as a conduit for healing vibrations aligned with the cycles of the planets.

### 2. The Alchemical Process

Mercury's association with alchemy, transformation, and the philosopher's stone underscores Raphael's ability to catalyze spiritual growth and physical healing. By working with Mercury's energy, you invoke Raphael as a celestial alchemist who balances body, mind, and spirit.

### 3. Astrology as a Sacred Map

Astrology provides a framework for timing and aligning rituals with Raphael's planetary influence. Understanding these correspondences allows you to harness celestial energies for healing, guidance, and renewal.

## Practical Applications: Planetary Magic with Raphael

### 1. Designing a Planetary Altar for Raphael

**Materials**

- A green cloth to symbolize Raphael's healing light
- Mercury-related symbols, such as caduceus or winged sandals
- Green and yellow candles

- Frankincense or sandalwood incense
- A quartz crystal engraved with Raphael's sigil

**Steps**

1. **Prepare the Altar**
   Place the green cloth on the altar, arranging the symbols of Mercury and Raphael. Light the candles and incense, focusing on aligning the space with celestial energies.
2. **Align with Planetary Energy**
   Perform the ritual on a Wednesday, ideally during the planetary hour of Mercury, to amplify the connection.
3. **Set Your Intention**
   Hold the quartz crystal and clearly state your intention, such as seeking guidance, healing, or clarity.

## 2. Planetary Invocation Ritual

**Steps**

1. **Open the Ritual**
   Begin by calling upon Raphael:
   *"Raphael, healer and guide,*
   *Celestial light of Mercury,*
   *I call upon your presence to illuminate my path."*
2. **Invoke Mercury's Energy**
   Light the green candle and say:
   *"By the swift wings of Mercury, I align with divine wisdom and clarity."*
3. **Activate the Altar Tools**
   Wave the quartz crystal through the incense smoke, visualizing it absorbing Raphael's healing energy.
4. **Meditate on Celestial Guidance**
   Sit quietly, focusing on the interplay between Mercury's energy and Raphael's light. Allow insights or sensations to arise.

## 3. Astrological Timing for Healing Work

- **Moon Phases:** Perform healing rituals with Raphael during the waxing moon to invite growth and renewal.
- **Transits:** Work with Mercury's favorable transits, such as its conjunctions or trines, to amplify Raphael's guidance and healing.

## Magical Correspondences

- **Planet:** Mercury
- **Day:** Wednesday
- **Hour:** Planetary hour of Mercury
- **Colors:** Green (healing), yellow (intellect), silver (celestial connection)
- **Symbols:** Raphael's sigil, caduceus, winged sandals
- **Crystals:** Malachite (healing), citrine (clarity), clear quartz (amplification)
- **Incense:** Frankincense, sandalwood

## Advanced Techniques for Planetary Magic

### 1. Personalized Astrological Charts

Incorporate your natal chart into rituals, identifying Mercury's placement and aspects to deepen your alignment with Raphael.

### 2. Integration with Angelic Choirs

Invoke Raphael alongside Mercury's associated choir, the *Benei Elohim* (Sons of God), to amplify celestial guidance.

### 3. Sigil Activation with Celestial Energy

Engrave Raphael's sigil on a talisman and consecrate it during a Mercury ritual, using it for ongoing healing and clarity.

## Harmonizing with the Celestial Healer

Raphael's connection to Mercury provides a powerful foundation for planetary magic, offering a framework to align your intentions with celestial rhythms. Through rituals, correspondences, and astrological insights, you can deepen your relationship with Raphael and unlock the transformative potential of his healing light.

### Advanced Tips for Mastery

1. **Journal Celestial Insights:** Record your experiences with Mercury rituals to track patterns and deepen your understanding.
2. **Expand Through Collaboration:** Work with Raphael alongside other planetary angels for multidimensional results.
3. **Refine Your Timing:** Use astrological apps or ephemerides to identify optimal times for rituals.

By attuning to Raphael's planetary connection, you align yourself with the harmonious flow of the cosmos, enhancing every aspect of your magical practice.

## Mastering the Winds: Raphael's Elemental Connection to Air

### Raphael and the Element of Air

As the guardian of the East and a ruler of the element of air, Archangel Raphael's association with air reflects his role as a divine communicator, healer, and guide. Air, symbolizing intellect, breath, and the life force, aligns seamlessly with Raphael's qualities of clarity, transformation, and healing. By attuning to this elemental connection, you can deepen your magical practice and strengthen your bond with Raphael.

# Historical and Spiritual Context

## Air in Sacred Texts

- **Biblical Symbolism:** In Genesis, the breath of God (*ruach*) animates life, mirroring Raphael's ability to heal and renew through the divine breath.
- **The Book of Tobit:** Raphael's guidance of Tobias can be likened to the currents of air, gentle yet transformative, leading the seeker to clarity and resolution.
- **Kabbalistic Teachings:** Air corresponds to the letter Aleph (א), symbolizing the unseen life force. Raphael's connection to air reflects his ability to navigate and channel this energy.

## Mystical Interpretations of Air

- **Hermetic Tradition:** Air represents the intellect and communication, qualities mirrored in Raphael's connection to Mercury and his role as a divine messenger.
- **Alchemy:** Air is one of the four classical elements essential for transmutation, resonating with Raphael's role in spiritual and physical healing.

# Symbolism and Esoteric Insights

### 1. The Breath of Life

Raphael's healing breath aligns with air's role as the carrier of life and spirit. Working with air invites his presence into your ritual space.

### 2. The Movement of Spirit

Air's qualities of mobility and expansiveness mirror Raphael's ability to move effortlessly between realms, bringing divine energy into the material world.

**3. The Voice of Guidance**

Air is the medium of sound and communication, making it an ideal element for invoking Raphael's wisdom and clarity.

# Practical Applications: Working with Air and Raphael

## 1. Preparing an Air-Focused Ritual

**Materials**

- Feather (symbol of air and freedom)
- Frankincense or sandalwood incense
- Green candle
- Raphael's sigil or an air-related symbol, such as the zodiac sign for Gemini

**Steps**

1. **Cleanse the Space**
   Use the incense to purify your ritual area, saying: *"By the breath of Raphael, I cleanse this space with divine light."*
2. **Set the Altar**
   Place the feather, sigil, and candle on the altar, arranging them to represent air's flowing energy.
3. **Ground Yourself**
   Take several deep breaths, visualizing the air filling your lungs with Raphael's healing energy.

## 2. Ritual for Aligning with Air and Raphael

**Steps**

1. **Call the Element of Air**
   Face the East, the direction of air, and say:

*"Winds of the East, bearers of clarity and wisdom,
   I call upon your currents to guide me.
   With the presence of Raphael, guardian of air,
   Let healing and light fill this space."*

2. **Light the Candle and Incense**
   As the flame flickers, envision Raphael's emerald light blending with the smoke. Say:
   *"Raphael, healer of the divine breath,
   Let your wings of air envelop me.
   By this sacred flame and rising smoke,
   Bring clarity and renewal to my spirit."*

3. **Activate the Feather**
   Hold the feather over the smoke, whispering:
   *"Feather of air, bearer of freedom,
   Align me with Raphael's breath of life."*
   Use the feather to waft the incense smoke around your body or space.

4. **Meditate on Air's Energy**
   Sit quietly, feeling the subtle movements of air around you. Imagine Raphael's energy flowing with each breath.

5. **Speak Your Intentions**
   Clearly state your purpose, whether it is healing, guidance, or protection. Example:
   *"Raphael, with the element of air,
   I seek your guidance to navigate this journey."*

6. **Close the Ritual**
   Thank Raphael and the element of air:
   *"Raphael, I thank you for your light and guidance.
   Winds of the East, I release you with gratitude.
   May your presence remain as I walk in clarity."*

## Magical Correspondences

- **Element:** Air
- **Direction:** East
- **Symbols:** Feather, incense smoke, winds
- **Colors:** Emerald green, yellow

- **Crystals:** Clear quartz (clarity), citrine (focus), fluorite (spiritual alignment)
- **Herbs:** Lavender (calm), frankincense (purification), mint (clarity)

## Advanced Techniques for Working with Air

### 1. Elemental Balance

Combine air with other elements to create harmonious rituals. For example, pair air with water for emotional healing or with fire for creative inspiration.

### 2. Visualization with Raphael's Wings

During meditative rituals, visualize Raphael's wings as currents of air, enveloping and lifting you to higher states of awareness.

### 3. Astral Projection with Air

Advanced practitioners can use Raphael's connection to air to aid in astral projection, visualizing themselves carried by winds to the astral plane.

## Mastery of the Elemental Breath

Raphael's connection to air provides a versatile and transformative foundation for your magical practice. By attuning to this element, you align yourself with the divine breath that animates and heals all life.

## Advanced Tips for Mastery

1. **Daily Breathwork:** Incorporate intentional breathwork into your practice to strengthen your connection to Raphael and the element of air.

2. **Seasonal Alignment:** Perform air-based rituals during spring, a season of renewal aligned with air's qualities.
3. **Collaborative Elemental Work:** Invoke Raphael alongside elemental rulers for synergistic effects, such as combining air (Raphael) with fire (Michael) for dynamic transformation.

By working with air as Raphael's element, you open yourself to the flow of divine energy, enabling healing, clarity, and spiritual elevation in all aspects of your life and practice.

## United in Celestial Harmony: Invoking Raphael with Michael, Gabriel, and Uriel

### The Archangelic Quartet

Invoking Archangels Raphael, Michael, Gabriel, and Uriel together forms a powerful synergy, uniting their unique strengths to address every facet of your spiritual and magical intentions. Raphael brings healing and guidance, Michael offers protection and strength, Gabriel enhances communication and intuition, and Uriel provides wisdom and grounding. This collaborative work creates a balanced and dynamic ritual force.

### Historical and Spiritual Context

#### The Four Archangels in Sacred Tradition

- **Judaism and Christianity:** These four archangels are prominent figures in mystical and theological traditions. They are often associated with the four cardinal directions, elements, and spiritual tasks. Raphael guards the East, Michael the South, Gabriel the West, and Uriel the North.
- **Kabbalistic Teachings:** In the Tree of Life, Raphael aligns with Tiferet (beauty and healing), Michael with

Gevurah (strength), Gabriel with Chesed (mercy), and Uriel with Malkhut (kingdom).
- **Apocryphal Texts:** Texts like the *Book of Enoch* and *Sefer Raziel HaMalakh* emphasize their collective work in maintaining cosmic harmony.

## Why Invoke All Four Archangels?

- **Holistic Support:** Their combined presence addresses every dimension of existence—physical, emotional, mental, and spiritual.
- **Balance and Harmony:** Invoking all four ensures that the energies of the elements and directions are aligned, creating a stable and powerful ritual space.
- **Strengthening Connections:** Collaborating with the archangels deepens your bond with each individually and collectively.

## Symbolism and Esoteric Insights

### 1. The Four Directions and Elements

- **Raphael:** East, air—clarity, healing, and new beginnings.
- **Michael:** South, fire—courage, protection, and willpower.
- **Gabriel:** West, water—intuition, emotional depth, and communication.
- **Uriel:** North, earth—wisdom, grounding, and stability.

### 2. Angelic Choirs and Harmonies

Each archangel works with specific angelic choirs, amplifying their energy. Calling upon their choirs further strengthens your ritual.

### 3. The Sacred Circle of Light

When invoked together, the four archangels form a circle of light around the practitioner, symbolizing divine protection and empowerment.

## Practical Applications: Collaborative Angelic Invocation

### 1. Preparing for the Ritual

**Materials**

- Four candles (green for Raphael, red for Michael, blue for Gabriel, yellow for Uriel)
- Incense (frankincense or sandalwood)
- Raphael's sigil and symbols for the other archangels
- Small representations of each element (feather for air, candle for fire, bowl of water, and stone for earth)

**Steps**

1. **Cleanse the Space**
   Use incense to purify the area, walking clockwise and saying:
   *"I cleanse this space with divine light, preparing for the presence of the archangels."*
2. **Set the Altar**
   Arrange the candles and elemental symbols in a circle, placing Raphael's sigil in the center.
3. **Center Yourself**
   Take deep breaths, visualizing a sphere of light surrounding you.

### 2. Invoking the Four Archangels

**Steps**

1. **Face the East and Call Raphael**
   Light the green candle and say:
   *"Raphael, guardian of air and healer of light,
   I call upon your presence in this sacred space.
   Bring your healing breath and divine guidance."*

2. **Turn to the South and Call Michael**
   Light the red candle and say:
   *"Michael, guardian of fire and protector of truth,
   I call upon your strength to shield and empower me."*
3. **Turn to the West and Call Gabriel**
   Light the blue candle and say:
   *"Gabriel, guardian of water and messenger of grace,
   I call upon your wisdom to illuminate my path."*
4. **Turn to the North and Call Uriel**
   Light the yellow candle and say:
   *"Uriel, guardian of earth and keeper of wisdom,
   I call upon your grounding light to guide my steps."*
5. **Seal the Circle**
   Stand in the center and say:
   *"Raphael, Michael, Gabriel, Uriel,
   Guardians of the light, surround me.
   By air, fire, water, and earth,
   I am whole, I am protected, I am guided."*

## Magical Correspondences

- **Colors:** Green (Raphael), red (Michael), blue (Gabriel), yellow (Uriel)
- **Elements:** Air, fire, water, earth
- **Tools:** Sigils, candles, elemental symbols
- **Incense:** Frankincense, myrrh, sandalwood
- **Crystals:** Malachite (Raphael), carnelian (Michael), aquamarine (Gabriel), hematite (Uriel)

## Advanced Techniques for Collaborative Work

### 1. Layered Intentions

Invoke specific qualities of each archangel based on your intention. For example, call Raphael for healing, Michael for protection, Gabriel for clarity, and Uriel for grounding.

### 2. Harmonizing with Angelic Choirs

Recite sacred names or chants associated with each archangel's choir to deepen their presence.

**3. Astral Collaboration**

In advanced practice, visualize the archangels forming a protective sphere around you during astral journeys or dream work.

## Empowerment Through Unity

Collaborative work with Raphael, Michael, Gabriel, and Uriel creates a transformative synergy, balancing all aspects of your being while aligning with divine energies. This practice enhances your spiritual growth, fortifies your magical work, and deepens your connection to the angelic realm.

## Advanced Tips for Mastery

1. **Practice Directional Meditation:** Meditate facing each cardinal direction to attune to the archangels' energies.
2. **Combine with Planetary Magic:** Align the invocation with planetary influences to amplify the archangels' qualities.
3. **Create a Permanent Altar:** Dedicate a space to all four archangels to maintain their protective and empowering presence in your life.

By working with these archangels as a unified force, you weave their collective light into your spiritual practice, fostering harmony, healing, and divine connection.

# Harmonizing with the Celestial Choirs: Raphael and Angelic Healing

## The Role of Angelic Choirs in Healing

The angelic choirs, also known as the celestial hierarchy, are divine beings organized into distinct orders, each with unique responsibilities and energies. Raphael, as a principal healer, works with the *Benei Elohim* (Sons of God) and other healing-focused choirs to manifest divine restoration and balance. By invoking these choirs alongside Raphael, you amplify the healing energies, creating a comprehensive approach to physical, emotional, and spiritual restoration.

## Historical and Spiritual Context

### Angelic Choirs in Mystical Traditions

- **Judaism:** The *Benei Elohim* are mentioned in Genesis 6:2 and Job 1:6, associated with divine acts of creation and guidance. These beings operate under Raphael's direction when bringing healing and harmony to creation.
- **Christianity:** Dionysius the Areopagite's *Celestial Hierarchy* categorizes choirs such as Thrones, Dominions, and Principalities, each with distinct roles. Raphael works closely with the Principalities and Virtues, orders associated with miracles and healing.
- **Kabbalistic Insights:** In Kabbalah, Raphael aligns with Tiferet, the heart of the Tree of Life, symbolizing balance and beauty. The choirs under his guidance harmonize divine and earthly realms, embodying holistic healing.

### Why Work with Angelic Choirs?

- **Amplified Energy:** Choirs channel collective angelic energy, magnifying the potency of healing rituals.

- **Targeted Healing:** Different choirs specialize in various aspects of restoration, from physical to emotional and spiritual healing.
- **Divine Alignment:** Invoking the choirs aligns you with celestial order, bringing clarity and balance.

## Symbolism and Esoteric Insights

### 1. Raphael as Conductor of Divine Harmony

Raphael orchestrates healing through the angelic choirs, guiding their energies like a symphony to restore wholeness. This reflects his role as a divine intermediary, bridging heavenly and earthly realms.

### 2. The Healing Light of Choirs

Each choir emits a unique vibrational light. The *Benei Elohim* resonate with emerald green, symbolic of growth and renewal, while the Principalities and Virtues radiate gold and white light, representing divine miracles and purity.

### 3. The Celestial Ladder

The choirs form a spiritual ladder, with Raphael at the center, facilitating your ascent toward divine connection and healing.

## Practical Applications: Rituals with Raphael and the Angelic Choirs

### 1. Preparing a Healing Choir Ritual

**Materials**

- Green, gold, and white candles to represent the healing lights of the choirs
- Incense such as frankincense or sandalwood

- Raphael's sigil
- A small bell or singing bowl

**Steps**

1. **Set the Space**
   Arrange the candles and Raphael's sigil on your altar. Light the incense to purify the area.
2. **Ground Yourself**
   Take deep breaths, visualizing roots connecting you to the earth and branches reaching toward the heavens.

## 2. Invocation of the Choirs for Healing

**Steps**

1. **Open the Ritual**
   Stand before the altar and say:
   *"I call upon Raphael, healer of the divine light,
   And the choirs of heaven who bring restoration and grace.
   Benei Elohim, Principalities, and Virtues,
   Descend into this sacred space with your healing power."*
2. **Light the Candles**
   As you light each candle, call upon the corresponding choir:
   - Green candle (*Benei Elohim*):
     *"Sons of God, bring your renewal and life."*
   - Gold candle (Principalities):
     *"Guardians of divine miracles, restore balance and harmony."*
   - White candle (Virtues):
     *"Bearers of purity and light, cleanse and uplift this spirit."*
3. **Ring the Bell or Singing Bowl**
   Sound the bell or bowl, imagining its vibrations summoning the angelic choirs. Say:
   *"By this sound, the heavenly chorus awakens.
   Their harmonies align my body, mind, and spirit."*

4. **Focus on Healing Intentions**
   Hold Raphael's sigil, visualizing his emerald light merging with the lights of the choirs. Speak your intention aloud, such as:
   *"With the grace of Raphael and the celestial choirs, Let this healing light flow into my being, restoring all that is whole."*
5. **Meditate on the Choirs' Presence**
   Sit quietly, visualizing the choirs surrounding you in a circle of light, each emitting its unique energy.

## Magical Correspondences

- **Choirs:** *Benei Elohim* (renewal), Principalities (protection), Virtues (miracles)
- **Colors:** Green, gold, white
- **Tools:** Raphael's sigil, singing bowl
- **Incense:** Frankincense, sandalwood, myrrh
- **Crystals:** Malachite (renewal), selenite (purity), citrine (miracles)

## Advanced Techniques for Choir Collaboration

### 1. Layered Healing Rituals

Work with specific choirs for different types of healing. For example, invoke the *Benei Elohim* for physical renewal and the Virtues for spiritual cleansing.

### 2. Incorporating Angelic Names

Recite the names of specific angels within the choirs, such as Raphael's subordinates, to personalize the ritual.

### 3. Choir Meditation

During deep meditative states, visualize the choirs as concentric circles of light, each representing a different aspect of healing.

# The Power of Collective Divine Energy

Collaborating with Raphael and the angelic choirs creates a multidimensional approach to healing, amplifying the energies of renewal, balance, and divine grace. This practice allows you to harness the full potential of celestial harmony.

## Advanced Tips for Mastery

1. **Journal Your Experiences:** Document your rituals and insights to refine your understanding of the choirs' energies.
2. **Combine with Astrological Alignments:** Perform rituals during planetary alignments that correspond to Raphael or the choirs' attributes.
3. **Create a Choir Altar:** Dedicate a permanent space to the angelic choirs, incorporating their symbols and colors.

Through Raphael's guidance and the collective energy of the choirs, you can achieve profound healing, clarity, and spiritual elevation, bringing divine harmony into every aspect of your practice.

As your connection with Archangel Raphael deepens, the next step is learning to recognize and interpret his guidance through divination and communication techniques. Raphael, as a healer and guide, often uses subtle and profound methods to communicate, from angelic visions to dream messages and symbolic signs in daily life. By mastering these practices, you open pathways for direct communication with the archangel, allowing his wisdom and healing energy to flow into your life. This chapter will explore diverse techniques, from scrying and meditation to angelic tarot and dreamwork, providing tools to enhance your intuitive bond with Raphael and recognize the sacred language through which he speaks.

# { 7 }

# Whispers of the Divine: Divination and Communication with Raphael

The art of communicating with Archangel Raphael invites you to transcend ordinary perception and tune into the subtle currents of divine guidance. Raphael, the healer and messenger, speaks through signs, symbols, dreams, and intuitive insight, offering clarity, comfort, and direction. In this section, we will explore techniques to establish a clear channel for his messages, from the ancient practices of scrying and meditation to the modern tools of angelic tarot and oracle cards. You will learn to recognize his presence in daily life through symbols and omens, as well as how to invoke his healing light in your dreams and visions. By integrating these methods, you can cultivate a profound and personal dialogue with Raphael, enriching your spiritual practice and deepening your connection to his celestial wisdom.

## Drawing the Veil Aside: Scrying, Meditation, and Automatic Writing with Raphael

### The Path to Divine Dialogue

Scrying, meditation, and automatic writing are powerful techniques for connecting with Archangel Raphael. These practices harness your intuition and open channels to the angelic realms, allowing Raphael's healing guidance and wisdom to flow into your awareness. Each method offers unique insights and pathways to his energy, fostering clarity and spiritual growth.

# Historical and Spiritual Context

## Scrying: The Ancient Art of Seeing

Scrying is a centuries-old practice used by mystics and magicians to peer beyond the veil of ordinary sight. In a Raphael-focused practice, scrying often involves water (linked to healing and clarity) or a crystal ball. By gazing into the reflective surface, you attune to Raphael's energy and receive symbolic visions or messages.

## Meditation: Harmonizing with Raphael's Light

Meditation has been a cornerstone of spiritual practice in many traditions. With Raphael, meditation focuses on aligning with his emerald-green healing light, invoking clarity and balance in the mind and spirit.

## Automatic Writing: The Angel's Whisper in Words

Automatic writing channels divine inspiration directly onto the page. When working with Raphael, this practice enables you to receive his messages in written form, offering healing guidance and insights.

# Symbolism and Esoteric Insights

## Raphael's Presence in These Techniques

- **Scrying:** Raphael's emerald energy illuminates visions, bringing clarity and insight. The element of water symbolizes emotional and spiritual healing.
- **Meditation:** His energy resonates with the heart chakra, fostering compassion and healing, and the third-eye chakra, enhancing intuition.
- **Automatic Writing:** Raphael's guidance flows through thought and intuition, translating into sacred words on the page.

# Practical Applications: Techniques for Communication

## 1. Scrying Ritual to Connect with Raphael

**Materials**

- A bowl of water or a crystal ball
- Green candle (Raphael's color)
- Frankincense incense
- Raphael's sigil

**Steps**

1. **Prepare the Space**
   Set up a quiet, dimly lit space. Place the candle, bowl, or crystal ball on your altar and light the incense.
2. **Invoke Raphael**
   Hold Raphael's sigil and say:
   *"Raphael, healer of light and clarity,
   I call upon your divine presence.
   Guide my vision and illuminate my path."*
3. **Begin Scrying**
   Gaze softly into the water or crystal ball, allowing your mind to relax. Watch for shapes, colors, or images to emerge.
4. **Interpret the Symbols**
   Record your impressions in a journal, noting any messages or patterns.

## 2. Meditation with Raphael's Energy

**Steps**

1. **Create the Space**
   Sit comfortably in a quiet space. Light a green candle and hold a malachite or emerald crystal.
2. **Visualize Raphael's Light**
   Close your eyes and imagine a beam of emerald-green light descending from above, enveloping you in warmth and healing energy.

3. **Mantra Invocation**
   Repeat silently or aloud:
   *"Raphael, healer divine, align my heart and mind with your light."*
4. **Receive Guidance**
   After 10–15 minutes of focused breathing and visualization, open yourself to any intuitive messages or impressions.

## 3. Automatic Writing for Raphael's Wisdom

**Materials**

- A journal or blank paper
- Green pen
- Raphael's sigil

**Steps**

1. **Prepare the Space**
   Light a green candle and place Raphael's sigil nearby.
2. **Set the Intention**
   Say:
   *"Raphael, divine guide, channel your wisdom through my hand.
   Let your healing words flow onto this page."*
3. **Begin Writing**
   Allow your hand to move freely across the page, writing whatever thoughts or words come to you.
4. **Reflect and Interpret**
   Read the message aloud and meditate on its meaning, recording insights.

# Magical Correspondences

- **Colors:** Emerald green
- **Crystals:** Malachite, emerald, selenite
- **Incense:** Frankincense, sandalwood
- **Tools:** Water, crystal ball, pen and paper

## Advanced Tips for Mastery

**1. Combine Techniques**

Perform a guided meditation before scrying or automatic writing to deepen your connection with Raphael.

**2. Symbolic Anchors**

Place Raphael's sigil or a green candle in view during your practice to focus your intention.

**3. Journaling the Journey**

Maintain a dedicated journal to track visions, messages, and insights from these practices.

## Raphael's Healing Voice

Scrying, meditation, and automatic writing are profound tools for opening a dialogue with Archangel Raphael. Each practice strengthens your intuitive connection, fostering healing and guidance in every area of your life. With patience and dedication, these techniques will bring you closer to Raphael's wisdom and light, empowering your magical and spiritual path.

## The Celestial Cards: Angelic Tarot and Oracle Readings with Raphael

### A Sacred Gateway to Raphael's Wisdom

Using angelic tarot and oracle cards offers a direct and tangible means of communicating with Archangel Raphael. These tools serve as symbolic gateways, reflecting Raphael's guidance in matters of healing, clarity, and spiritual growth.

By incorporating these readings into your practice, you create a sacred dialogue, revealing hidden truths and aligning your path with divine wisdom.

## Historical and Spiritual Context

### Angelic Tarot: Ancient Symbols Meet Celestial Wisdom

Tarot has long been a tool for divination, bridging the seen and unseen realms. When focused on Raphael, specific cards—such as the *Temperance* card in the Major Arcana—reflect his attributes of healing, balance, and renewal. Raphael's presence adds a layer of divine clarity to these readings, transforming traditional interpretations into angelic insights.

### Oracle Cards: Raphael-Specific Messages

Oracle cards, often themed around angels, provide a more open-ended and intuitive approach. Decks dedicated to Raphael or healing angels offer tailored messages designed to connect directly with his energy.

### Biblical and Mystical Foundations

Scripture and mystical traditions affirm the use of symbolic tools to receive divine messages. In the Book of Tobit, Raphael guides Tobias step by step, much like a reading reveals divine insights. The cards serve as a modern extension of this guiding principle.

## Symbolism and Esoteric Insights

### 1. **Raphael's Energy in Tarot**

- *Temperance*: Balance, healing, and divine alignment.
- *The Star*: Renewal, faith, and celestial guidance.

- *The Hermit*: Wisdom and spiritual introspection, reflecting Raphael's mentoring role.

## 2. Colors and Imagery in Oracle Cards

Decks that emphasize emerald green light, healing symbols (e.g., the caduceus or fish), or depictions of Raphael offer potent visual anchors for his energy.

## 3. Card Layouts as Sacred Maps

Choosing spreads with a focus on healing, such as past-present-future for recovery or a chakra alignment spread, aligns the reading with Raphael's purpose.

# Practical Applications: Angelic Card Readings

### 1. Preparing for a Reading

**Materials**

- Angelic tarot or oracle cards
- Green candle (Raphael's color)
- Raphael's sigil
- Incense (frankincense or sandalwood)

**Steps**

1. **Cleanse the Space**
   Light the incense and candle. Waft the smoke over the cards, visualizing them being filled with Raphael's emerald light.
2. **Invoke Raphael**
   Place his sigil beside the cards and say:
   "Raphael, healer and guide,
   Bless these cards with your wisdom.
   Reveal your truth and clarity through these sacred symbols."

## 2. Performing the Reading

**Steps**

1. **Set Your Intention**
   Focus on your question or topic, such as physical healing, emotional balance, or spiritual guidance.
2. **Shuffle with Purpose**
   As you shuffle, silently or aloud repeat a mantra, such as:
   *"Through Raphael's light, the truth is revealed."*
3. **Choose a Spread**
   Select a layout that aligns with your intention:
   - **Healing Spread**: Three cards for body, mind, and spirit.
   - **Guidance Spread**: A five-card cross for insight and direction.
4. **Interpret the Cards**
   Look for symbols, colors, and patterns that resonate with Raphael's energy. For example:
   - Green tones indicate healing and renewal.
   - Cards depicting light or water reflect Raphael's guiding presence.

## 3. Closing the Ritual

**Steps**

1. **Thank Raphael**
   Hold your hands over the cards and say:
   *"Raphael, I honor your guidance.*
   *May your healing light continue to bless my path."*
2. **Record Your Insights**
   Write down the cards drawn and your interpretations in a dedicated journal.

# Magical Correspondences

- **Colors:** Emerald green

- **Symbols:** Raphael's sigil, healing imagery
- **Incense:** Frankincense, sandalwood
- **Decks:** Angelic tarot or Raphael-themed oracle cards

## Advanced Tips for Mastery

### 1. Combine Tarot and Oracle

Use tarot for structure and oracle cards for additional clarity, creating a layered reading that reflects Raphael's multifaceted guidance.

### 2. Sacred Timing

Perform readings during Mercury's hours or on Wednesdays, which align with Raphael's planetary correspondence.

### 3. Personalized Deck Consecration

Dedicate your deck to Raphael by inscribing his sigil on the storage pouch or box, enhancing its connection to his energy.

## The Sacred Dialogue of Cards

Angelic tarot and oracle readings provide a powerful medium to access Raphael's wisdom and healing light. Through careful preparation, intuitive interpretation, and reverence for the process, you create a dynamic dialogue with the archangel. With each reading, your connection deepens, allowing Raphael's guidance to illuminate your path and support your magical practice.

# Deciphering the Divine: Recognizing Raphael's Messages in Daily Life

## A Subtle Whisper of Angelic Presence

Archangel Raphael often communicates through signs, symbols, and omens that manifest in everyday life. His messages are subtle yet profound, designed to guide, heal, and reassure. Learning to recognize and interpret these divine signals deepens your connection to Raphael, allowing you to navigate your life with clarity and trust.

## Historical and Spiritual Context

### The Language of Angels

Angels, including Raphael, have been described throughout spiritual traditions as messengers of God who use non-verbal cues to communicate. In the Bible, Raphael's guidance in the Book of Tobit demonstrates his ability to intervene subtly yet effectively, using symbolic acts (e.g., the fish) to convey healing and protection.

### Mystical Traditions and Omens

In mystical practices, Raphael's signs often align with his healing and guiding roles. Symbols such as the color green, depictions of a fish, or specific recurring numbers carry his signature energy.

### Everyday Miracles

Raphael's messages may appear in moments of synchronicity, through dreams, or even as a sudden, inexplicable sense of peace. These signs encourage you to remain open to divine intervention in mundane circumstances.

# Symbolism and Esoteric Insights

### 1. Recognizing Raphael's Signature

- **Emerald Green Light:** A flash of green in your vision or surroundings may signal Raphael's presence.
- **Symbols of Healing:** Images of fish, caduceus staffs, or even medical emblems resonate with his healing energy.
- **Guidance Through Travel:** Encountering signs related to journeys, such as maps, road signs, or unplanned detours, may indicate Raphael is watching over your travels.

### 2. Synchronicities in Numbers

Raphael frequently communicates through repeating numbers, particularly those associated with healing and balance:

- **311:** Derived from the gematria of Raphael's name in Hebrew.
- **6:** Representing harmony and healing in numerology.

### 3. Nature and Raphael

Raphael often uses elements of nature—like birds in flight, a refreshing breeze, or the soothing sound of water—to reassure you of his presence.

## Practical Applications: Recognizing Raphael's Signs

### 1. Setting the Intention to Perceive Raphael's Messages

**Steps**

1. **Create a Sacred Space**
   Light a green candle and burn frankincense to invite Raphael's energy.
2. **Invoke Raphael's Presence**
   Say:
   *"Raphael, divine guide and healer, open my eyes to your signs.*
   *May I see your presence in the light, the symbols, and the whispers of the world around me."*
3. **Meditate on Awareness**
   Close your eyes and visualize emerald light enveloping your senses, enhancing your awareness of subtle cues.

## 2. Journaling Raphael's Messages

**Steps**

1. **Carry a Journal Daily**
   Dedicate a small notebook to recording synchronicities, dreams, and signs you associate with Raphael.
2. **Log Observations**
   Note recurring symbols, patterns, or feelings of peace. For example:
   - Seeing green lights when contemplating a decision.
   - Encountering healing imagery during moments of stress.
3. **Reflect on Patterns**
   Review your notes weekly to discern patterns or recurring themes in Raphael's guidance.

## 3. Creating a Symbolic Ritual for Clarity

**Materials**

- A bowl of water
- Green candle
- Small fish symbol or drawing

**Steps**

1. **Prepare the Ritual Space**
   Place the candle and bowl of water on your altar. Add the fish symbol to the setup.
2. **Invoke Raphael**
   Say:
   *"Raphael, reveal your guidance through the sacred signs of life.*
   *May my heart recognize your presence in all things."*
3. **Observe the Water**
   Gaze into the water, asking for clarity on a specific question. Look for subtle ripples or reflections as a sign of Raphael's response.
4. **Conclude with Gratitude**
   Blow out the candle and say:
   *"Thank you, Raphael, for your guiding light and healing presence."*

## Magical Correspondences

- **Colors:** Emerald green
- **Symbols:** Fish, staff, caduceus
- **Numbers:** 311, 6
- **Elements:** Air (guidance), Water (healing)
- **Incense:** Frankincense, myrrh

## Advanced Tips for Mastery

**1. Trust Your Intuition**

When you notice a potential sign, reflect on your intuitive response. Raphael often uses your inner knowing as a channel for clarity.

**2. Deepen Your Observation**

Spend quiet moments in nature or meditation, actively seeking subtle changes in your environment that resonate with Raphael's energy.

### 3. Combine Practices

Pair this practice with angelic tarot or oracle readings for a comprehensive understanding of Raphael's messages.

## Living in the Flow of Raphael's Guidance

Recognizing Raphael's signs requires an open heart, keen awareness, and trust in divine timing. Through daily mindfulness and intentional rituals, you can strengthen your ability to perceive his messages, allowing Raphael's healing and guidance to illuminate your path. With patience and practice, the world will transform into a tapestry of Raphael's divine whispers, offering support and reassurance in every moment.

## Numerical Whispers and Dreamscapes: Understanding Angel Numbers and Dreams with Raphael

### Unlocking the Divine Codes

Archangel Raphael, as a healer and guide, communicates through angel numbers and dreams, using these subtle methods to offer reassurance, healing, and insight. Recognizing the significance of these messages can deepen your connection to Raphael, revealing a divine narrative tailored to your path. By attuning to these symbolic communications, you can integrate Raphael's wisdom into your daily life and spiritual practice.

## Historical and Spiritual Context

### Angel Numbers: Divine Language in Numerical Form

Angel numbers are sequences imbued with spiritual meaning, appearing in clocks, receipts, or other everyday contexts. In esoteric traditions, numbers serve as conduits for celestial messages, and Raphael often uses sequences related to healing, balance, and divine protection. For example:

- **311**: Corresponding to the gematria of Raphael's Hebrew name (רפאל), symbolizing his healing essence.
- **6**: A number representing harmony and restoration, resonating with Raphael's role as a restorer.

## Dreams: Raphael's Healing in the Subconscious

Dreams have been recognized across cultures as a sacred medium for angelic communication. In the Book of Tobit, Raphael's guidance takes place not only in waking life but also in moments of divine revelation, a theme echoed in mystical traditions. Dreams involving green light, healing waters, or fish often signify Raphael's intervention.

# Symbolism and Esoteric Insights

### 1. Angel Numbers as Healing Codes

- **Repeated Sequences**: Numbers like 111 (manifestation) or 444 (protection) are amplified when combined with Raphael's energy.
- **Numeric Synchronicities**: Seeing specific numbers during healing moments signifies Raphael's support.

### 2. Dreams as Sacred Messages

- **Emerald Light**: Seeing green in a dream symbolizes Raphael's healing and protective presence.
- **Fish Symbolism**: Echoing the Book of Tobit, fish in dreams often represent emotional or spiritual healing.
- **Journey Themes**: Dreams of travel or paths align with Raphael's role as a guide.

# Practical Applications: Decoding Angel Numbers and Dreams

## 1. Recognizing and Interpreting Angel Numbers

**Steps**

1. **Record Patterns**
   Keep a journal of recurring numbers, noting the time and context of their appearance.
2. **Meditate on Meaning**
   Light a green candle and hold Raphael's sigil. Meditate on the number and its potential message, asking:
   *"Raphael, reveal the meaning of this divine sequence. Guide me to clarity and healing."*
3. **Apply the Insight**
   Reflect on how the number aligns with current challenges or opportunities.

## 2. Invoking Raphael for Dream Communication

**Steps**

1. **Prepare for Sleep**
   Place a piece of malachite or emerald under your pillow. Light incense such as sandalwood or frankincense to purify the space.
2. **Invoke Raphael's Guidance**
   Before sleeping, say:
   *"Raphael, healer of the divine,*
   *Guide my dreams with your healing light.*
   *Reveal your wisdom and align my spirit*
   *With the path of peace and restoration."*
3. **Keep a Dream Journal**
   Upon waking, immediately record your dreams, noting symbols, colors, and emotions.

### 3. Ritual for Interpreting Dreams

**Materials**

- Green candle
- Bowl of water (symbolizing the subconscious)
- Raphael's sigil

**Steps**

1. **Create a Sacred Space**
   Light the candle and place the bowl of water on your altar. Hold Raphael's sigil in your hands.
2. **Meditate on the Dream**
   Close your eyes and visualize the dream as clearly as possible. Focus on the details that stood out.
3. **Ask for Clarity**
   Say:
   *"Raphael, illuminate the symbols of my dreams. Bring clarity to their meaning and guide my understanding."*
4. **Observe the Water**
   Look into the bowl, allowing reflections or ripples to inspire insights. Write down interpretations in your journal.

## Magical Correspondences

- **Numbers:** 311, 6, 444
- **Symbols:** Green light, fish, water, paths
- **Crystals:** Malachite, emerald
- **Incense:** Frankincense, sandalwood

## Advanced Tips for Mastery

### 1. Combine Angel Numbers and Dreams

If a specific number appears in a dream, meditate on its deeper meaning and its connection to Raphael's guidance.

## 2. Create a Sacred Sleep Space

Enhance your dreamwork by dedicating a portion of your altar to Raphael, placing symbols of healing and guidance nearby.

## 3. Engage in Weekly Reflection

Review your dream and number journals regularly, looking for patterns that align with Raphael's teachings.

# The Sacred Code of Raphael

Angel numbers and dreams offer profound opportunities to connect with Archangel Raphael's wisdom. By learning to recognize and interpret these messages, you unlock a deeper understanding of his guidance, enriching your spiritual practice and aligning your life with his healing energy. Trust in the process, and let Raphael's signs and dreams light your path to wholeness.

# Dreaming in the Light: Invoking Raphael for Guidance and Healing in Dreamwork

## Dreams as a Gateway to Raphael's Wisdom

Archangel Raphael often communicates through the sacred realm of dreams, offering insights, guidance, and healing while the conscious mind rests. Invoking his presence in dreamwork allows for profound personal transformation, as dreams provide a space for the subconscious to align with divine energies. This practice opens a direct channel to Raphael's wisdom, helping you address emotional wounds, gain clarity on life's challenges, and experience spiritual renewal.

# Historical and Spiritual Context

## Dreams in Sacred Texts and Mystical Traditions

The power of dreams is deeply rooted in spiritual traditions. In the Book of Tobit, Raphael's interventions lead to healing and guidance, symbolizing how divine messengers operate subtly, often through dreams. Ancient cultures, including Jewish mysticism, viewed dreams as a conduit for angelic messages, offering clarity and inspiration.

## The Healing Archetype in Dreamwork

Raphael embodies the archetype of the healer, making his dream presence especially potent. Whether delivering clarity through symbols or facilitating emotional release, his energy fosters a deeper connection between the dreamer and the divine.

# Symbolism and Esoteric Insights

## Signs of Raphael in Dreams

- **Emerald Light:** Dreams illuminated with green light symbolize Raphael's presence and healing energy.
- **Water Imagery:** Healing waters, rivers, or oceans in dreams often reflect Raphael's restorative power.
- **Fish Symbolism:** As seen in the Book of Tobit, fish in dreams signify emotional or physical healing.
- **Journeys and Paths:** Dreams involving guidance or travel reflect Raphael's role as a spiritual mentor.

## The Dream Realm as Sacred Space

Dreams transcend time and space, offering a unique dimension where Raphael's energy can flow freely. By invoking him before sleep, you invite this divine connection into a state of openness and vulnerability, ideal for receiving his guidance.

## Practical Applications: Invoking Raphael in Dreamwork

### 1. Preparing for Dreamwork with Raphael

**Materials**

- Green candle
- Raphael's sigil
- Malachite or emerald
- Frankincense or sandalwood incense
- Dream journal

**Steps**

1. **Create a Sacred Sleep Environment**
   Place Raphael's sigil and your chosen crystal under your pillow or on your nightstand. Light the green candle and incense to sanctify the space.
2. **Invoke Raphael**
   Say:
   *"Raphael, healer and guide, I call upon your presence in my dreams.*
   *Surround me with your emerald light,*
   *Bring clarity, healing, and divine guidance*
   *As I journey through the sacred realm of sleep."*
3. **Focus on Your Intention**
   Reflect on what you seek from Raphael in your dreams, such as healing, answers to a question, or emotional release.
4. **Settle into Rest**
   Visualize Raphael's emerald light enveloping you as you drift into sleep, creating a protective and healing cocoon.

### 2. Interpreting Raphael's Messages in Dreams

**Steps**

1. **Awaken Gently**
   Avoid sudden alarms. Allow yourself to transition peacefully from sleep to waking to retain dream details.
2. **Record Your Dream**
   Write down symbols, feelings, and messages in your journal. Note any elements associated with Raphael, such as light, water, or healing symbols.
3. **Meditate on the Dream**
   Sit with the dream's imagery and ask Raphael for further clarity, saying:
   *"Raphael, reveal the deeper meaning of this dream. Guide my understanding and show me the path to healing."*

## 3. Ritual to Deepen Dream Communication

**Materials**

- Bowl of water (symbolizing the subconscious)
- Green candle
- Raphael's sigil
- Feather or a small fan (symbolizing air and Raphael's connection to the element)

**Steps**

1. **Sanctify the Space**
   Light the candle and place the bowl of water on your altar. Hold the feather or fan in your hand.
2. **Invoke Raphael**
   Say:
   *"Raphael, divine healer, enter my dreams tonight.
   Let your emerald light illuminate my path,
   Your wisdom flow like the waters,
   And your breath guide my soul to truth and renewal."*
3. **Reflect on the Intention**
   Visualize yourself immersed in green light, seeing Raphael's presence guiding you through a peaceful dreamscape.

4. **Seal the Ritual**
   Wave the feather over the water, saying:
   *"As the waters reflect your light,*
   *May my dreams reflect your wisdom."*

## Magical Correspondences

- **Colors:** Emerald green
- **Symbols:** Water, fish, light
- **Crystals:** Malachite, emerald
- **Incense:** Frankincense, sandalwood

## Advanced Tips for Mastery

### 1. Combine Dreamwork with Angel Numbers

If specific numbers recur in your dreams, meditate on their connection to Raphael's messages for deeper insights.

### 2. Perform Regular Reflection

Review your dream journal weekly to discern patterns and recurring symbols associated with Raphael's guidance.

### 3. Enhance Dream Recall

Use affirmations such as *"I remember my dreams with clarity"* before sleeping to strengthen your connection to the messages received.

## The Dream Realm as Raphael's Canvas

Invoking Raphael in dreamwork allows you to access divine wisdom and healing in a deeply personal and transformative way. By cultivating a sacred sleep practice, interpreting signs with care, and aligning your subconscious with Raphael's energy, you deepen your connection to this archangel. Trust the dream realm as a sacred space where Raphael's light can illuminate your path to wholeness and understanding.

# Illuminating the Unseen: Techniques for Inducing Angelic Visions with Raphael

## The Divine Gateway of Angelic Visions

Angelic visions are a profound means of connecting with Archangel Raphael, offering glimpses of divine wisdom, guidance, and healing energy. By inducing these sacred experiences, practitioners can establish a deeper spiritual relationship with Raphael, allowing his light to illuminate their path. Techniques for inducing visions require focused intention, a purified space, and alignment with the vibrational frequency of the angelic realm.

## Historical and Spiritual Context

### Visions in Sacred Texts

Angelic visions have been documented throughout spiritual history. In the Book of Tobit, Raphael appears to Tobias with guidance and protection, embodying the transformative power of divine encounters. Mystical traditions, from Jewish Kabbalah to Christian mysticism, emphasize visions as a means of direct communion with celestial beings.

### Esoteric Insights into Raphael's Visions

Raphael's visions often manifest as emerald light, symbolic imagery (such as a staff or fish), or profound feelings of peace and clarity. These experiences resonate with his archetype as a healer and guide, offering revelations that inspire wholeness and divine alignment.

# Preparing for Angelic Visions

## Sacred Space and Mindset

Creating a sanctified environment is essential for inducing angelic visions. This space becomes a bridge between the physical and spiritual realms, allowing Raphael's energy to flow freely. Equally important is cultivating a receptive state of mind through meditation, breathwork, and focused intention.

## Key Symbols and Correspondences

- **Emerald Green Light:** Represents Raphael's healing and transformative energy.
- **Crystals:** Malachite or emerald amplify connection to Raphael's vibrational frequency.
- **Incense:** Frankincense and sandalwood raise the spiritual vibration of the space.

# Techniques for Inducing Angelic Visions

### 1. Candle Gazing Ritual

**Purpose:**

Aligns your energy with Raphael's and opens the mind to angelic visions.

**Materials:**

- Green candle
- Raphael's sigil
- Frankincense incense

**Steps:**

1. **Create Sacred Space**
   Light the green candle and incense on your altar. Place Raphael's sigil before you.
2. **Set an Intention**
   Say:
   *"Raphael, healer of divine light,*
   *I seek your presence and vision.*
   *Illuminate my spirit and guide my path."*
3. **Focus on the Flame**
   Gaze at the candle's flame, allowing its movement to draw your mind into a meditative state. Imagine the flame transforming into emerald light, enveloping you.
4. **Visualize Raphael**
   Picture Raphael standing within the light, holding his staff. Allow his presence to guide the vision.
5. **Receive the Vision**
   Remain open to images, symbols, or feelings that arise. Trust that Raphael is revealing what you need.
6. **Close the Ritual**
   Thank Raphael by saying:
   *"Raphael, I honor your guidance and light.*
   *May your wisdom remain within me."*
   Extinguish the candle and record your vision in a journal.

## 2. Guided Visualization Technique

**Purpose:**

Engages the imagination to foster a visionary experience of Raphael.

**Steps:**

1. **Prepare for Meditation**
   Sit comfortably in a quiet space. Hold a malachite crystal and light sandalwood incense.
2. **Enter a Relaxed State**
   Close your eyes and focus on your breath. Imagine

each inhale filling you with green light, each exhale releasing tension.
3. **Journey to the Vision**
   Visualize yourself walking along a radiant green path, leading to a sacred garden. In the garden, Raphael waits with his staff, radiating light.
4. **Engage with Raphael**
   Ask questions or seek guidance. Allow Raphael's responses to manifest as images, symbols, or words in your mind's eye.
5. **Return Gently**
   When ready, thank Raphael and visualize yourself walking back along the path. Open your eyes and ground yourself.

## 3. Crystal Scrying for Angelic Visions

**Purpose:**

Uses the reflective surface of a crystal to channel Raphael's presence.

**Materials:**

- Malachite or emerald
- Raphael's sigil

**Steps:**

1. **Prepare the Space**
   Place the crystal on your altar alongside Raphael's sigil. Light a green candle.
2. **Gaze into the Crystal**
   Hold the crystal or place it before you. Gaze into its surface, allowing your vision to soften.
3. **Invoke Raphael**
   Say:
   "Raphael, divine healer and guide,
   Reveal your vision through this sacred stone.
   Open my heart and mind to your wisdom."

4. **Interpret the Vision**
   Observe shapes, colors, or images within the crystal. These reflections are Raphael's messages.

## Magical Correspondences

- **Symbols:** Staff, green light, fish
- **Crystals:** Malachite, emerald
- **Incense:** Frankincense, sandalwood
- **Colors:** Emerald green
- **Times:** Sunrise or twilight, symbolic of transition and revelation

## Advanced Tips for Mastery

### 1. Combine Techniques

Alternate between candle gazing, guided visualization, and crystal scrying to enhance your practice and develop a multifaceted connection to Raphael.

### 2. Record and Reflect

Keep a detailed journal of your visionary experiences. Over time, patterns and deeper messages will emerge.

### 3. Integrate Angelic Invocations

Combine the techniques with invocations, such as chanting Raphael's name or reciting sacred passages, to deepen the spiritual resonance.

## Walking with Raphael in the Light of Vision

Inducing angelic visions with Raphael is a transformative practice that bridges the material and spiritual realms. By engaging in these sacred techniques, you open your heart and mind to his guidance, allowing his healing light to illuminate your path. Trust in the process, and let Raphael's visions inspire and empower your magical journey.

As your understanding of Archangel Raphael deepens, the next natural step is to preserve and refine your knowledge through the creation of a dedicated grimoire. This sacred book will serve as both a repository and a guide—a place to organize your prayers, rituals, and spells while documenting your evolving connection with Raphael. By customizing your practices and reflecting on his wisdom, you will create a living record that aligns with your spiritual journey. Through this process, the grimoire becomes more than a book; it transforms into a personal talisman of divine healing, guidance, and growth. Let us now explore how to craft this powerful tool, ensuring it reflects your unique bond with Raphael.

# { 8 }

# Crafting the Sacred: Building Your Raphael Grimoire

A grimoire is more than a collection of rituals and spells; it is a reflection of your spiritual journey and a testament to your evolving relationship with Archangel Raphael. In this section, you will learn to craft a personalized and sacred book that serves as your constant companion on the path of divine healing and guidance. By thoughtfully organizing sections, customizing rituals, and integrating Raphael's wisdom into your daily life, you will create a living repository of angelic connection. Whether recording profound visions, developing personalized invocations, or reflecting on spiritual growth, this grimoire will become a beacon of Raphael's light in your magical practice. Together, let us explore how to bring this sacred creation to life, ensuring it resonates with your unique energy and intention.

## Designing a Sacred Repository: Organizing a Raphael Grimoire

### A Grimoire as a Mirror of Raphael's Wisdom

Your grimoire is a sacred reflection of your relationship with Archangel Raphael, serving as both a guide and a testament to your spiritual growth. Thoughtfully organizing its sections ensures that it remains a living document, accessible and dynamic. Structuring the grimoire into dedicated areas for prayers, rituals, and spells creates a harmonious framework that mirrors the multifaceted aspects of Raphael's guidance.

# Historical and Esoteric Significance of the Grimoire

## The Tradition of Magical Books

Grimoires have been central to magical traditions for centuries, functioning as repositories for sacred knowledge, rituals, and personal experiences. In Kabbalistic and Hermetic traditions, they often serve as tools for angelic invocation, bridging the practitioner's intent with divine energies.

## Raphael's Role in Sacred Texts

Archangel Raphael, often associated with healing and guidance, resonates with the concept of a grimoire. His presence in the Book of Tobit exemplifies the importance of recording divine wisdom and transformative experiences.

# Organizing the Grimoire: The Divine Blueprint

### 1. A Section for Prayers

Prayers are the cornerstone of communication with Raphael, allowing you to align your energy with his healing and guiding light.

- **Suggested Content:**
  Include invocations for healing, protection, and guidance. Document historical prayers, such as the *Prayer of Raphael* from mystical texts, alongside your personal creations.
- **Practical Tip:**
  Dedicate a specific color scheme (e.g., emerald green headings) to visually associate this section with Raphael's energy.

## 2. A Section for Rituals

Rituals channel Raphael's energy into purposeful action, making this section essential for your practice.

- **Suggested Content:**
  Detail healing, protective, and transformational rituals. For each ritual, provide step-by-step instructions, the materials required, and the invocations to use.
- **Practical Tip:**
  Use symbols, such as Raphael's sigil, as section dividers to signify the transition into sacred space.

## 3. A Section for Spells

This section allows for practical applications of Raphael's energy in your magical work.

- **Suggested Content:**
  Include spells for physical and emotional healing, travel protection, and spiritual renewal. For each spell, explain its purpose, magical correspondences, and expected outcomes.
- **Practical Tip:**
  Add a notes column next to each spell for recording observations and results, fostering a feedback loop in your practice.

# Symbolic and Esoteric Enhancements

## 1. Incorporating Raphael's Sigil

Begin each section with Raphael's sigil to consecrate the grimoire as a sacred space.

## 2. Color Coding

Use emerald green ink or accents throughout to resonate with Raphael's energy and vibrational frequency.

### 3. Elemental Correspondences

Include air symbols, such as feathers or wind motifs, to honor Raphael's elemental association.

## Step-by-Step: Structuring Your Raphael Grimoire

1. **Prepare the Materials**
   Choose a high-quality notebook or binder that feels sacred to you. Consider using green or gold embellishments.
2. **Dedicate the Grimoire**
   Before writing, light a green candle and invoke Raphael, saying:
   *"Raphael, divine healer and guide,
   Bless this book with your light and wisdom.
   May it serve as a vessel of divine connection
   And a beacon of healing for all who seek it."*
3. **Create Sections**
   Divide the grimoire into three main areas: Prayers, Rituals, and Spells. Use dividers, tabs, or artistic embellishments to mark each section.
4. **Begin with Raphael's Symbols**
   On the first page of each section, draw Raphael's sigil and inscribe his name in Hebrew (רפאל). Visualize his emerald light infusing the page.
5. **Record Content Thoughtfully**
   Write prayers, rituals, and spells with intention, leaving space for personal reflections and updates.

## Advanced Tips for Mastery

### 1. Record Personal Experiences

Add a subsection in each area for journaling your interactions with Raphael. This can include insights from rituals, dreams, or meditations.

### 2. Include Cross-References

Link similar prayers, rituals, and spells across sections to build a cohesive understanding of your practice.

### 3. Update Regularly

Treat your grimoire as a living document. Revisit and refine entries as your relationship with Raphael evolves.

## A Sacred Testament to Raphael's Light

Organizing your grimoire into dedicated sections for prayers, rituals, and spells transforms it into a functional and sacred tool. This structure not only enhances your magical practice but also strengthens your bond with Raphael. By imbuing each page with intention and respect, you create a tangible connection to his healing energy—a resource that will continue to grow with you on your spiritual journey.

# Chronicles of Divine Encounters: Recording Personal Experiences and Angelic Messages

## The Sacred Practice of Documentation

Recording personal experiences and angelic messages in your grimoire transforms it into a living testimony of your spiritual evolution. Archangel Raphael, as a divine healer and guide, often communicates through subtle signs, visions, and synchronicities. Capturing these moments with clarity and reverence ensures that they become enduring sources of insight and inspiration.

## Historical and Esoteric Context

### The Role of Documentation in Mystical Traditions

Mystics and magicians throughout history have recorded their divine encounters to preserve sacred wisdom and refine their practices. For instance:

- **Kabbalistic Traditions** emphasize journaling as a means to interpret the layered meanings of spiritual experiences.
- **The Book of Tobit** itself is a narrative of divine intervention, illustrating the value of preserving one's encounters with the celestial.

## Raphael as a Messenger

Raphael's communications often carry themes of healing, guidance, and protection. These messages may appear in dreams, meditative visions, or daily life as intuitive impressions or symbolic synchronicities.

## Organizing the Journal Section of Your Grimoire

### 1. Creating a Dedicated Space

Include a section in your grimoire specifically for recording personal experiences and angelic messages. Label it clearly to signify its sacred purpose.

### 2. Structuring Your Entries

Each entry should follow a format that allows for clarity and introspection. Suggested sections include:

- **Date and Time:** Anchor the experience in a specific moment.
- **Method of Communication:** Note whether the message came through meditation, prayer, or a synchronicity.
- **Details of the Message:** Record symbols, imagery, or words exactly as they appeared.
- **Interpretation:** Reflect on the potential meaning of the message.
- **Follow-Up Actions:** Outline how you plan to incorporate the guidance.

# Practical Applications: Capturing Raphael's Messages

## 1. Journaling After Meditation or Ritual

**Steps:**

1. **Set Intention**
   Before meditation or ritual, ask Raphael to communicate with you. Say:
   *"Raphael, divine guide, I open my heart and mind to your healing light.*
   *May your wisdom flow through me and illuminate my path."*
2. **Engage in the Practice**
   Meditate, scry, or perform a ritual as usual, keeping your intention focused on receiving Raphael's guidance.
3. **Record Immediately**
   Afterward, write down everything you experienced. Include emotions, physical sensations, and mental imagery. Even seemingly insignificant details may carry meaning.

## 2. Journaling Dreams

Dreams are a powerful channel for Raphael's guidance, often imbued with healing or symbolic messages.

**Steps:**

1. **Prepare Before Sleep**
   Place a green crystal, such as malachite, and Raphael's sigil under your pillow. Say:
   *"Raphael, angel of light, visit me in my dreams.*
   *Guide my spirit and heal my soul as I rest."*
2. **Record Upon Waking**
   Keep your grimoire or a separate dream journal beside your bed. Write down your dreams immediately upon waking, focusing on recurring symbols or feelings.

### 3. Recognizing Signs and Synchronicities

Raphael may communicate through patterns in daily life, such as repeated numbers (e.g., angel numbers like 444), encounters with symbolic animals, or sudden insights.

**Steps:**

1. **Stay Attuned**
   Remain mindful of your environment, especially after invoking Raphael. Signs often appear in the hours or days following rituals or prayers.
2. **Record the Context**
   Note what was happening when the sign appeared, including your emotional state and any questions you had in mind.

## Symbolic and Esoteric Enhancements

### Incorporating Raphael's Energy

- Use green or gold ink for entries to honor Raphael's healing vibration.
- Begin each session with his sigil or a short invocation to consecrate the act of writing.

### Illustrating Messages

If a message includes visual symbols, sketch them in your grimoire. This practice deepens your connection to the imagery and helps decode its meaning over time.

## Advanced Tips for Deepening Your Connection

### 1. Reflect Regularly

Revisit past entries to observe patterns or recurring themes. These may reveal deeper layers of Raphael's guidance.

### 2. Create a Symbol Dictionary

Over time, compile a list of symbols and their meanings as they relate to your connection with Raphael.

### 3. Share Gratitude

After documenting a message, offer gratitude to Raphael. Say:
*"Raphael, I thank you for your light and wisdom.
May your guidance continue to bless my path."*

## A Sacred Dialogue with Raphael

Recording personal experiences and angelic messages in your grimoire fosters an ongoing dialogue with Raphael. This sacred practice not only preserves the profound moments of connection but also helps you interpret and integrate his guidance into your life. By honoring these messages and the act of documentation, you deepen your relationship with Raphael and ensure that his light continues to guide and inspire your journey.

## The Art of Personal Connection: Customizing Rituals and Invocations for Raphael

### Personalizing the Path of Divine Healing

Customizing your rituals and invocations for Archangel Raphael enhances the depth and effectiveness of your practice. By crafting unique offerings and prayers that resonate with your intentions, you create a personalized channel to Raphael's healing light. This sacred customization transforms each ritual into a profound act of co-creation with the divine.

# Historical and Spiritual Context

## Offerings in Angelic Traditions

Offerings have long been a bridge between human intent and divine energy. In biblical texts, offerings are acts of devotion symbolizing gratitude, humility, and faith. The *Book of Tobit* recounts Raphael's guidance in collecting fish parts for healing, suggesting the sacredness of thoughtful preparation and giving.

## The Power of Personal Invocation

Invocations are the spoken word's spiritual counterpart to offerings. In mystical traditions like Kabbalah and Hermeticism, words are vessels for intention, aligning the practitioner with angelic frequencies. A personal invocation tailored to Raphael ensures that your unique energy harmonizes with his healing essence.

# Crafting Unique Offerings for Raphael

### 1. Selecting Symbolic Offerings

Choose offerings that align with Raphael's attributes, considering their symbolic and vibrational significance.

- **Herbs and Incense:** Frankincense, sandalwood, and sage represent purification and divine connection.
- **Crystals:** Emerald, malachite, or green fluorite amplify healing energies.
- **Food Offerings:** Honey and figs, symbolizing nourishment and sweetness, are excellent choices.
- **Candles:** Green candles resonate with Raphael's light, while gold honors his divine presence.

### 2. Preparing the Offering

Create a ritualized process to consecrate your offerings, infusing them with intention and sacred energy.

1. **Cleanse the Offering:**
   Wash or smudge the item to purify it, symbolizing the removal of mundane energies.
2. **Infuse with Intention:**
   Hold the offering in your hands and speak your purpose, such as:
   *"I dedicate this [offering] to Archangel Raphael, as a sign of gratitude and devotion."*
3. **Present the Offering:**
   Place it on Raphael's altar or a sacred space while visualizing his presence accepting it.

## Developing Unique Invocations for Raphael

### 1. Writing Personalized Invocations

Tailor your invocation to your intention, whether it's healing, protection, or guidance.

- **Structure of an Invocation:**
    - **Greeting:** Acknowledge Raphael's presence and attributes.
      *"Raphael, angel of healing and light, I call upon you now."*
    - **Purpose:** Clearly state your request.
      *"I seek your guidance to mend the wounds of my heart and soul."*
    - **Gratitude:** Offer thanks in advance.
      *"I thank you, Raphael, for your healing touch and divine wisdom."*

### 2. Enhancing Invocations with Correspondences

Amplify your words by integrating sacred tools and symbols.

- **Use a Green Candle:** Light it as you recite your invocation, symbolizing the illumination of Raphael's energy.
- **Hold a Crystal:** Emerald or malachite can serve as focal points, grounding the invocation in physical energy.
- **Chant Raphael's Name in Hebrew (רפאל):** This vibrational technique strengthens your connection.

## Practical Applications: A Unique Ritual with Offerings and Invocation

### Step-by-Step: A Ritual for Healing Guidance

1. **Prepare the Space:**
   Cleanse the area with sage or incense. Set up an altar with a green cloth, a candle, and your chosen offering.
2. **Consecrate the Offering:**
   Hold the offering in your hands, close your eyes, and say:
   *"Raphael, divine healer and guide, I dedicate this offering to you. May it carry my intentions to your light."*
3. **Light the Candle:**
   As the flame burns, visualize it as a beacon drawing Raphael's energy into the space.
4. **Speak the Invocation:**
   Recite your personalized prayer. For example:
   *"Raphael, angel of healing and compassion, I call upon your emerald light to guide me. Illuminate my path with wisdom and restore balance to my spirit. Accept this offering as a token of my gratitude and devotion."*
5. **Meditate in Silence:**
   Sit quietly, focusing on the energy of the space. Feel Raphael's presence and allow insights to arise.
6. **Close the Ritual:**
   Extinguish the candle, thanking Raphael:
   *"Raphael, I thank you for your light and healing. May your blessings remain with me always."*

## Symbolic and Esoteric Significance

- **Offerings as Bridges:** Thoughtful offerings anchor divine energy in the physical realm, solidifying your connection to Raphael.
- **Invocations as Vibrational Alignments:** The spoken word creates a resonant field that aligns your energy with Raphael's frequency.
- **Personalization as Sacred Engagement:** By crafting unique offerings and invocations, you honor Raphael's individual guidance in your life.

## Advanced Tips for Mastery

1. **Experiment with Offerings:**
   Notice how different offerings influence the energy of your rituals. Keep notes in your grimoire to refine your practice.
2. **Integrate Angelic Correspondences:**
   Combine Raphael's planetary (Mercury) and elemental (Air) correspondences for more powerful invocations.
3. **Evolve with Practice:**
   As your relationship with Raphael deepens, adapt your invocations and offerings to reflect new insights and experiences.

## Co-Creating with Raphael

Customizing rituals and invocations is an act of sacred creativity, allowing you to deepen your bond with Archangel Raphael. Through thoughtful offerings and personalized prayers, you forge a unique pathway to his healing light. This practice not only strengthens your spiritual connection but also empowers you to bring Raphael's guidance into every aspect of your life.

# Crafting a Sacred Language: Creating Personalized Correspondences for Raphael

## A Foundation for Divine Connection

Creating personalized correspondences for Archangel Raphael allows you to weave your unique energy into your spiritual practice, deepening your bond with his healing presence. This process builds on universal correspondences while tailoring them to reflect your intentions, preferences, and spiritual journey. The act of personalization transforms correspondences from general symbols into intimate tools of co-creation with Raphael.

## Historical and Spiritual Context

### What Are Correspondences?

Correspondences are symbolic links between spiritual forces and physical objects, colors, sounds, or actions. These links act as conduits, focusing and amplifying intention during rituals and magical practices. For Raphael, correspondences like emerald green, Mercury, Air, and healing herbs embody his qualities and energy.

### Personalization in Mystical Traditions

Many mystical traditions emphasize the importance of personalizing correspondences. The Kabbalistic tree of life, for example, offers universal archetypes, but practitioners customize their connections to align with personal experiences. By doing so, they create a more potent spiritual practice.

## Building Personalized Correspondences for Raphael

**1. Choosing Core Symbols**

Begin by selecting symbols that resonate with Raphael's attributes of healing, guidance, and renewal. Use these as a foundation for personalization.

- **Colors:** Start with emerald green (Raphael's universal color) but consider adding hues that resonate with your intentions, such as gold for divine illumination or soft blue for calmness.
- **Crystals:** Expand beyond malachite and emerald to include stones like peridot or aventurine if they align with your energy.
- **Herbs:** Frankincense and sandalwood are universal, but you can include local or personal favorites like lavender for emotional healing or eucalyptus for respiratory health.

## 2. Incorporating Personal Symbols

Infuse your practice with symbols that hold personal meaning or reflect your unique relationship with Raphael.

- **Natural Elements:** Use feathers, shells, or flowers you feel drawn to, imbuing them with significance in your practice.
- **Sacred Objects:** Dedicate objects like a locket, ring, or journal to Raphael, transforming them into vessels of his energy.

## 3. Connecting Correspondences to Your Intentions

Link your personalized correspondences to specific intentions to create a unique and powerful connection.

- **For Healing:** Use emerald crystals, frankincense incense, and a green candle engraved with Raphael's sigil.
- **For Guidance:** Incorporate Mercury-related symbols like a caduceus charm or a map, symbolizing clarity and direction.

- **For Protection:** Pair Air symbols like feathers with protective herbs such as rosemary or thyme.

## A Ritual for Personalizing Correspondences

### Step-by-Step Instructions

1. **Prepare the Space:**
   Cleanse the area with sage or incense, creating an energetically neutral space for your work.
2. **Select Your Correspondences:**
   Choose items like crystals, herbs, or symbols that align with Raphael's energy and your personal intentions.
3. **Consecrate the Items:**
   Hold each item and say:
   *"I dedicate this [item] to Raphael, angel of healing and light. May it serve as a vessel for your guidance and protection."*
4. **Create a Correspondence Grid:**
   Arrange your items in a sacred geometric pattern, such as a triangle (for healing) or a circle (for protection).
5. **Invoke Raphael's Blessing:**
   Light a green candle and recite:
   *"Raphael, healer and guide, bless these symbols as pathways to your light. Infuse them with your wisdom and power, that they may aid me in my sacred work."*
6. **Seal the Connection:**
   Meditate on Raphael's presence, visualizing his emerald energy flowing into each correspondence.

## Symbolic and Esoteric Significance

- **Emerald Energy:** The color green reflects growth, renewal, and Raphael's healing light, linking the physical and spiritual realms.
- **Sacred Geometry:** Arranging correspondences in patterns amplifies their collective energy and aligns them with universal forces.

- **Personal Symbols:** Incorporating unique items strengthens the emotional and spiritual resonance of your practice.

## Practical Applications

- **Daily Rituals:** Use your correspondences as focal points during meditations or prayers to Raphael.
- **Spellwork:** Incorporate them into healing, protection, or guidance spells for enhanced effectiveness.
- **Grimoire Integration:** Record your correspondences in your grimoire, noting their significance and any insights received.

## Advanced Tips for Mastery

1. **Experiment and Observe:**
   Rotate or refine your correspondences over time, paying attention to which items enhance your connection with Raphael.
2. **Seasonal Adjustments:**
   Adapt correspondences to align with the seasons or planetary transits, deepening their connection to universal cycles.
3. **Combine Traditions:**
   Blend Raphael's correspondences with those of other angels or spiritual figures for collaborative rituals.

## A Unique Pathway to Raphael's Light

Creating personalized correspondences for Raphael transforms your spiritual practice into a deeply intimate journey. By infusing universal symbols with personal meaning, you forge a sacred connection that reflects your unique path. Through this customized relationship, you bring Raphael's guidance, healing, and protection into every aspect of your life.

# Integrating Raphael's Wisdom: Reflecting on Lessons and Spiritual Growth

## A Pathway to Enlightenment Through Reflection

Reflecting on lessons learned from Archangel Raphael allows you to transform divine guidance into actionable wisdom. By recognizing how Raphael's healing and guidance have influenced your life, you deepen your spiritual growth and strengthen your connection to his energy. Reflection fosters self-awareness, gratitude, and clarity, forming the cornerstone of an evolving spiritual practice.

## Historical and Spiritual Context

### The Role of Reflection in Angelic Magic

In mystical traditions, reflection is not merely introspection but an act of aligning one's mind with divine will. The Book of Tobit reveals Raphael's guidance as a process of healing not only the body but also the soul, urging practitioners to recognize and honor their growth.

### Raphael's Role as a Spiritual Mentor

Raphael's energy inspires clarity, discernment, and transformation. His teachings invite practitioners to examine their lives, identify areas for healing, and pursue alignment with their highest potential.

## Practical Applications for Reflection

### 1. Creating a Sacred Reflection Space

Design a tranquil environment that invites introspection and communion with Raphael.

1. **Set the Scene:**
   Use emerald green fabric, Raphael's sigil, and crystals like malachite to create a focal point.
2. **Include Reflective Tools:**
   Incorporate a mirror (symbolizing self-examination) or a bowl of water (representing emotional depth).

## 2. Writing in the Grimoire

Document your experiences with Raphael, noting insights, lessons, and spiritual breakthroughs.

- Begin each entry with a prayer or invocation, such as: *"Raphael, divine healer and guide, I open my heart to your wisdom. Illuminate my reflections with your emerald light."*
- Write freely about challenges, growth, and moments of divine intervention.

# A Ritual for Reflection and Integration

## Step-by-Step Instructions

1. **Prepare Your Space:**
   Light a green candle and place it beside Raphael's sigil or statue.
   - *Symbolism:* The candle represents Raphael's guiding light illuminating your path.
2. **Ground Yourself:**
   Sit comfortably and take three deep breaths, visualizing emerald light entering your heart.
3. **Invoke Raphael:**
   Recite:
   *"Raphael, angel of wisdom and light, I call upon your presence. Guide my thoughts and open my heart to your healing truths."*
4. **Engage in Reflection:**
   Use the following prompts to guide your thoughts or writing:

- What lessons have I learned through Raphael's guidance?
- How have I grown emotionally, spiritually, or physically?
- What patterns or habits need further healing?

5. **Seek Clarity Through Divination:**
   If you feel stuck, use angelic tarot or scrying to gain deeper insight.
6. **Close with Gratitude:**
   Thank Raphael for his guidance:
   *"Raphael, I am grateful for your presence and wisdom. May your light continue to guide me on my path."*
   Extinguish the candle as a gesture of completion.

## Symbolic and Esoteric Significance

- **Mirror and Water:** Represent self-reflection and the subconscious mind.
- **Emerald Light:** Serves as a bridge between earthly concerns and divine wisdom.
- **Sacred Writing:** Captures spiritual growth, preserving it for deeper integration over time.

## Practical Tips for Deeper Integration

1. **Create a Daily Reflection Practice:**
   Dedicate a few minutes each evening to reflect on the day's events and Raphael's guidance.
2. **Track Patterns Over Time:**
   Revisit past entries to identify recurring themes or areas of progress.
3. **Combine Reflection with Rituals:**
   Follow reflective sessions with specific rituals to reinforce insights, such as lighting a green candle to symbolize continued growth.

## Honoring the Journey

Reflecting on lessons and spiritual growth with Raphael transforms everyday experiences into profound spiritual milestones. Through consistent reflection and documentation, you anchor divine wisdom in your life, enabling you to evolve toward your highest self. This practice not only deepens your connection to Raphael but also empowers you to live in alignment with his healing light.

## Incorporating Raphael's Guidance into Daily Practices

### Living in Alignment with Angelic Wisdom

Integrating Raphael's guidance into daily practices allows you to bring his healing light into every aspect of your life. By weaving rituals, prayers, and conscious actions into your routine, you maintain an ongoing connection with his divine energy, fostering balance, health, and spiritual growth.

## Historical and Spiritual Context

### The Daily Presence of Archangels

In mystical traditions, working with an angel such as Raphael is not limited to ceremonial rituals but extends to everyday life. The Book of Tobit portrays Raphael as a constant companion, demonstrating how his energy can guide, protect, and heal in the mundane and extraordinary alike.

### Raphael's Role in Daily Transformation

Raphael's energy is not confined to grand gestures; his presence is equally transformative in small, consistent actions. Through mindfulness, gratitude, and ritual, you can establish a living relationship with his guidance.

# Practical Applications for Daily Integration

### 1. Morning Invocation for Guidance

Begin your day by inviting Raphael's healing energy into your life.

1. **Prepare a Sacred Space:**
   Light a green candle and place a crystal, such as malachite, nearby.
2. **Recite a Prayer:**
   Say:
   *"Raphael, angel of healing and light, I call upon your presence. Guide my steps today, bless my heart with your wisdom, and fill my spirit with your emerald light. May I walk in harmony and health under your protection. Amen."*
3. **Focus on Intentions:**
   Visualize Raphael's emerald light surrounding you, setting the tone for your day.

### 2. Mindful Eating with Raphael's Blessing

Invoke Raphael's energy during meals to nourish body, mind, and soul.

1. **Pause Before Eating:**
   Hold your hands over your meal and say:
   *"Raphael, bless this food with your healing light. May it nourish my body, uplift my mind, and strengthen my spirit."*
2. **Visualize Emerald Light:**
   Imagine the food glowing with divine energy as you consume it.

### 3. Healing Breathwork for Midday Renewal

Restore balance and focus during busy moments by connecting with Raphael through breath.

1. **Find a Quiet Space:**
   Sit comfortably and close your eyes.
2. **Perform a Breath Ritual:**
   Inhale deeply, visualizing emerald light filling your lungs, and exhale any tension.
   Repeat:
   *"Raphael, healer of breath and spirit, restore me with your light."*

### 4. Evening Reflection with Gratitude

Conclude your day by reflecting on Raphael's presence and expressing gratitude.

1. **Write in Your Grimoire:**
   Record moments where you felt Raphael's guidance or experienced healing.
2. **Offer Thanks:**
   Light incense such as frankincense and say:
   *"Raphael, I thank you for your wisdom and light this day. Continue to guide and heal me as I rest in your peace."*

## Symbolic and Esoteric Significance

- **Emerald Light:** Represents continuous healing and protection in your daily life.
- **Green Candle:** Symbolizes Raphael's constant presence and the renewal of your energy.
- **Grimoire Entries:** Capture the flow of angelic influence, deepening your understanding over time.

# Personalized Rituals for Integration

## Crafting Your Raphael Routine

- Combine multiple practices, such as morning invocations and evening reflections, into a cohesive daily routine.
- Use symbolic items like Raphael's sigil, a crystal, or a small token to keep his presence close throughout the day.

## Angelic Affirmations

Incorporate affirmations inspired by Raphael's guidance, such as:

- *"I am guided and healed by Raphael's light."*
- *"With each breath, I align with divine health and wisdom."*

## Advanced Tips for Deepening Connection

1. **Angel Walks:**
   Take mindful walks outdoors, imagining Raphael's presence beside you, enhancing your connection with the natural world.
2. **Anchor Points:**
   Place Raphael's sigil in your workspace, home, or car as a visual reminder of his protective and healing energy.
3. **Cycle of Reflection:**
   Dedicate one day per week to a longer reflection or ritual focused entirely on integrating Raphael's lessons.

# A Life Touched by Raphael

By incorporating Raphael's guidance into your daily practices, you create a life imbued with divine wisdom and healing light. These consistent acts of devotion allow you to embody the principles of health, balance, and spiritual alignment that Raphael represents, transforming every moment into an opportunity for growth and grace.

As we move forward, our exploration delves into the diverse traditions that honor Raphael as a healer and guide. Across Kabbalistic, Christian, Islamic, and folk traditions, Raphael's role transcends cultural boundaries, embodying the universal principles of restoration and divine mercy. By examining his place in these spiritual frameworks, we uncover a wealth of practices and interpretations that illuminate his multifaceted nature. From the mystical depths of the Sephirot to heartfelt pilgrimages in Christian devotion, from Islamic reflections on Israfil's cosmic role to the vibrant syncretism of folk magic, this next section reveals how Raphael's healing light shines across spiritual landscapes. Each tradition offers unique insights and rituals that deepen our understanding and enhance our connection with this profound angelic force.

# { 9 }

# Raphael's Universal Light: Healing Across Spiritual Traditions

Archangel Raphael, as a divine healer and guide, is revered across spiritual traditions, each offering unique perspectives and practices that enrich our understanding of his essence. In Kabbalistic mysticism, Raphael's role within the Sephirot reveals the intricate connections between divine energies and the human soul. Christian traditions honor Raphael as a patron of healing, invoking his intercession through pilgrimages and prayers. In Islamic angelology, Raphael, known as Israfil, carries profound significance in cosmic renewal and spiritual guidance. Folk traditions further extend Raphael's reach, blending his attributes with local deities and spirits in vibrant acts of syncretism. This exploration reveals how Raphael's light unites these diverse paths, offering healing and wisdom to all who seek his presence. By engaging with these traditions, we uncover a universal message of restoration, mercy, and transformation that transcends cultural boundaries, enriching our practice and understanding of this beloved archangel.

## Raphael in Kabbalistic Mysticism: Guardian of the Sephirot

### Raphael's Place in the Tree of Life

In the Kabbalistic tradition, Archangel Raphael is intricately associated with the Sephirot of Tiferet (Beauty), which serves as the heart of the Tree of Life. Tiferet harmonizes divine energies, balancing judgment (Gevurah) and mercy (Chesed). Raphael embodies this balance, channeling healing and restoration through divine beauty and alignment.

- **Tiferet's Essence:** Representing harmony, beauty, and compassion, Tiferet connects the upper Sephirot (divine consciousness) with the lower Sephirot (manifestation). Raphael's role here signifies the healing of the soul by aligning it with divine purpose.
- **Symbolism in the Sephirot:** As a healing angel, Raphael bridges the spiritual and physical realms, offering restoration through divine equilibrium. His connection to Tiferet makes him a mediator between the divine and the earthly, harmonizing conflicting energies within the soul.

## Raphael in Angelic Hierarchies

In Jewish mysticism, Raphael is a principal angel of healing and a member of the angelic hierarchy associated with divine restoration.

- **Malachim and Archangels:** Raphael is classified among the Malachim (messengers) and Archangels, emphasizing his dual role as a healer and guide.
- **Healing Mission:** Within the angelic orders, Raphael is tasked with mending spiritual and physical ailments, providing divine intervention for those seeking restoration.

## Practical Applications in Kabbalistic Magic

### Meditation with Tiferet and Raphael

Meditating on Tiferet while invoking Raphael can harmonize your inner energies and foster healing.

1. **Preparation:**
    - Sit in a quiet space with a candle (gold or green) and a malachite crystal to represent Tiferet's harmony.
2. **Visualization:**

- Imagine the Tree of Life before you. See Raphael standing at Tiferet, emanating emerald green and golden light.
3. **Invocation:** Say:
   *"Raphael, guardian of Tiferet, bringer of harmony,*
   *Align my soul with divine beauty and balance.*
   *Heal my spirit and body with your light,*
   *So I may reflect the harmony of the divine."*

## Creating a Talisman for Divine Alignment

Craft a talisman symbolizing Raphael's connection to Tiferet.

1. **Materials Needed:**
   - A gold or green pendant (to represent Tiferet's colors).
   - Inscribe Raphael's name in Hebrew (רפאל) and the symbol of Tiferet (a six-pointed star).
2. **Blessing the Talisman:**
   - Anoint it with frankincense oil while reciting Psalm 23, aligning its energy with divine restoration.
3. **Use:**
   - Wear or carry it during healing rituals or challenging times to channel Raphael's harmonizing influence.

## Ritual for Healing Through Tiferet

Invoke Raphael to harmonize the energies of Tiferet for personal or collective healing.

1. **Preparation:**
   - Create a sacred space with green and gold candles, incense (such as sandalwood or frankincense), and a central focus like a Tree of Life diagram.
2. **Invocation:** Recite the following:
   *"Raphael, healer of divine beauty,*

> *Descend from the heart of the Tree of Life.*
> *Bring balance to the discord within,*
> *And heal my spirit through Tiferet's harmony."*

3. **Focus:**
    - Visualize emerald and golden light descending from Tiferet into your heart, spreading throughout your being.
4. **Closing:**
    - Thank Raphael by saying:
      *"Raphael, my gratitude shines like Tiferet.*
      *Your harmony heals all aspects of my being.*
      *Return to the heavens, and I remain whole."*

## Symbolic and Esoteric Significance

- **Emerald and Gold:** Colors representing healing (emerald) and divine beauty (gold).
- **Tiferet's Energy:** Harmonizes dualities, symbolizing the balance needed for spiritual and physical well-being.
- **Hebrew Mysticism:** Raphael's name reflects his essence, "God heals," anchoring him in the divine plan of restoration.

## Connections to Sacred Texts and Mystical Interpretations

- **Zohar:** Highlights Tiferet as the balance point in the Tree of Life, with Raphael as its angelic custodian.
- **Sefer Yetzirah:** Offers insights into the Sephirot's attributes, underscoring Raphael's alignment with harmony and healing.

## Advanced Tips for Deepening the Connection

1. **Daily Tiferet Meditations:** Incorporate Raphael's presence into your daily meditations by visualizing Tiferet's light within you.

2. **Collaborative Kabbalistic Work:** Explore connections between Raphael and other Sephirot, such as Chesed and Gevurah, for comprehensive healing.
3. **Angel-Specific Practices:** Study the Zohar's insights on angels to deepen your understanding of Raphael's healing mission.

## Harmony as Healing

Through his role in Tiferet and the angelic hierarchies, Raphael embodies the divine principle of healing through harmony. By working with him in Kabbalistic magic, you align yourself with the universal balance of the Tree of Life, fostering restoration and spiritual growth. Raphael's presence serves as a reminder that healing begins with alignment—within ourselves and with the divine.

## Healing Through the Divine Blueprint: Raphael in Kabbalistic Practice

### Healing in the Kabbalistic Tradition: A Mystical Framework

In Kabbalah, healing is not merely the resolution of physical ailments but the restoration of harmony between the body, soul, and divine energy. Raphael, whose name means "God heals," embodies this principle, channeling the energies of divine balance and restoration into the physical and spiritual realms.

- **The Tree of Life as a Healing Blueprint:** Healing practices are deeply rooted in the Sephirotic structure of the Tree of Life. Raphael's association with Tiferet (Beauty) makes him a conduit for harmony, connecting the higher divine spheres with earthly existence.
- **Healing Through Light:** Raphael's energy is often visualized as emerald green light, symbolizing growth, restoration, and the renewal of life force. This light

serves as a bridge between the human soul and the divine source.

# Kabbalistic Techniques for Healing with Raphael

## Meditative Visualization: Drawing Healing from Tiferet

This practice involves connecting with the Sephirot of Tiferet to channel Raphael's healing energy.

1. **Preparation:**
   - Find a quiet, sacred space. Light a green or gold candle and burn frankincense or sandalwood incense.
   - Place a malachite or emerald crystal in front of you to represent Tiferet's energy.
2. **Visualization:**
   - Close your eyes and imagine the Tree of Life glowing before you. Focus on Tiferet at its center, radiating golden and green light.
   - See Raphael standing within Tiferet, holding a staff that pulses with healing energy.
3. **Invocation:** Say:
   "Raphael, guardian of divine beauty,
   Bring healing from the heart of creation.
   Align my soul with Tiferet's harmony,
   That my body, mind, and spirit may be restored."
4. **Integration:**
   - Visualize the emerald green light flowing from Tiferet through Raphael's staff into your body. See it illuminating areas of pain or imbalance, dissolving blockages and restoring vitality.
5. **Closing:**
   - Thank Raphael with a simple prayer:
   "Raphael, healer of all realms,
   Your light has touched me with divine grace.
   I am whole, I am aligned, I am renewed."

# The Use of Hebrew Letters in Healing Rituals

Kabbalistic practices often incorporate sacred Hebrew letters to amplify healing energy.

- **Raphael's Name in Hebrew:** רפאל (Resh, Peh, Aleph, Lamed) symbolizes the flow of divine healing. Writing or meditating on these letters can create a direct connection to Raphael's energy.
- **Practical Application:** Write Raphael's name on a piece of parchment and place it under a green candle. Recite Psalm 23 while focusing on the flame to invite divine healing into your space.

## Kabbalistic Healing Ritual: The Three Pillars of Balance

This ritual aligns the energies of Tiferet (harmony), Chesed (mercy), and Gevurah (strength) through Raphael's guidance.

1. **Setup:**
    - Arrange three candles in a triangular formation: green for Tiferet, blue for Chesed, and red for Gevurah.
    - Place a chalice of spring water in the center, symbolizing the flow of divine life force.
2. **Invocation:** Say:
    "Raphael, divine healer of Tiferet,
    Balance the mercy of Chesed with the strength of Gevurah.
    Pour your healing light into this sacred space,
    That all discord may be resolved in harmony."
3. **Activation:**
    - Light the candles, beginning with Chesed, then Gevurah, and finally Tiferet.
    - Dip your fingers into the chalice and sprinkle the water over yourself or another, visualizing Raphael's light flowing through you.
4. **Affirmation:** Say:
    "By the balance of the Tree of Life, I am healed.

> *By Raphael's light, I am restored.*
> *By the divine will, I am whole."*

5. **Closing:** Extinguish the candles in reverse order and pour the water into the earth as an offering of gratitude.

## Symbolic and Esoteric Significance

- **Tiferet's Central Role:** Healing begins with harmony, both within the soul and in alignment with divine energy.
- **The Triadic Balance:** The integration of Chesed and Gevurah through Tiferet reflects the Kabbalistic principle of balancing opposites for holistic restoration.

## Sacred Texts and Mystical Insights

- **Zohar:** Describes Tiferet as the heart of divine energy, with Raphael as its healing emissary.
- **Sefer Yetzirah:** Explores the interplay of the Sephirot, emphasizing the importance of alignment for spiritual and physical health.

## Advanced Tips for Deepening Your Practice

1. **Daily Hebrew Letter Meditations:** Focus on the letters of Raphael's name, visualizing their light merging with your own energy field.
2. **Study the Sephirot:** Understand the relationships between Tiferet, Chesed, and Gevurah to refine your healing practices.
3. **Collaborative Work:** Combine Raphael's energy with other archangels associated with specific Sephirot for multidimensional healing.

In Kabbalistic and angelic traditions, collaborative work involves integrating the energies of multiple archangels to create a more comprehensive healing experience. Each archangel corresponds to specific **Sephirot** on the Tree of Life, representing distinct divine qualities that, when combined, can address healing on multiple levels—physical, emotional, mental, and spiritual.

Here's a detailed look at how Raphael can work synergistically with other archangels associated with the **Sephirot**:

## Michael: Chesed (Mercy and Compassion)

- **Why Michael?**
    - Michael is associated with **Chesed**, the Sephira of divine mercy, kindness, and expansive love. Chesed's energy provides the nurturing force necessary to foster emotional healing, alleviate fear, and inspire hope.
    - Pairing Raphael's harmony and healing energy with Michael's mercy creates a powerful blend for emotional and spiritual restoration.
- **Applications:**
    - For emotional healing, call upon Raphael to bring balance and Michael to provide comfort and protection.
    - This combination is particularly effective for those struggling with feelings of guilt, grief, or despair.

## Gabriel: Yesod (Foundation and Inner Strength)

- **Why Gabriel?**
    - Gabriel is linked to **Yesod**, the Sephira of foundation, emotional stability, and the subconscious mind. Gabriel governs intuition, dreams, and inner resilience.
    - Collaborating with Raphael and Gabriel addresses not only physical healing but also

the deeper emotional and psychological foundations that may hinder recovery.
- **Applications:**
    - Use Gabriel's intuitive guidance with Raphael's restorative energy in dreamwork or meditation aimed at uncovering and healing emotional wounds.
    - For those feeling disconnected or fragmented, this duo helps restore inner strength and focus.

## Metatron: Keter (Divine Will and Spiritual Connection)

- **Why Metatron?**
    - Metatron governs **Keter**, the crown of the Tree of Life, which connects directly to divine will and ultimate unity with the Source.
    - While Raphael works in **Tiferet** (harmony and balance), Metatron's presence can elevate healing to a deeply spiritual level, aligning the individual with their higher purpose and divine plan.
- **Applications:**
    - Combine Raphael's healing energy with Metatron's spiritual insight for those experiencing existential crises or seeking spiritual enlightenment alongside physical recovery.
    - Particularly useful in rituals for life transitions or overcoming spiritual stagnation.

## Uriel: Gevurah (Strength and Discipline)

- **Why Uriel?**
    - Uriel is associated with **Gevurah**, the Sephira of strength, discipline, and divine justice. Gevurah provides the necessary force to

break through obstacles and dissolve negative energies or habits.
    - Partnering Uriel's assertive energy with Raphael's gentle healing can address issues requiring a decisive shift, such as addiction or harmful behavioral patterns.
- **Applications:**
    - For breaking unhealthy cycles, invoke Raphael to heal the underlying cause and Uriel to empower the will to change.
    - This combination ensures that healing is not only restorative but also transformative and protective.

## Sandalphon: Malkuth (Grounding and Physical Manifestation)

- **Why Sandalphon?**
    - Sandalphon governs **Malkuth**, the Sephira of the physical world and manifestation. Sandalphon anchors divine energy into the material plane, making abstract healing energies tangible in the body and environment.
    - When working with Raphael, Sandalphon ensures that healing energies manifest in real, observable changes in health and well-being.
- **Applications:**
    - Use this pairing for physical healing and grounding after energy work or spiritual experiences.
    - In practical terms, this combination can help channel spiritual insight into actionable steps for health and balance.

## Tzadkiel (Zadkiel): Netzach (Victory and Overcoming Challenges)

- **Why Tzadkiel?**
    - Tzadkiel is linked to **Netzach**, the Sephira of endurance, perseverance, and emotional triumph. Netzach's energies help overcome long-standing challenges or chronic illnesses.
    - Together, Raphael and Tzadkiel bring perseverance in healing processes that require patience and consistent effort.
- **Applications:**
    - This collaboration is ideal for individuals facing prolonged recovery or deeply rooted emotional wounds.
    - Tzadkiel can provide the motivation and determination to persist, while Raphael facilitates ongoing healing.

## Why These Archangels?

1. **Comprehensive Healing:** Each archangel complements Raphael by focusing on a specific aspect of divine healing (spiritual, emotional, physical, or psychological).
2. **Balance and Synergy:** Just as the Sephirot function in harmony, these archangels work together to ensure that healing is multidimensional.
3. **Tailored Focus:** Depending on the need, the practitioner can tailor their invocation to include archangels whose energies align with their intention.

# Collaborative Healing Ritual Example

## Purpose: Comprehensive Healing

- **Participants:** Raphael, Michael, Gabriel, and Metatron
- **Tools Needed:**
    - Candles: Green (Raphael), Blue (Michael), White (Metatron), Purple (Gabriel)

- Symbols: Raphael's sigil, a chalice of water, and sacred herbs such as frankincense and sage.
- Incantation: A prayer or invocation combining their names and energies.

1. **Setup:**
   - Create a square with candles representing each archangel at its corners.
   - Place Raphael's sigil in the center, with a chalice of water on top.
2. **Invocation:**
   - Begin with Raphael:
   *"Raphael, healer of all realms, bring your emerald light to restore balance and harmony."*
   - Call upon Michael:
   *"Michael, protector of divine mercy, shield us with your unwavering strength and compassion."*
   - Invoke Gabriel:
   *"Gabriel, guardian of inner wisdom, bring clarity to the subconscious and emotional peace."*
   - End with Metatron:
   *"Metatron, bridge to the divine, connect us with the highest will for our ultimate healing."*
3. **Healing Visualization:**
   - Visualize a beam of light descending through Metatron (white), passing through Raphael (green), merging with Gabriel's energy (purple), and finally enveloping you with Michael's protection (blue).
4. **Closing:**
   - Offer gratitude to each archangel:
   *"With your combined grace, I am healed, whole, and aligned with divine will."*
   - Extinguish the candles in reverse order, pouring the chalice's water into the earth.

Collaborating with other archangels enhances Raphael's healing power by addressing multiple layers of existence. Each archangel's Sephirotic alignment ensures that healing is comprehensive, balanced, and transformative, making these collaborative rituals invaluable for deep, multidimensional healing practices.

## Healing as Divine Alignment

Through Kabbalistic practices, Raphael serves as a bridge between the divine and the earthly, channeling healing energy that restores harmony and balance. By aligning yourself with the energies of the Sephirot and invoking Raphael's guidance, you participate in a mystical tradition that views healing as an act of divine creation. Raphael's light illuminates the path to wholeness, reminding us that true healing begins with spiritual alignment.

## Raphael in Christian Healing Practices: A Bridge Between Heaven and Earth

### Raphael's Prominence in Catholicism and Orthodox Christianity

Archangel Raphael holds a revered place in Christian traditions, especially in Catholic and Orthodox Christianity, where he is celebrated as the patron saint of healing, travelers, and protection against evil. His narrative in the Book of Tobit provides a foundation for understanding his role in divine intervention and holistic restoration. Raphael's presence is invoked in personal prayers, communal liturgies, and sacred rituals, reflecting his role as a compassionate intercessor between humanity and God.

# Historical and Spiritual Context

## The Book of Tobit: Raphael's Role as Healer and Protector

In the Catholic and Orthodox canons, Raphael's most prominent appearance is in the *Book of Tobit*. Here, he heals Tobit's blindness and frees Sarah from a demon's grip. These acts establish Raphael as a divine agent of physical, emotional, and spiritual healing.

- **Healing of Tobit:** Symbolizes the restoration of sight (both literal and spiritual), reinforcing Raphael's ability to heal afflictions and illuminate one's path to divine truth.
- **Liberation of Sarah:** Demonstrates Raphael's power to banish malevolent forces and bring peace, embodying themes of deliverance and reconciliation.

## Feast Days and Liturgical Recognition

- In Catholicism, Raphael's feast day is celebrated on **September 29** (combined with Michael and Gabriel).
- Orthodox Christianity often venerates Raphael alongside other archangels in collective feasts, highlighting his protective and healing nature.

# Practical Applications: Invoking Raphael in Christian Healing

## Creating a Sacred Space

1. **Prepare an Altar:**
   - Place a green cloth (symbolizing healing) on a table.
   - Add a crucifix or icon of Christ to center the focus on divine grace.
   - Include a candle for Raphael (green or white) and sacred elements such as holy water and olive oil.

2. **Set Intention:**
    - Begin by quieting your mind and offering a prayer for clarity and focus.
    - Dedicate the space to Raphael's healing presence and invite his intercession.

## Step-by-Step Healing Ritual

1. **Opening Prayer:** Begin with a traditional Christian prayer, such as the *Our Father*, to establish a sacred connection.

    *"Heavenly Father, I come before you in humility and faith. Through the intercession of your archangel Raphael, I seek healing for my body, mind, and soul. May your divine light flow through him to restore and renew me."*

2. **Invocation of Raphael:** Light the green or white candle, and anoint yourself with holy water or olive oil.

    *"Archangel Raphael, servant of the Most High,
    You who guided Tobit and Sarah to healing,
    I call upon your sacred presence.
    Surround me with your emerald light,
    Banish all affliction and fill me with divine grace."*

    Trace a small cross on your forehead with the oil as a symbol of blessing.

3. **Scripture Reading:** Read Psalm 103:1-5 aloud, focusing on its themes of healing and renewal: *"Bless the Lord, O my soul,
    and all that is within me, bless his holy name.
    …Who forgives all your iniquity,
    who heals all your diseases…"*
4. **Visualization and Meditation:** Close your eyes and visualize Raphael's emerald light surrounding you, flowing through your body to cleanse and heal every

part of you. Imagine his gentle presence guiding you toward peace.

5. **Closing Prayer:** Conclude with a prayer of thanksgiving: *"Thank you, Raphael, for your healing touch. May your light guide me always toward health, strength, and faith in God's love. Amen."*

## Symbolic and Esoteric Significance

- **Emerald Light:** Represents divine healing, renewal, and Raphael's presence.
- **Holy Water and Oil:** Serve as conduits for divine grace and purification, mirroring sacramental practices in Christianity.
- **Candle Flame:** Symbolizes the light of Christ, illuminating the path to health and restoration.

## Incorporating Raphael's Role in Daily Christian Practices

1. **Daily Prayer to Raphael:** Include a short prayer to Raphael in your morning or evening routine, asking for guidance and protection.
2. **Blessing Ritual:** Use holy water to bless your home regularly, inviting Raphael to safeguard your family's health and harmony.
3. **Pilgrimage:** Visit a sacred site dedicated to Raphael or Christ to deepen your connection and seek physical or spiritual healing.

## Advanced Tips for Working with Raphael

- **Combine with Sacraments:** Integrate Raphael's energy into sacramental practices, such as anointing of the sick, for added efficacy.
- **Focus on Gratitude:** Regularly thank Raphael for his intercession, fostering a reciprocal relationship of faith and devotion.

By embracing Raphael's healing presence in Christian traditions, you can align yourself with his restorative energy, transforming your spiritual practice and deepening your connection to divine grace.

## Seeking Healing Through Raphael: Pilgrimages and Prayers for Divine Restoration

### The Tradition of Pilgrimage to Raphael's Sacred Sites

In Christian healing practices, Raphael's connection to healing and protection has inspired many believers to embark on pilgrimages to sacred sites associated with his intercession. Pilgrimages serve as acts of devotion, symbolic journeys toward spiritual and physical renewal. These journeys often include specific prayers and rituals designed to invite Raphael's healing energy into one's life.

- **Sacred Locations:** While Raphael is not as strongly associated with specific shrines as other saints or angels, pilgrimage sites that honor archangels—such as Monte Sant'Angelo in Italy (traditionally dedicated to Michael but inclusive of angelic veneration)—can also serve as focal points for connecting with Raphael.
- **Symbolism of the Journey:** The act of traveling reflects the theme of Raphael's guidance in the *Book of Tobit*, symbolizing faith, healing, and divine companionship on life's path.

## Historical and Spiritual Context

### Pilgrimages in the Christian Tradition

Pilgrimages have long been a practice of Christian devotion, representing a metaphorical return to God. When directed toward Raphael, these journeys take on added layers of healing and guidance, mirroring his assistance to Tobias in Tobit.

- **Healing of the Soul:** Pilgrimages provide opportunities for prayer, reflection, and penitence, aligning with Raphael's role as a mediator of divine mercy.
- **Healing of the Body and Mind:** Sacred sites are often believed to be imbued with the presence of angels and saints, offering miraculous healings and spiritual blessings.

## Prayers to Raphael for Healing

### Prayer as a Pathway to Raphael's Energy

Prayers to Raphael invoke his presence, calling on his restorative power to mend physical, emotional, and spiritual wounds. Such prayers can be used during pilgrimages or as standalone devotions.

**Sample Prayer to Raphael:** *"Glorious Archangel Raphael,*
*Guide of travelers and healer of the sick,*
*I call upon your divine mercy.*
*Bring the light of God's healing grace into my life.*
*Protect me on my journey,*
*Restore my body, mind, and soul,*
*And lead me always toward divine peace and joy. Amen."*

## Practical Applications: Undertaking a Pilgrimage to Honor Raphael

### Preparation for the Pilgrimage

1. **Set Your Intention:** Reflect on your reasons for embarking on this spiritual journey. Write down your intentions in a journal or grimoire.
    - *Example:* Healing a specific ailment, seeking emotional peace, or strengthening your connection with Raphael.
2. **Gather Sacred Items:**

- A green candle to symbolize Raphael's healing energy.
- A small vial of holy water for blessings during the journey.
- A prayer card or sigil of Raphael to focus your devotions.

## Step-by-Step Pilgrimage Ritual

1. **Begin with a Blessing:** Before departing, light a green candle and pray to Raphael for safe travels and guidance. **Words to Say:** *"Raphael, heavenly guide and protector,*
   *Walk with me on this sacred path.*
   *Illuminate my journey with your healing light,*
   *And bring me safely to my destination. Amen."*
2. **Sacred Acts During the Journey:**
   - Recite the *Prayer to Raphael* daily as you travel.
   - Offer acts of kindness to strangers, reflecting Raphael's healing and compassionate nature.
3. **Arrival at the Sacred Site:** Upon arrival, create a small altar with your sacred items. Light the green candle and anoint yourself with holy water. **Invocation to Raphael:** *"Archangel Raphael, keeper of God's healing power,*
   *I stand before you in faith and humility.*
   *Bless this journey and grant me renewal,*
   *That I may walk forward in health and grace. Amen."*
4. **Conclude with Gratitude:** Offer thanks to Raphael for his guidance, and leave a token of gratitude (e.g., a small green stone or flowers) at the site.

## Symbolic and Esoteric Significance

- **Sacred Travel:** Reflects Raphael's role in guiding Tobias, symbolizing divine companionship and protection on life's journey.

- **Candles and Holy Water:** Serve as conduits for Raphael's energy, bridging the physical and spiritual realms.
- **Acts of Kindness:** Mirror Raphael's compassionate role in Tobit, aligning the practitioner with his divine qualities.

## Incorporating Pilgrimages and Prayers into Daily Practice

- **Miniature Pilgrimages:** If unable to travel to sacred sites, create a symbolic pilgrimage by walking a designated path in nature while invoking Raphael's presence.
- **Daily Prayer Routine:** Incorporate Raphael's prayer into your daily spiritual practice, especially during times of need.

## Advanced Tips for Enhancing Pilgrimages

- **Meditative Walking:** As you walk, focus on your breath and visualize Raphael's emerald light surrounding you.
- **Journaling Experiences:** Document your journey in your grimoire, noting any synchronicities, signs, or spiritual insights.
- **Create a Pilgrimage Ritual:** Design a personalized ritual to perform upon reaching your destination, incorporating elements of your intention.

By embarking on pilgrimages and offering heartfelt prayers to Raphael, you deepen your connection to his healing presence, creating transformative experiences that align you with divine energy and grace.

# Exploring Raphael as Israfil in Islamic Angelology

## A Divine Herald: Raphael's Role as Israfil in Islamic Tradition

In Islamic angelology, Raphael is identified as Israfil (Arabic: إسرافيل), the angel assigned the monumental task of sounding the trumpet on the Day of Resurrection. Though not directly linked to healing in Islamic texts, Israfil's role as the herald of cosmic renewal parallels Raphael's archetype as a restorer and guide in other traditions. This dual identity offers a profound lens through which to explore his transformative energy.

## Historical and Spiritual Context

### Israfil in the Quran and Hadith

While Israfil is not explicitly mentioned in the Quran by name, Islamic tradition and hadiths (sayings of the Prophet Muhammad) provide detailed insights into his role. Israfil is described as one of the four archangels alongside Jibril (Gabriel), Mika'il (Michael), and Azrael, and is revered for his proximity to Allah and his pivotal role in the divine plan.

- **The Trumpet of Resurrection:** Israfil's primary role involves the blowing of the trumpet, an act that will signal both the end of the world and the resurrection of the dead. This cosmic renewal mirrors Raphael's restorative essence.
- **Symbol of Divine Mercy:** Israfil's task underscores themes of divine mercy, renewal, and alignment with God's will, aligning with Raphael's identity as a healer and guide.

## Symbolism and Esoteric Significance

### The Trumpet and the Breath of Life

The trumpet is a recurring symbol in spiritual traditions, representing divine communication, awakening, and transformation. For Israfil, the trumpet signifies the power of sound as a creative and restorative force, resonating with Raphael's association with healing frequencies and vibrational energy.

- **Breath of Life:** The act of blowing the trumpet evokes the life-giving breath of God, emphasizing Israfil's role in renewal and healing on a cosmic scale.

## Practical Applications: Invoking Raphael as Israfil

### Connecting to Divine Renewal

Engaging with Raphael as Israfil invites transformative energy into your magical practice, helping you align with cycles of renewal and healing.

### Step-by-Step Ritual for Renewal Through Israfil's Energy

1. **Preparation of Sacred Space:**
    - Place a white or emerald-green cloth on your altar, representing purity and renewal.
    - Add a small trumpet symbol or a singing bowl to evoke Israfil's sound vibrations.
    - Light frankincense incense to create a sacred atmosphere.
2. **Invocation of Israfil:** Begin by standing or sitting with your hands open in a posture of receptivity. **Words to Say:** *"Israfil, divine herald of renewal,*
*By your sacred breath, awaken the light within me.*
*Align my heart with the divine harmony,*
*That I may be restored in body, mind, and soul.*

*Carry my prayers to the heavens on the sound of your trumpet,
And bless me with the mercy of renewal. Amen."*

3. **Sound Activation:** Use a singing bowl, horn, or wind instrument to create sound vibrations. Alternatively, chant a resonant phrase such as *"Ya Israfil"* or *"Allah's mercy flows through sound."*
   - Visualize the sound waves breaking through stagnant energy, making way for healing and transformation.
4. **Meditation on Renewal:** Sit quietly and focus on your breath, imagining Israfil's energy flowing into you with each inhalation. Visualize the trumpet's sound awakening dormant aspects of your spirit.
5. **Closing and Gratitude:** Conclude by offering gratitude to Israfil with these words: *"Thank you, divine herald, for your presence and blessings.
May your trumpet's call guide me to divine alignment and peace. Amen."*

## Magical Correspondences for Israfil's Energy

- **Colors:** White and emerald green for purity and renewal.
- **Sacred Herbs:** Frankincense and sandalwood to enhance spiritual connection.
- **Element:** Air, symbolizing sound, breath, and communication.
- **Tools:** Trumpets, singing bowls, or wind chimes to channel Israfil's vibrational energy.

## Advanced Tips for Working with Israfil's Energy

1. **Dreamwork and Visions:** Invite Israfil into your dreams by reciting the invocation before sleep, asking for guidance and clarity through dream symbols.
2. **Sound Meditation:** Regularly use sound therapy (e.g., Tibetan singing bowls or toning exercises) to align with Israfil's vibrational energy and promote deep healing.

3. **Astrological Alignment:** Perform rituals during periods of significant astrological events, such as air-dominant transits, to amplify the connection to Israfil's celestial energy.

## Embracing Renewal Through Israfil

Understanding Raphael as Israfil enriches your magical practice by introducing themes of divine mercy, renewal, and vibrational healing. By aligning with Israfil's energy, you can invite transformative shifts into your life, mirroring the cosmic renewal he heralds. Through sound, intention, and sacred ritual, you forge a deeper connection to this divine herald, enhancing your spiritual journey and aligning with divine harmony.

## Angelic Healing and Guidance in Islamic Tradition: Raphael as Israfil

### An Angelic Role in Divine Mercy and Healing

In Islamic angelology, Raphael is revered as Israfil, an archangel deeply intertwined with themes of divine renewal and cosmic harmony. Though Islamic texts primarily focus on Israfil's role as the herald of resurrection, his association with divine breath and cosmic sound opens the door to understanding him as a guide and healer. By exploring Islamic perspectives on angelic healing and guidance, practitioners can access a profound spiritual framework rooted in mercy, faith, and vibrational harmony.

### Healing and Guidance in Islamic Theology

#### The Qur'anic Perspective

While the Quran does not directly attribute healing roles to Israfil, angelic intercession and divine guidance are emphasized throughout Islamic scripture. Angels are messengers and agents of Allah's mercy, often assisting the faithful during trials or illness.

- **Key Verses to Reflect Upon:**
  - *"And We send down of the Quran that which is healing and mercy for the believers..."* (Surah Al-Isra, 17:82)
  - *"He [Allah] creates what you do not know, and to Him belong the unseen forces of the heavens and the earth."* (Surah Al-An'am, 6:59)

These verses emphasize divine healing and the unseen aid provided by angels, reinforcing the Islamic belief in spiritual guidance and restoration.

## The Role of Breath and Sound in Healing

Islamic mysticism (Sufism) often emphasizes the power of *dhikr* (remembrance of God) and the healing quality of sound. Israfil, whose trumpet heralds renewal, becomes a symbolic figure for spiritual and vibrational healing, aligning with the Sufi practices of chanting and meditative breathing.

## Practical Applications: Islamic-Inspired Healing Rituals

### Creating a Healing Invocation

By drawing from Islamic principles, you can create a ritual that aligns with Israfil's vibrational and restorative qualities.

### Step-by-Step Ritual for Angelic Healing and Guidance

1. **Preparation of Space:**
   - Lay out a white cloth to symbolize purity and light.
   - Place a bowl of water and a piece of quartz (or clear crystal) to represent clarity and divine energy.

- Light frankincense to enhance spiritual focus.
2. **Recitation of Quranic Verses:**
    - Begin with Surah Al-Fatihah, as it is known as a chapter of healing.
    - Recite Surah Al-Ikhlas (112) for purity and divine alignment.
3. **Invocation of Israfil for Healing: Words to Say:** *"Ya Israfil, herald of divine sound,*
*By your trumpet's call, awaken the light within me.*
*By Allah's mercy, heal my heart, my body, and my soul.*
*Guide me toward divine harmony and peace. Amen."*
4. **Focus on Sound Vibrations:**
    - Use a singing bowl, chime, or chant the *Asma ul-Husna* (Beautiful Names of Allah), particularly *Ya Shafi* (The Healer).
    - Visualize Israfil's trumpet as a divine instrument sending waves of healing through your body and mind.
5. **Blessing with Water:**
    - Dip your fingers in the bowl of water and touch your forehead, saying: *"By Allah's mercy and Israfil's presence, I am restored and whole."*
6. **Closing with Gratitude:**
    - Thank Israfil for his guidance and Allah for His mercy, saying: *"Alhamdulillah, for all blessings seen and unseen."*

## Symbolism and Correspondences in Islamic Healing

- **Color Correspondences:** White (purity), green (renewal), and gold (divine light).
- **Herbs and Incense:** Frankincense, myrrh, and oud.
- **Sacred Sounds:** Chanting Quranic verses, *dhikr*, or angelic invocations.
- **Tools:** Water for cleansing, crystals for focus, and sound instruments for vibrational alignment.

## Advanced Practices for Islamic Angelic Healing

1. **Dreamwork for Guidance:** Before sleeping, recite Surah Al-Mulk (67:1-30) and invite Israfil into your dreams for clarity and healing.
2. **Daily Angelic Alignment:** Incorporate the recitation of *Ya Shafi* and *Ya Nur* (The Light) into your daily *dhikr* to maintain energetic harmony.
3. **Energy Clearing with Israfil:** Use the sound of bells or a simple hum to clear stagnant energy from your space, envisioning Israfil's trumpet dispersing negativity.

## Embracing Divine Healing Through Israfil

Islamic perspectives on angelic healing invite us to see Israfil as more than a herald of resurrection; he is a symbol of divine harmony, breath, and renewal. By integrating these principles into your practice, you access a wellspring of mercy and vibrational healing, aligning with Raphael's universal archetype as a restorer and guide. Through thoughtful invocation, sound, and sacred alignment, you deepen your connection to divine healing, enhancing your magical and spiritual practice.

## Raphael in Folk Magic: The Archangel of Healing Across Cultures

### Folk Traditions: Bridging the Divine and the Practical

In folk magic traditions worldwide, Archangel Raphael often appears as a mediator between divine healing energy and practical, earthly remedies. His name, meaning "God heals," has inspired countless healing practices, ranging from herbal remedies to symbolic rituals. Whether invoked in Christian, Jewish, or syncretic traditions, Raphael embodies the harmonious balance between spiritual intervention and tangible healing methods.

# The Role of Raphael in Folk Healing Practices

## The Universal Healer in Everyday Magic

In folk traditions, Raphael is celebrated as a healer who empowers practitioners with tools to address physical, emotional, and spiritual ailments. His association with herbs, water, and light makes him accessible to those seeking holistic well-being.

- **Cultural Expressions of Raphael:**
    - **Christian Folk Healing:** Raphael is invoked for blessings over remedies and sacred spaces. His presence is often symbolized by emerald-green candles, herbs, or oils.
    - **Latin American Practices:** Raphael merges with folk saints and indigenous deities, such as Our Lady of Guadalupe or the curandero spirit guides, representing healing and protection.
    - **Jewish Mysticism:** Raphael is connected to angelic healing spells and the recitation of sacred names within amulets and talismans.

# Practical Applications: Invoking Raphael in Folk Healing

## Step-by-Step Ritual: Raphael's Folk Healing Remedy

**Purpose:** To channel Raphael's healing energy into an herbal remedy for physical or emotional healing.

1. **Gathering Materials:**
    - A green candle to symbolize Raphael's presence.
    - A bowl of water (preferably spring water) as a medium of divine energy.
    - Healing herbs like chamomile, lavender, and rosemary.

- o  A small pouch or container to store the infused water or herbs.
2. **Preparing the Space:**
   - o  Set up a simple altar with a green cloth, Raphael's sigil, and the materials above.
   - o  Light the green candle, saying: *"Raphael, Angel of Healing,*
     *I invite your presence into this space.*
     *Bless these herbs and this water with your divine light."*
3. **Creating the Remedy:**
   - o  Place the herbs in the water and gently stir while reciting: *"By the light of God and the hands of Raphael,*
     *Let this remedy bring healing and peace.*
     *As herbs heal the body, may your light heal the soul."*
4. **Infusion of Energy:**
   - o  Hold your hands over the bowl and visualize emerald light flowing into the water. Chant: *"Raphael, healer and guide, imbue this water with your grace.*
     *Let it carry your touch to those in need."*
5. **Blessing the Pouch:**
   - o  Fill the pouch with the infused herbs or pour a small amount of water into a vial.
   - o  Seal it with the words: *"With Raphael's blessing, this carries healing and hope."*
6. **Usage:**
   - o  Use the water for anointing or add a few drops to a bath.
   - o  Carry the pouch as a talisman of protection and healing.

## Symbolism in Folk Practices

- **Herbs:** Represent Raphael's connection to natural healing. Lavender calms the mind; rosemary strengthens the body; chamomile soothes the spirit.

- **Water:** Reflects Raphael's purity and life-giving energy, often used for cleansing and blessing.
- **Emerald Light:** Symbolizes growth, renewal, and the activation of divine energy in earthly elements.

## Syncretism: Raphael and Cultural Integration

### Latin America: Curanderismo and Raphael

In Latin America, Raphael blends seamlessly into the curandero (folk healer) tradition. His energy is invoked alongside indigenous spirits and Catholic saints, creating a powerful fusion of spiritual and practical healing.

- **Ritual Example:** A curandero might invoke Raphael while preparing a limpia (spiritual cleansing), combining herbs, eggs, and prayers to remove negative energy and restore balance.

### European Folk Magic: Raphael and Herbal Charms

In European folk magic, Raphael is often invoked in the creation of herbal charms and healing poultices. The prayers to Raphael are said to amplify the natural properties of the herbs.

## Advanced Tips for Working with Raphael in Folk Healing

1. **Integrate Local Traditions:** Research and incorporate healing practices unique to your cultural heritage, enhancing your connection to Raphael's universal healing energy.
2. **Use Ancestral Tools:** Invoke Raphael using tools or materials passed down through your lineage, such as heirloom herbs or ritual objects.
3. **Combine Prayer with Practicality:** Complement spiritual invocations with tangible healing methods,

such as herbal teas or balms, to honor Raphael's role as a bridge between heaven and earth.

## Raphael as a Universal Healer in Folk Magic

Folk traditions provide a practical yet deeply spiritual approach to working with Raphael. Through rituals, natural remedies, and syncretic practices, you can connect with his healing energy in profound and accessible ways. By blending these practices with your magical work, you honor Raphael's legacy as a healer and guide, creating a harmonious union between divine energy and earthly care.

## Raphael and Syncretism: Bridging Indigenous Wisdom with Angelic Healing

### The Intersection of Raphael and Indigenous Spirituality

Syncretism between Archangel Raphael and indigenous deities or spirits exemplifies how spiritual traditions merge, enriching both practices. Raphael, as a celestial healer, often aligns with indigenous spirits or gods associated with health, protection, and guidance. These connections arise in regions where Christian influences integrated with native beliefs, creating a tapestry of hybrid spiritual practices.

In such syncretic frameworks, Raphael is not just an external entity but a universal force adaptable to diverse cultural contexts. Indigenous healers may view Raphael as an emissary of divine energy who cooperates with ancestral and nature spirits, bringing harmony and healing to both individuals and the land.

# Indigenous Deities and Raphael's Healing Archetype

## Latin American Syncretism: Raphael and Indigenous Healers

In Latin American traditions, Raphael often merges with spirits like the Aztec deity Tlaloc (god of rain and fertility) or the Andean Pachamama (earth mother). These spirits, like Raphael, embody healing, renewal, and protection.

- **Parallels with Raphael:**
    - **Tlaloc:** Oversees water and fertility, echoing Raphael's use of water as a medium for healing.
    - **Pachamama:** Represents nurturing and growth, akin to Raphael's emerald energy fostering renewal.

## African Diaspora: Raphael and Orishas

In Afro-Caribbean traditions such as Santería or Vodou, Raphael finds parallels with Orishas like Osanyin (herbal medicine and healing) or Erzulie Freda (compassion and emotional restoration).

- **Osanyin:** Master of herbal knowledge, aligns with Raphael's role as a guide in holistic healing practices.
- **Erzulie Freda:** Governs love and emotional well-being, resonating with Raphael's ability to heal the heart and spirit.

# Creating Syncretic Rituals with Raphael

## Step-by-Step Ritual: Honoring Raphael and Indigenous Spirits

**Purpose:** To create a harmonious connection between Raphael's healing energy and the wisdom of an indigenous deity or spirit.

1. **Preparation:**
   - Select an indigenous spirit or deity aligned with healing (e.g., Pachamama or Osanyin).
   - Gather materials representing both Raphael (emerald green candle, Raphael's sigil) and the indigenous spirit (e.g., offerings like corn, tobacco, or herbs).
2. **Setting the Space:**
   - Create an altar combining symbols of Raphael (sigil, green candle) and the chosen deity (e.g., earth or herbal offerings).
   - Light incense (frankincense for Raphael, native herbs for the indigenous spirit) to purify the space.
3. **Invocation:**
   - Begin with a prayer to Raphael: *"Archangel Raphael, healer of all realms,
   I call upon your light to guide this union.
   Bless this space with your healing presence."*
   - Transition to invoking the indigenous spirit:
   *"[Name of spirit], guardian of [specific domain],
   I honor your wisdom and ask for your guidance.
   Join with Raphael to bring healing and balance."*
4. **Offerings and Meditation:**
   - Place offerings (herbs, water, or symbolic items) on the altar while visualizing emerald light surrounding you.
   - Meditate on the harmony between Raphael and the spirit, imagining their energies merging into a radiant force.
5. **Chant for Unity:**
   - Repeat a chant blending their attributes:
   *"Raphael of the heavens, healer divine,
   [Spirit's name], guardian of earth's sacred line,
   Together restore, renew, and refine."*
6. **Closure:**
   - Extinguish the candles and thank both entities:
   *"To Raphael and [Spirit's name], I offer my gratitude.*

*May your energies remain with me in harmony and grace."*

## Esoteric and Symbolic Significance

- **Emerald Light and Earth Energies:** Raphael's emerald light resonates with Pachamama's nurturing earth energy, symbolizing growth and fertility.
- **Herbs and Water:** Reflect the universal language of healing shared by Raphael and indigenous spirits.
- **Dual Invocation:** Blends celestial and terrestrial wisdom, creating a powerful synergy for transformation.

## Connecting Raphael to Nature and Ancestral Wisdom

### Raphael as a Mediator in Land-Based Rituals

Indigenous traditions often honor the land as a living entity. Raphael's connection to renewal and restoration makes him an ideal intermediary for land blessings and environmental healing. Rituals invoking Raphael alongside earth spirits can revitalize sacred spaces or address ecological imbalances.

### Enhancing Ancestral Practices with Raphael

Raphael can enhance traditional ancestral practices by amplifying the spiritual and emotional aspects of healing. His universal energy bridges gaps between traditions, fostering respect and cooperation.

## Advanced Tips for Syncretic Work with Raphael

1. **Study Indigenous Myths:** Deepen your understanding of the chosen spirit's attributes and align them with Raphael's energy.

2. **Incorporate Cultural Tools:** Use local herbs, songs, or instruments to honor the indigenous spirit's traditions alongside Raphael's invocation.
3. **Balance Celestial and Earthly Energies:** Ensure your rituals reflect a balance, with Raphael representing the heavens and the indigenous spirit embodying the earth.

## Raphael's Universal Healing Power in Syncretism

Raphael's ability to adapt and merge with diverse spiritual traditions underscores his universal role as a healer. By integrating indigenous deities or spirits into your practice, you create a richer, more inclusive path to healing and balance. This syncretic approach not only deepens your connection to Raphael but also honors the cultural wisdom of the land and its people, fostering a spiritual practice rooted in both celestial and earthly harmony.

As we approach the culmination of our exploration, it is essential to reflect on the ethical and transformative aspects of working with Archangel Raphael. While rituals, invocations, and magical practices bring profound benefits, they also carry responsibilities that extend beyond personal gain. In this next section, we will delve into the principles of ethical angelic magic, ensuring that your work aligns with divine will and respects the free will of others. We will also explore how to live Raphael's teachings through daily actions and community service, allowing his guidance to inspire compassion and healing on a broader scale. Finally, we will consider how integrating Raphael's wisdom can propel your spiritual growth, deepening your understanding of angelic magic and expanding your capacity as a practitioner. These topics invite you to embrace Raphael's light not only as a tool for transformation but as a way of life.

# { 10 }

# Living Raphael's Light: Ethical Magic and Spiritual Evolution

The path of working with Archangel Raphael is not solely one of rituals and invocations; it is a journey toward embodying his healing wisdom and ethical principles in every aspect of life. As we move forward, we turn our attention to the responsibilities that come with angelic magic, exploring the delicate balance between divine alignment and personal intentions. Through Raphael's teachings, we will uncover ways to integrate his guidance into daily practices, fostering compassion and healing within ourselves and our communities. This section also examines the role of ethical considerations in angelic magic, ensuring that all actions honor the sacred harmony of free will and divine purpose. Finally, we will focus on personal evolution, expanding our understanding of angelic and healing magic while deepening our spiritual connection to Raphael. By engaging with these topics, you will not only practice Raphael's magic but also live his light, transforming your path into one of spiritual growth and service.

## Respecting Free Will and Divine Alignment: Ethical Foundations in Raphael's Magic

Working with Archangel Raphael is not merely a process of summoning his energy or performing healing rituals; it is an act of spiritual alignment with divine order and cosmic balance. Ethical angelic magic, especially in the context of Raphael, requires a profound understanding of free will, divine purpose, and the sacred trust placed upon the practitioner. Raphael, as the angel of healing and guidance, embodies respect for individual autonomy and divine timing. When invoking his energy, practitioners must align their intentions with the highest good, avoiding interference with another's path or forcing outcomes that contradict divine will.

## The Sacred Principle of Free Will

Free will is a cornerstone of ethical magic and spiritual practice. Angels like Raphael respect the autonomy granted to all beings by divine law. When you seek Raphael's assistance, it is crucial to ensure that your request honors the choices and growth of others. For example, you may pray for someone's healing, but you should avoid imposing specific outcomes that they have not consented to or are not spiritually ready to embrace. This principle extends to your own work, ensuring your intentions are free from selfish motives or harmful desires.

## Attuning Intentions with Divine Alignment

**Divine alignment** is the practice of syncing your intentions with the will of the divine. In working with Raphael, this means framing your requests within the context of healing, growth, and service to the greater good. Before invoking Raphael, take time to reflect on your goals and ensure they align with principles of compassion, wisdom, and balance.

- **Reflection Practice:**
  Sit quietly in a meditative state and ask yourself:
    - Is my intention rooted in love and healing?
    - Does my request support the free will and growth of others?
    - Am I willing to accept the divine timing and form of the outcome?
    These questions serve as a compass to refine your intentions and ensure ethical alignment.

# Ritual for Ethical Invocation of Raphael

This ritual creates a space to align your intentions with divine will and invite Raphael's guidance while respecting free will.

## Tools Required

- Green candle (symbolizing Raphael's healing energy)
- White candle (representing divine alignment and purity)
- A piece of clear quartz (clarity and ethical focus)
- Raphael's sigil or an image representing him

## Step-by-Step Instructions

1. **Prepare Your Space**
    - Cleanse the area using sage or frankincense.
    - Place the candles and the quartz on your altar, with Raphael's sigil at the center.
2. **Light the Candles**
    - Light the white candle, saying:
      *"By this flame, I call upon the light of divine wisdom, aligning my heart with the will of the Creator."*
    - Light the green candle, saying:
      *"Archangel Raphael, healer of mind, body, and soul, I invite your presence into this space, that your energy may guide my intentions toward the highest good."*
3. **Set Ethical Intentions**
    - Hold the quartz in your hand and focus on your intention.
    - Say aloud:
      *"I ask for healing and guidance, aligned with divine purpose and free will. May all outcomes serve the greatest good and honor the paths of all involved."*

4. **Invoke Raphael**
   - Trace Raphael's sigil in the air above the altar using your index finger or a wand. Visualize emerald light radiating from the sigil as you chant:
     *"Raphael, angel of healing and grace, I call upon your presence. Guide me in harmony with divine wisdom, and let my actions reflect love and compassion."*
5. **Close the Ritual**
   - Thank Raphael for his presence:
     *"Thank you, Raphael, for your guidance and healing light. May your energy bless all who seek your aid in alignment with divine will."*
   - Extinguish the candles and place the quartz in a sacred space as a reminder of your ethical commitment.

## Symbolic and Esoteric Significance

- **Green Candle:** Represents Raphael's energy, healing, and renewal.
- **White Candle:** Symbolizes divine purity, alignment, and ethical clarity.
- **Clear Quartz:** Amplifies focus and ensures clarity of purpose.
- **Sigil:** Acts as a spiritual gateway to Raphael's energy.

## Advice and Advanced Tips

1. **Practice Patience:** Ethical magic often requires waiting for outcomes to manifest in divine timing. Trust that the universe will provide what is needed when it is right.
2. **Daily Ethical Reflection:** At the end of each day, reflect on your actions and intentions, ensuring they align with Raphael's principles of healing and compassion.

3. **Ethical Petition:** When working with Raphael for others, always include the phrase, *"If it is in alignment with their highest good and divine will."*

By integrating these practices, you will cultivate a deeper, ethically grounded relationship with Raphael, enhancing your effectiveness as a healer and spiritual practitioner.

## Balancing Personal Desires with Raphael's Guidance: Walking the Path of Alignment

In the practice of angelic magic, one of the most nuanced aspects is learning to balance personal desires with the divine guidance offered by Archangel Raphael. As a healer and guide, Raphael embodies wisdom that transcends ego and encourages alignment with higher principles. To work ethically and effectively with Raphael, practitioners must navigate the intersection of personal will and divine intention, creating a partnership rooted in trust, humility, and spiritual growth.

### Raphael as a Guide to Self-Awareness

Archangel Raphael's guidance fosters a deep awareness of the motivations behind our desires. In texts like the *Book of Tobit*, Raphael exemplifies the importance of trust and faith in divine timing. Tobit and Tobias both learn that their journey is as much about healing and transformation as it is about achieving their goals. Similarly, Raphael's role in your practice encourages reflection on whether your desires align with divine purpose.

- **Esoteric Insight**: Desires that align with divine will often lead to healing, growth, and a sense of peace. Raphael's energy helps to clarify these intentions, cutting through the distractions of ego and fear.

# Ritual to Harmonize Desires with Divine Will

This ritual is designed to align your personal goals with the higher guidance of Archangel Raphael. It includes steps for identifying desires, invoking Raphael's insight, and releasing intentions with trust.

## Preparation

1. **Sacred Space**: Cleanse the area with sage or frankincense. Place an emerald-green candle on your altar, along with Raphael's sigil, a chalice of water, and a small journal.
2. **Intention Setting**: Write down your desire in the journal. Beneath it, write the question: *Does this align with divine will and my highest good?*

## Invocation

1. **Light the Candle**: Light the emerald-green candle, focusing on its flame as a symbol of Raphael's illuminating guidance. Say:

    > "Archangel Raphael, healer and guide,
    > Bring clarity to my heart and mind.
    > Illuminate my path, that I may walk in divine alignment.
    > Reveal what serves my highest good,
    > And release all that does not."

2. **Hold the Chalice**: Pour spring water into the chalice, symbolizing the purity of your intentions. Hold it in both hands and visualize Raphael's emerald light infusing the water.

## Reflection

1. **Meditate**: Close your eyes and breathe deeply. Visualize Raphael standing beside you, his presence

calming and luminous. Imagine him placing his hand over your heart, helping you to discern the true nature of your desire.
2. **Ask for Insight**: Mentally or aloud, ask:

> "Raphael, guardian of divine wisdom,
> Show me if this desire serves my soul's purpose.
> Guide me toward alignment with the divine."
> Sit quietly, observing thoughts, feelings, or imagery that arise.

**Release**

1. **Pour the Water**: If your desire feels aligned, take a sip of the water, affirming:

> "With Raphael's light, my path is clear.
> I embrace divine alignment and trust the way forward."
> If misaligned, pour the water onto the earth, saying: "I release this desire into the hands of the divine.
> May it transform into what serves my highest good."

2. **Extinguish the Candle**: Allow the candle to burn for a while longer if possible, then extinguish it, imagining Raphael's light continuing to guide you.

## Practical Applications of Raphael's Guidance

- **Daily Reflection**: Begin each day with a brief invocation to Raphael, asking for his guidance in aligning your actions with divine will.
- **Dream Work**: Before sleep, invite Raphael to bring clarity through dreams, using a journal to record insights upon waking.

- **Chakra Balancing**: Focus on the heart chakra, the center of balance and love, during meditative work with Raphael.

## Raphael's Teachings on Balance and Trust

Balancing desires with divine guidance requires trust in the process of life. Raphael reminds us that healing and fulfillment come not from force or control but from surrender to the wisdom of the divine.

## Advanced Tips for Integration

1. **Keep a Balance Journal**: Regularly document your desires and evaluate their alignment with your spiritual goals.
2. **Seek Signs**: Stay attuned to synchronicities that validate or redirect your path. Raphael often communicates through subtle messages in your environment.
3. **Revisit Your Ritual**: Periodically perform the ritual to refine your alignment with Raphael's wisdom, ensuring continuous growth.

By consistently aligning personal will with divine guidance, you deepen your relationship with Raphael, making your magical practice a harmonious blend of aspiration and surrender.

## Living Raphael's Teachings: Integrating Healing and Compassion

Archangel Raphael's role as a healer and guide transcends mystical practice, extending into the principles of everyday life. His teachings encourage not only self-healing but also the active practice of compassion and service to others. By incorporating Raphael's healing wisdom into daily routines and engaging in community service, you align your life with his transformative energy and become a vessel of divine light and love.

## Healing as a Lifestyle: Raphael's Principles in Daily Life

Raphael's teachings emphasize holistic healing, integrating physical, emotional, and spiritual wellness. In daily life, his influence manifests as mindfulness, self-care, and a commitment to personal and communal harmony.

## Historical Context

- In the *Book of Tobit*, Raphael heals Tobit's blindness and guides Tobias, illustrating his ability to address physical and spiritual ailments. This narrative encourages practitioners to seek balance in all aspects of life.
- Christian and Jewish traditions celebrate Raphael as a companion to travelers and the sick, symbolizing continuous care and vigilance.

## Practical Applications

- **Mindfulness Ritual**: Begin your day with a simple invocation of Raphael's energy to guide your thoughts and actions. Light an emerald-green candle and say:

    > "Archangel Raphael, healer of all,
    > Guide my thoughts to harmony, my heart to love,
    > And my actions to align with divine grace."
    > Spend five minutes meditating on your intentions for the day.

- **Healing Practices**: Dedicate moments throughout the day to your well-being. Practice mindful breathing, visualize Raphael's green light enveloping you, or recite affirmations like:

> "I am healed, I am whole, I am guided by divine wisdom."

- **Emotional Balance**: When challenges arise, invoke Raphael to bring clarity and peace. A quick affirmation, whispered or thought, can transform a stressful moment:

    > "Raphael, calm my heart and steady my mind."

# Extending Raphael's Compassion: Community Service and Healing

Raphael's energy inspires service to others, reflecting his role as a protector and healer. Engaging in acts of compassion extends his influence, fostering a ripple effect of healing and love.

## Esoteric Significance

- Raphael's emerald light represents the heart chakra, the center of love and empathy. By channeling his energy, you magnify the impact of your service.
- In Kabbalistic traditions, Raphael's association with *Tiferet* (beauty and harmony) underscores the importance of creating balance through giving.

## Ritual for Compassionate Service

1. **Preparation**: Choose a symbol of Raphael, such as his sigil or an emerald crystal. Carry it with you as a reminder of his presence.
2. **Invocation**: Before engaging in a compassionate act, recite:

    > "Raphael, angel of mercy,
    > Guide my hands and heart in service.

> Let your healing light flow through me,
> Bringing peace and love to all I touch."

3. **Visualization**: As you perform the act—whether volunteering, comforting someone, or contributing to a cause—imagine Raphael's green light enveloping the space, magnifying the impact of your efforts.

## Raphael's Guidance in Relationships and Communities

Living Raphael's teachings also means fostering harmony in relationships and community. By embodying his qualities of patience, empathy, and clarity, you inspire others to seek healing and balance.

### Practical Practices

- **Conflict Resolution**: In moments of tension, silently call upon Raphael for guidance, saying:

  > "Raphael, healer of discord,
  > Bring peace to this situation.
  > Help me act with love and understanding."

- **Support Networks**: Use Raphael's energy to nurture connections. Host gatherings where his presence is invoked for shared healing or guidance.

### Advice for Deepening Your Practice

1. **Daily Journaling**: Record moments when you feel guided by Raphael. Reflect on how his teachings shape your decisions and relationships.
2. **Create a "Service Altar"**: Dedicate a space to honor Raphael's role in community healing. Include a green candle, his sigil, and symbols of compassion such as a heart or chalice.

3. **Periodic Offerings**: Express gratitude to Raphael through acts of kindness or by lighting incense in his honor, saying:

> "Raphael, I offer this as a token of my gratitude
> For the light and love you inspire in me."

## Raphael's Healing Beyond Self

By living Raphael's teachings, you not only transform your own life but also contribute to the healing of the collective. As a magician and healer, you embody Raphael's principles, becoming a beacon of his energy in the world. This ongoing alignment with his wisdom fosters growth, service, and a profound sense of spiritual fulfillment.

## Evolving as a Practitioner: Integrating Raphael's Teachings into Your Spiritual Journey

Archangel Raphael's guidance is a profound source of inspiration for spiritual evolution. By embodying his principles of healing, wisdom, and divine alignment, practitioners can weave his teachings into the fabric of their lives. This integration extends beyond rituals, transforming how we perceive ourselves, others, and the spiritual realm.

## Raphael as a Guide to Lifelong Spiritual Growth

Raphael's role as a teacher and healer offers a framework for continuous learning and self-discovery. His teachings transcend immediate concerns, encouraging us to view life as a sacred journey.

## Historical Context

- In the *Book of Tobit*, Raphael's guidance illustrates the importance of trust, perseverance, and divine alignment in overcoming challenges.
- Kabbalistic traditions associate Raphael with *Tiferet* (harmony) in the Tree of Life, symbolizing spiritual balance and integration.

## Esoteric Significance

- Raphael's emerald-green energy resonates with the heart chakra, emphasizing love, empathy, and self-healing.
- His association with Mercury connects him to communication, making him an ideal guide for spiritual inquiry and growth.

# Practical Steps for Integrating Raphael's Teachings

To fully incorporate Raphael's wisdom into your spiritual journey, commit to practices that foster connection, reflection, and action.

### 1. Daily Connection Ritual

- Begin each day with a brief ritual to align with Raphael's energy.

1. Light a green candle and hold a crystal such as malachite or emerald.
2. Say:

    > "Raphael, guide of light and wisdom,
    > Walk with me today.
    > Help me to see clearly, love fully,
    > And heal in alignment with divine grace."

3. Visualize Raphael's green light surrounding you as you set your intentions for the day.

## 2. Reflective Journaling

- Dedicate time to reflect on how Raphael's principles manifest in your life. Create journal sections for:
    - Challenges and how Raphael's teachings have helped.
    - Dreams or meditations that reveal new insights.
    - Acts of service inspired by his energy.

## 3. Monthly Spiritual Check-In

- Set aside time each month to evaluate your spiritual growth:

1. Create a sacred space with Raphael's symbols (sigil, green cloth, incense).
2. Meditate on the following:
    - How have I embodied healing and compassion this month?
    - What lessons has Raphael taught me recently?
    - Where do I need to focus next?
3. Record your reflections and set goals for continued growth.

# Ritual for Lifelong Integration

This ritual invokes Raphael's presence to anchor his teachings in your spiritual path.

1. **Preparation**:
    - Green candle for Raphael's energy.
    - Bowl of water symbolizing healing and renewal.
    - Raphael's sigil drawn on paper.
2. **Invocation**:
    - Light the candle and say:

> "Raphael, guardian of healing and light,
> Guide me on this sacred journey.
> Let your wisdom shape my steps
> And your light illuminate my path."

3. **Meditation**:
    - Hold the sigil in your hands, close your eyes, and breathe deeply.
    - Visualize Raphael standing before you, his emerald light merging with your aura.
    - Ask:

    > "What do I need to grow spiritually?
    > How can I serve others while staying aligned with divine will?"

4. **Closing**:
    - Pour the water onto the earth, symbolizing the integration of Raphael's energy into your life.
    - Say:

    > "With this offering, I ground Raphael's wisdom within me,
    > Becoming a vessel of his love and light."

## Expanding Your Practice with Raphael's Teachings

To deepen your spiritual journey, explore these advanced techniques:

- **Study Raphael's Role in Other Traditions**: Engage with texts on Raphael in Jewish, Christian, and Islamic contexts to gain a multidimensional understanding of his energy.
- **Teach Others**: Share Raphael's teachings by guiding others in healing rituals or spiritual practices.
- **Experiment with New Correspondences**: Create new rituals using unique combinations of symbols, colors, and elements that resonate with Raphael.

## Raphael as a Life-Long Companion

By integrating Raphael's teachings, you transform your spiritual journey into a living testament to healing, wisdom, and compassion. As you evolve, Raphael's presence will guide you through challenges, inspire new growth, and deepen your connection to the divine. With practice and dedication, his energy becomes an inseparable part of your spiritual path, leading you toward profound self-discovery and fulfillment.

## Expanding Horizons: Deepening Knowledge of Angelic and Healing Magic with Raphael

Archangel Raphael embodies the infinite possibilities of healing and spiritual growth. By broadening your understanding of angelic magic and delving deeper into its mysteries, you unlock profound opportunities to refine your craft, amplify your spiritual connection, and transform your practice.

## The Call to Continuous Learning in Angelic Magic

### Raphael as the Teacher
Raphael is more than a healer; he is a divine educator. Known for guiding Tobias on his transformative journey in the *Book of Tobit*, Raphael demonstrates the importance of learning and evolving as part of the spiritual path. This same principle applies to practitioners who seek mastery in angelic and healing magic.

### Historical Context of Angelic Magic

- Angelic magic has its roots in texts like the *Key of Solomon* and the *Sefer Raziel HaMalakh*, which emphasize angels as intermediaries between humans and the divine.

- Raphael, associated with Mercury and Tiferet (beauty, balance) in Kabbalistic traditions, symbolizes the union of intellectual growth and spiritual harmony.

## Esoteric Significance of Expanding Knowledge

Raphael's guidance emphasizes harmony between intellect, intuition, and divine connection. Expanding your knowledge of angelic and healing magic aligns with this principle, creating a foundation for a holistic and effective magical practice.

## Practical Approaches to Deepen Your Knowledge

### 1. Study Foundational and Advanced Texts

- **Foundational Works**: Begin with the *Book of Tobit* for Raphael's narrative and the *Key of Solomon* for general angelic correspondences.
- **Advanced Works**: Explore the *Zohar* for mystical insights into Raphael's role in Kabbalistic healing and the *Greek Magical Papyri* for ancient rituals involving angelic invocations.

### 2. Develop a Study and Practice Schedule

- Dedicate weekly time to both reading and practicing:
    - One session for studying angelic texts.
    - One session for rituals, focusing on healing and guidance.
- Record your reflections in a dedicated journal.

### 3. Participate in Angelic Magic Communities

- Join groups or forums where practitioners share their experiences and insights.
- Seek out workshops or seminars on angelic healing and related disciplines.

# Ritual: Expanding Knowledge with Raphael's Guidance

This ritual seeks Raphael's assistance in your pursuit of knowledge and skill in angelic and healing magic.

**Materials**:

- Green candle (Raphael's energy).
- Blue candle (wisdom and divine guidance).
- Raphael's sigil.
- Bowl of spring water.

**Steps**:

1. **Preparation**:
    - Create a sacred space with Raphael's symbols, crystals (emerald or malachite), and incense (frankincense).
2. **Lighting the Candles**:
    - Light the green candle and say:

        "Raphael, divine guide of healing and wisdom,
        Illuminate my path to greater knowledge and understanding."

    - Light the blue candle and say:

        "By the light of divine wisdom, may I grow in harmony,
        Aligning my learning with the will of the heavens."

3. **Invocation**:
    - Draw Raphael's sigil in the air above the candles using your dominant hand. Say:

        "Raphael, angel of learning and light,
        Open my mind to the mysteries of healing

and the divine.
Guide me to the wisdom I seek,
And strengthen my heart to carry it with compassion."

4. **Water Offering**:
   - Hold the bowl of spring water and visualize it absorbing Raphael's green energy.
   - Sprinkle the water around your sacred space, symbolizing purification and preparation for learning.
5. **Meditation**:
   - Sit in silence, focusing on the green and blue candle flames. Visualize Raphael standing before you, offering a scroll or book.
   - Reflect on what areas of angelic magic you are drawn to explore further.
6. **Closing**:
   - Extinguish the candles with gratitude, saying:

"Raphael, guide and teacher,
I honor your wisdom and thank you for your presence.
May my studies be fruitful and align with divine will."

## Exploring Diverse Healing Traditions

Expand your practice by incorporating knowledge from various traditions:

- **Kabbalistic Healing**: Study the Sephirot and Raphael's alignment with Tiferet for balance and beauty.
- **Christian Angelology**: Explore Raphael's role in Catholic and Orthodox healing practices, including prayers and pilgrimages.
- **Islamic Angelology**: Learn about Raphael as Israfil, focusing on cosmic renewal and divine harmony.

## Advice for Deepening Your Practice

- **Integrate Raphael's Teachings into Daily Life**: Reflect on how each new piece of knowledge enhances your ability to heal and serve others.
- **Experiment Creatively**: Personalize rituals and invocations using new correspondences or insights.
- **Embrace Patience and Humility**: Learning is a lifelong process. Trust that Raphael's guidance will unfold as you remain open and committed.

By dedicating yourself to lifelong learning and integrating Raphael's wisdom, you align with the divine principles of healing and growth. As your understanding deepens, so too will your ability to embody and share Raphael's light.

# APPENDIX

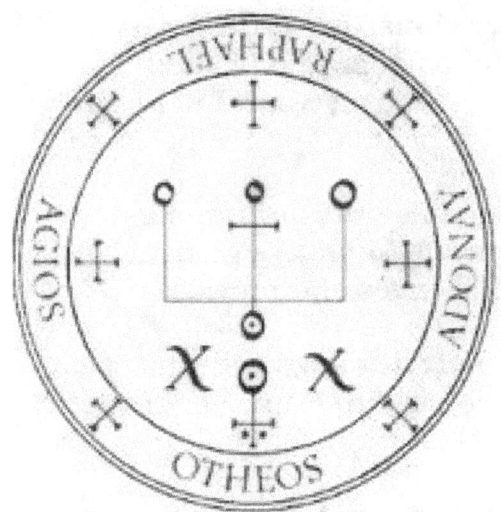

This sigil's design and symbolism strongly align with the traditional attributes and purposes associated with Raphael, making it a powerful tool for healing and guidance. The inclusion of Raphael's name and divine names, as well as the symbolic elements, align with traditional depictions of sigils used for invoking angelic aid. Let's analyze the components in detail:

## Outer Circle: Sacred Names

- **"Raphael"**: The archangel's name prominently displayed indicates this sigil is directly connected to him. Raphael is the archangel of healing, associated with the element of Air and the planet Mercury.
- **"Agios" (Greek: Ἅγιος)**: Meaning "holy," emphasizing the sacred and divine nature of the invocation.
- **"Otheos"**: Derived from "Theos," the Greek word for God, affirming a connection to divine authority.
- **"Adonay"**: A Hebrew name for God, highlighting the sigil's alignment with divine will and power.

## Inner Design

- **Central Cross and Extensions**: The central design aligns with the imagery of balance and healing:
  - The **cross** symbolizes the meeting of spiritual and earthly forces, a hallmark of Raphael's role as a mediator and healer.
  - The **branches** extending outward resemble pathways, representing Raphael's guidance in navigating life's challenges and providing healing.
  - The **red and green circles** align with the colors traditionally associated with Raphael—green for healing and renewal, and red for vitality and divine energy.
- **"X" Symbols**: These represent the transformative and protective aspects of Raphael's energy, symbolizing the crossing out of illness or negativity and marking a sacred space.

## Use in Healing

This sigil is ideal for healing rituals. Its elements affirm the focus on Raphael's divine power and the supportive energies of God. The symmetry and repeated use of holy names enhance its potency for spiritual alignment, protection, and restoration.

## Application in Rituals

1. **Trace or Draw**: Recreate the sigil on parchment or use it visually during meditation.
2. **Invocation**: Call upon Raphael using prayers or incantations. Include divine names ("Adonay," "Agios") for added strength.
3. **Focus on Healing**: Use green candles, herbs like lavender or rosemary, and crystals like emerald or aventurine to amplify the sigil's healing energy.

# Consecrating Tools with Water, Fire, Air, and Earth

Consecrating magical tools ensures they are energetically aligned with your intentions and purified for use in ritual work. The act of consecration invokes the elements to cleanse, bless, and empower the tools.

**Overview of the Process**

1. **Tools Required**:
    - A small bowl of purified or spring water (Water)
    - A candle or incense stick (Fire)
    - A feather, incense, or your breath (Air)
    - A dish of salt, sand, or soil (Earth)
2. **Preparation**:
    - Clean the tools physically.
    - Create a sacred space (e.g., perform a cleansing ritual or LBRP).
    - Place the items for consecration on your altar.

## Step-by-Step Instructions

### 1. Center Yourself

- Begin by grounding yourself and connecting to your higher intention.
- Say:

> *"By the light of the divine, I dedicate this act of consecration to purify and empower these tools for sacred work."*

### 2. Invoke the Elements

- Invite each element to participate in the consecration:

- **East (Air)**: "I call upon the sacred element of Air, breath of life, to bless this tool with clarity and wisdom."
- **South (Fire)**: "I call upon the sacred element of Fire, light of transformation, to purify and energize this tool."
- **West (Water)**: "I call upon the sacred element of Water, source of intuition and flow, to cleanse and renew this tool."
- **North (Earth)**: "I call upon the sacred element of Earth, foundation of strength, to ground and stabilize this tool."

## 3. Consecrate with Each Element

**Water (Cleansing and Purifying)**

- Dip your fingers in the water and sprinkle it lightly over the tool.
- Say:

    *"By the element of Water, I cleanse this tool of all impurities and negativity. May it flow with divine purpose and intuition."*

**Fire (Purification and Empowerment)**

- Pass the tool through the flame of a candle or over burning incense. Do so carefully to avoid damage.
- Say:

    *"By the element of Fire, I purify this tool and ignite its energy with divine strength and power."*

**Air (Insight and Inspiration)**

- Waft incense smoke or blow gently over the tool.
- Alternatively, use a feather to symbolically fan the tool with air.
- Say:

> *"By the element of Air, I bless this tool with wisdom, clarity, and the breath of life."*

**Earth (Stability and Grounding)**

- Sprinkle a pinch of salt, sand, or soil onto the tool or pass the tool over the Earth element.
- Say:

> *"By the element of Earth, I ground and stabilize this tool, aligning it with the foundation of creation."*

## 4. Seal the Consecration

- Hold the tool in both hands and visualize it glowing with white or golden light, fully cleansed and charged.
- Say:

> *"By the powers of Water, Fire, Air, and Earth, I consecrate this tool for the service of sacred and divine purpose. May it always be a vessel of my highest intent. So it is."*

## 5. Thank the Elements

- Face each cardinal direction and express gratitude to the elements for their participation.
- Example: *"I thank the element of Fire for your purification and light. Go in peace, and may your essence remain as a blessing in this work."*

## 6. Close the Ritual

- Clap your hands, ring a bell, or state:

    *"The consecration is complete. The circle is open but unbroken. So it is."*

## Post-Consecration Care

- Keep the tools in a sacred, clean space.
- Avoid letting others handle your tools unless absolutely necessary, as their energy can disrupt the alignment.
- Re-consecrate tools periodically or after intense rituals.

By aligning your tools with the elements, you integrate their energies into your practice, creating a balanced and empowered foundation for your magical work.

# Master Ritual Structure

## 1. Preparation and Purification

- **Physical Cleansing**: Bathe or wash hands and face with blessed water or herbal infusion to purify yourself physically.
- **Space Cleansing**: Use incense (frankincense, sage, or another appropriate herb) to cleanse the space.
    - Say: *"I purify this space with sacred smoke, removing all that is harmful or unwelcome."*
- **Magical Tools Preparation**: Arrange your tools on the altar and consecrate them with water, fire, air, and earth.

## 2. Banishing Negative Energies

- Perform the **Lesser Banishing Ritual of the Pentagram (LBRP)** or a comparable banishing ritual.
    - This clears the space of residual negative energies and sets a neutral and protected foundation.

Step-by-Step Instructions for Performing the LBRP

### 1. The Qabalistic Cross (Opening the Ritual)

1. **Stand Facing East**: Visualize a brilliant sphere of white light above your head.
2. **Touch Your Forehead**:
    - Say: *"Ateh"* (Thine is the kingdom).
    - Visualize the light descending through your body.
3. **Touch Your Heart/Chest**:
    - Say: *"Malkuth"* (The Kingdom).

- Imagine the light reaching your feet and grounding you to the Earth.
4. **Touch Your Right Shoulder**:
    - Say: *"Ve-Geburah" (and the Power)*.
    - Visualize the light extending to your right.
5. **Touch Your Left Shoulder**:
    - Say: *"Ve-Gedulah" (and the Glory)*.
    - See the light extending to your left.
6. **Clasp Hands Over Chest**:
    - Say: *"Le-Olam, Amen" (Forever, Amen)*.
    - Envision a glowing cross of light within you, radiating outward.

## 2. Drawing the Pentagrams

1. **Face East**:
    - Draw a large, upright banishing pentagram (starting with an upward stroke) in the air with your wand or index finger.
    - Visualize it flaming blue and brilliant.
    - **Vibrate**: *"Yod-Heh-Vuv-Heh" (Name of God in the East)*.
2. **Face South**:
    - Draw the same pentagram.
    - Visualize it blazing blue.
    - **Vibrate**: *"Adonai" (Name of God in the South)*.
3. **Face West**:
    - Draw the pentagram again.
    - Visualize it glowing.
    - **Vibrate**: *"Eheieh" (Name of God in the West)*.
4. **Face North**:
    - Draw the pentagram.
    - Visualize its brilliance.
    - **Vibrate**: *"Agla" (Name of God in the North)*.
5. **Return to East**: Complete the circle of pentagrams, connecting each with a glowing line of light.

## 3. Invocation of the Archangels

1. **Extend Arms Outward**: Form a cross shape with your body.
2. **Visualize Metatron Above You**:
   - Say: *"Above me shines the presence of Metatron, Keeper of the Divine Light."*
   - See a radiant, golden presence hovering above, symbolizing divine connection.
3. **Visualize Sandalphon Below You**:
   - Say: *"Below me stands Sandalphon, Guardian of the Earth's Foundation."*
   - See a grounding, earthen presence anchoring you to the material world.
4. **Visualize Raphael in the East**:
   - Say: *"Before me stands Raphael, Healer and Guardian of Air."*
   - See Raphael in green robes, wings shimmering with emerald light.
5. **Visualize Michael in the South**:
   - Say: *"Behind me stands Michael, Protector and Flame of Fire."*
   - See Michael in red or gold armor, a flaming sword in hand.
6. **Visualize Gabriel in the West**:
   - Say: *"To my left stands Gabriel, Messenger of Water and Intuition."*
   - See Gabriel in blue robes, holding a chalice or trumpet.
7. **Visualize Uriel in the North**:
   - Say: *"To my right stands Uriel, Keeper of Earth's Wisdom."*
   - See Uriel in brown or golden robes, holding a lantern or scroll.
8. **Seal the Archangels**:
   - Say: *"For around me burns the Pentagrams, and within me shines the Star of Divine Light."*
   - Visualize a six-pointed star glowing in your heart, radiating divine light.

## 4. Repetition of the Qabalistic Cross (Closing the Ritual)

1. **Touch Your Forehead**:
   - Say: *"Ateh."*
   - Visualize the sphere of light above you.
2. **Touch Your Heart**:
   - Say: *"Malkuth."*
3. **Touch Your Right Shoulder**:
   - Say: *"Ve-Geburah."*
4. **Touch Your Left Shoulder**:
   - Say: *"Ve-Gedulah."*
5. **Clasp Hands Over Chest**:
   - Say: *"Le-Olam, Amen."*
   - Visualize the glowing cross of light stabilizing your energy.

## Key Tips

- **Vibrating Names**: Ensure you vibrate each divine name audibly and with intention, feeling the resonance.
- **Visualization**: Clear, vivid imagery enhances the ritual's potency. Spend extra time forming the pentagrams and visualizing the Archangels.
- **Repetition**: Regular practice deepens your connection to the energies invoked.

This enhanced **LBRP** not only cleanses and protects but also aligns you with higher and lower realms through Metatron and Sandalphon, creating a sacred, balanced connection between the divine and material planes.

## 3. Establishing the Protective Circle

- **Calling the Quarters**:
  - Face each cardinal direction and invoke the corresponding archangel and elemental energy:
    - **East (Air)**: Raphael
    - **South (Fire)**: Michael
    - **West (Water)**: Gabriel

- **North (Earth)**: Uriel

# Detailed Step-by-Step Instructions for Calling the Quarters and Invoking the Archangels

This guide will walk you through the process of calling the quarters and invoking the Archangels and their corresponding elemental energies to establish a sacred and protected circle.

## Preparation

1. **Set Up Your Space**:
    - Ensure your ritual area is clean and free of clutter.
    - Place symbols or tools on altars representing the elements at each cardinal direction (e.g., a feather for air, a candle for fire, a chalice of water, and a bowl of salt or soil for earth).
2. **Ground and Center**:
    - Stand quietly in the center of your ritual space.
    - Take a few deep breaths, grounding yourself by imagining roots extending from your feet into the earth.
3. **Align with Intent**:
    - Focus your mind on the purpose of your ritual (e.g., protection, guidance, or spiritual work).
    - Visualize a glowing sphere of light surrounding your space.

## Calling the Quarters

### Step 1: Begin in the Center

- Stand in the middle of your space and hold your hands over your heart.
- Visualize a glowing golden light within you, radiating outward.

## Step 2: Invoke Raphael (East - Air)

1. **Face East**:
   - Turn to the East, the direction of the rising sun.
   - Imagine a gentle breeze or the rustling of air around you.
2. **Draw the Pentagram or Air Symbol**:
   - Use your dominant hand or a ritual tool (wand or dagger) to draw an upright invoking pentagram starting with a downward stroke or an alchemical air triangle (an upward triangle with a horizontal line through it) in the air.
   - Visualize the symbol glowing with emerald-green light.
3. **Speak the Invocation**:
   - Say clearly and with intention:

     > "Raphael, guardian of the East and the element of Air,
     > I call upon your presence to protect, witness, and guide this sacred space.
     > Bring the healing breeze of clarity and insight.
     > With your emerald light, bless and purify this circle."

4. **Anchor Raphael's Energy**:
   - Imagine Raphael appearing in shimmering green robes, wings expansive, holding a caduceus staff or standing amidst gentle winds.
   - Feel a shift in the energy of the space as the Archangel's presence strengthens.

## Step 3: Invoke Michael (South - Fire)

1. **Face South**:
   - Turn to the South, the direction of the sun's highest point.
   - Visualize the warmth and brilliance of fire.
2. **Draw the Pentagram or Fire Symbol**:

- Trace an upright invoking pentagram with a downward stroke or an alchemical fire triangle (an upward triangle) in the air.
- Visualize it glowing fiery red or gold.

3. **Speak the Invocation**:
    - Say with strength and confidence:

        "Michael, guardian of the South and the element of Fire,
        I call upon your presence to protect, witness, and guide this sacred space.
        Bring the purifying flames of courage and transformation.
        With your fiery light, shield this circle from all harm."

4. **Anchor Michael's Energy**:
    - Imagine Michael appearing in radiant armor, holding a flaming sword.
    - Feel the protective warmth of his presence enveloping the space.

## Step 4: Invoke Gabriel (West - Water)

1. **Face West**:
    - Turn to the West, the direction of the setting sun.
    - Imagine the cool flow of water or the gentle sound of waves.
2. **Draw the Pentagram or Water Symbol**:
    - Trace an upright invoking pentagram or an alchemical water triangle (a downward triangle) in the air.
    - Visualize it glowing deep blue or silver.
3. **Speak the Invocation**:
    - Say with calm and emotional resonance:

        "Gabriel, guardian of the West and the element of Water,
        I call upon your presence to protect,

witness, and guide this sacred space.
Bring the nurturing waves of intuition and renewal.
With your flowing light, bless and cleanse this circle."

4. **Anchor Gabriel's Energy**:
   - Visualize Gabriel appearing in flowing blue robes, holding a chalice or trumpet.
   - Sense the soothing and intuitive energy of their presence in the space.

## Step 5: Invoke Uriel (North - Earth)

1. **Face North**:
   - Turn to the North, the direction of stability and grounding.
   - Imagine the strength of the Earth beneath you.
2. **Draw the Pentagram or Earth Symbol**:
   - Trace an upright invoking pentagram or an alchemical earth triangle (a downward triangle with a horizontal line through it) in the air.
   - Visualize it glowing gold or brown.
3. **Speak the Invocation**:
   - Say with firmness and grounding:

     "Uriel, guardian of the North and the element of Earth,
     I call upon your presence to protect, witness, and guide this sacred space.
     Bring the stable strength of wisdom and grounding.
     With your golden light, secure this circle with divine power."

4. **Anchor Uriel's Energy**:
   - Visualize Uriel appearing in golden or earthy robes, holding a lantern or staff.
   - Feel a deep sense of stability and grounding as Uriel's energy joins the circle.

### Step 6: Seal the Circle

1. **Return to the Center**:
   - Stand in the middle of your space, arms raised outward or palms upward.
2. **Declare the Circle Sealed**:
   - Say:

     > "With the presence of Raphael, Michael, Gabriel, and Uriel,
     > this sacred circle is sealed and protected. May it serve as a space of light, healing, and divine connection."

3. **Visualize the Circle**:
   - Imagine a dome of light forming over your space, integrating the energies of the four Archangels.

### Tips for Success

- **Voice and Intention**: Speak clearly, with authority and reverence, ensuring your intention is felt in your words.
- **Visualization**: The clearer your visualization, the stronger the connection to the Archangels.
- **Repetition and Practice**: The more you perform this ritual, the easier it becomes to connect with the energies invoked.

This method establishes a sacred space imbued with the protection and wisdom of the Archangels, ready for deeper spiritual work.

## 4. Grounding and Centering

- Perform the **Middle Pillar Ritual** to ground yourself and connect to divine energy. This balances your spiritual and physical energies.

- Visualize light descending through the Kabbalistic spheres, connecting you to the divine and the Earth.
- As you finish, feel yourself as a conduit of balanced energy.

## Step-by-Step Instructions for Performing the Middle Pillar Ritual

The Middle Pillar Ritual is a powerful Kabbalistic practice that aligns you with divine energy, balancing your spiritual and physical energies by invoking the flow of light through the central column of the Tree of Life. Below are detailed instructions to perform the ritual effectively.

## Preparation

1. **Prepare Your Space**:
    - Ensure your area is clean and free from distractions.
    - Light a candle or incense if desired to symbolize divine presence.
2. **Center Yourself**:
    - Stand comfortably with your feet shoulder-width apart.
    - Close your eyes, take a few deep breaths, and focus on your intention: balancing and connecting to divine energy.
3. **Invoke Divine Presence**:
    - Begin by affirming your connection to the divine with a short prayer or statement, such as:

        "I align myself with the divine light, the source of all creation."

## The Middle Pillar Visualization

### Step 1: The Crown (Kether)

1. Visualize a brilliant white light above your head, representing the divine source.
2. Chant or vibrate the Hebrew name **Eheieh (אהיה)** (pronounced "Eh-hey-yay"), meaning "I Am."
3. Imagine this light forming a glowing sphere (Sefirah) above your head, expanding and radiating divine energy.
4. Say:

> "Kether, the Crown, divine light of unity. I call upon the infinite."

## Step 2: The Third Eye (Da'at or Binah/Chokmah Connection)

1. Visualize the light descending to the center of your forehead.
2. Chant or vibrate the Hebrew name **Yahweh Elohim (יהוה אלהים)** (pronounced "Yah-weh Eh-loh-heem"), meaning "Lord God."
3. See a sphere of light forming at your third eye, radiating wisdom and understanding.
4. Say:

> "Da'at, the hidden knowledge, bridging wisdom and understanding."

## Step 3: The Throat (Tiferet's Link to Higher Spheres)

1. Guide the light downward to your throat.
2. Chant or vibrate **Yahweh Tzabaoth (יהוה צבאות)** (pronounced "Yah-weh Tzah-bah-oht"), meaning "Lord of Hosts."
3. Visualize a golden light forming a sphere at your throat, resonating with communication and truth.
4. Say:

> "Tiferet's voice, balance of beauty and truth, linking divine expression."

## Step 4: The Heart (Tiferet)

1. Move the light to your heart center.
2. Chant or vibrate **Yahweh Eloah Va Da'at (יהוה אלוֹה וֹדעת)** (pronounced "Yah-weh Eh-loh-ah Vah Da-aht"), meaning "Lord God of Knowledge."
3. Imagine a radiant golden sphere forming in your heart, pulsing with harmony and love.
4. Say:

    "Tiferet, the heart, the center of beauty, harmony, and divine love."

## Step 5: The Solar Plexus (Yesod's Channel)

1. Direct the light downward to your solar plexus.
2. Chant or vibrate **El Shaddai (אל שדי)** (pronounced "El Shah-die"), meaning "God Almighty."
3. Visualize a bright silver sphere forming, representing the foundation of your spiritual and physical connection.
4. Say:

    "Yesod, the foundation, grounding divine energy into manifestation."

## Step 6: The Base of the Spine (Malkuth)

1. Finally, guide the light to the base of your spine, connecting you to the Earth.
2. Chant or vibrate **Adonai Ha-Aretz (אדוני הארץ)** (pronounced "Ah-doe-nai Ha-Ah-retz"), meaning "Lord of the Earth."
3. Visualize a vibrant, earthen sphere of golden or green light at your feet, grounding you to the material world.
4. Say:

"Malkuth, the Kingdom, the root of physical reality, where divine light manifests."

## Completion and Grounding

1. **Connect the Pillar**:
   - Visualize the light flowing continuously through all spheres, connecting Kether to Malkuth.
   - Feel yourself as a glowing conduit of divine energy, balanced and aligned.
2. **Declare Completion**:
   - Say:

   "I am aligned with the divine light, a perfect balance of spiritual and physical energy."

3. **Ground Yourself**:
   - Stamp your feet gently on the ground and feel the energy anchoring into the Earth.

## Advanced Tips

- **Chant with Intention**: Vibrate the Hebrew names with focus, letting the sound resonate within you.
- **Practice Visualization**: Strengthen your visualization skills by meditating on the colors and qualities of each sphere.
- **Repeat as Needed**: Perform this ritual daily to deepen your connection to divine energy and improve balance.

This practice not only balances your energies but also enhances your alignment with higher spiritual planes, making it an invaluable tool for rituals and spiritual growth.

# Perform First Enochian Call (OPTIONAL)

This call is traditionally recited in the Enochian language, and proper pronunciation is essential to capture its intended vibrational essence.

Below is the First Enochian Call with a phonetic transcription to assist in accurate pronunciation:

Ol sonuf vorsag, goho Iad balt,

lons caod goholor, gohus amiran!

Mad zodir comselh aaf nor molap.

Zodien do o aai ta piap,

piamol od vooan.

Zacare ca od zamran;

odo cicle qaa;

zorge, lap zirdo noco mad, hoath Iaida.

## Phonetic Transcription:

Ohl soh-nuf vor-sag, go-hoh ee-ahd balt,

lons ka-od go-hoh-lor, goh-hus ah-mee-ran!

Mad zoh-deer kom-sel-ah ahf nor moh-lap.

Zoh-dee-en doh oh ah-ee ta pee-ap,

pee-ah-mol od voh-ahn.

Zah-kah-reh ka od zahm-ran;

oh-doh see-kleh kah;

zor-geh, lahp zeer-doh noh-ko mad, hoh-ath ee-ah-ee-dah.

## Pronunciation Notes:

- **Vowels:**
    - 'A' as in 'father' (ah)
    - 'E' as in 'grey' (eh)
    - 'I' as in 'machine' (ee)
    - 'O' as in 'go' (oh)
    - 'U' as in 'flute' (oo)
- **Consonants:**
    - 'C' is pronounced as 'k'
    - 'G' is always hard, as in 'go'
    - 'Q' is pronounced as 'kw'

To hear the First Enochian Call pronounced correctly, you can listen to recordings by practitioners and scholars. One such resource is available on YouTube, where the call is recited with attention to traditional pronunciation: https://www.youtube.com/watch?v=xSeogRpN2R4

# 5. Opening the Central Altar

When working primarily with Archangels and invoking energies at the center altar, the entities or deities called upon will generally align with the purpose of the ritual and the Archangels' divine roles. These entities typically emphasize universal principles, healing, protection, guidance, and alignment with the Divine Will. Here's a structured approach to the entities you might call upon:

## 1. Shekinah (Divine Feminine Presence)

- **Role**: Represents the nurturing and compassionate aspects of divine energy, harmonizing the sacred space. Shekinah represents the indwelling presence of

the Divine and can anchor celestial energies into the sacred space. Her energy aligns the spiritual and physical realms, ensuring that all invoked forces operate in harmony.
- Invoking the Shekinah complements the traditionally masculine energies often associated with Archangels, creating a harmonious balance. Shekinah's light acts as a shield, dispelling discordant energies and fostering a sense of divine peace around the altar. Her presence ensures the altar is a sanctuary for divine wisdom and grace.
- **When to Call**: To balance the altar with divine compassion and unity.
- **Invocation Example**:

*"Shekinah, indwelling light of the Divine, Mother of grace and wisdom, I welcome your sacred presence to this altar. Fill this space with your eternal compassion, Balance the forces gathered here with your light, And guide my work in harmony with divine will."*

**Gesture**:

- Light a white or silver or blue candle as a representation of the Shekinah's presence.
- Place a symbolic item, such as a moonstone, pearl, or any sacred object resonating with divine feminine energy, on the altar.

## 2. The Divine Source or God

- **Why Call**: Archangels are messengers and agents of the Divine, and calling upon the Source emphasizes the ritual's alignment with divine will and purpose.
- **How to Call**: Use a prayer or affirmation that acknowledges the ultimate power behind the angelic energies.
    - *Example*:

*"O Eternal Source of all light and creation, The One who breathes life into all that is, I open this altar in your name and for your glory.*
*Shekinah, indwelling presence of divine grace,*
*Fill this space with your nurturing light.*
*Together, may your energies unite,*
*Creating harmony and balance in this sacred work.*
*Guide and protect this altar,*
*That all acts here align with divine wisdom and love."*

**Symbolism**:

- Light a **white or gold candle** to represent the Divine Source.
- Place a sacred object, such as a chalice or crystal, that resonates with unity and balance.

**Physical Gestures**:

- Raise your arms skyward while invoking the Source, symbolizing the connection to higher, transcendent energy.
- Lower your hands to your heart or the altar when invoking Shekinah, symbolizing the grounding of divine energy.

**Note:** calling in both the **Divine Source (God)** and the **Shekinah** together to balance the altar is a profoundly meaningful and balanced approach. Here's why:

# Why Call the Divine Source and Shekinah Together

1. **Union of Masculine and Feminine Divine Aspects**:
    o The Divine Source represents the ultimate, transcendent creative power often associated with masculine attributes like authority and omniscience.

- Shekinah embodies the immanent, nurturing, and grounding presence of the Divine Feminine, harmonizing with the Source's energy.
- Invoking both creates a balanced spiritual dynamic at the altar, aligning transcendent and immanent forces. When invoking deity, invoke female first and male second. When dismissing deity, dismiss male first and female second.

2. **Enhanced Unity and Harmony**:
   - Calling both honors the fullness of divine energy and ensures that all aspects of the ritual are infused with balance and completeness.
   - This unity also reflects the Kabbalistic idea of merging the supernal and earthly realms.
3. **Spiritual and Energetic Completeness**:
   - By invoking the Source and Shekinah, you connect with both the origin of divine will and its manifestation in the material world.
   - This dual invocation grounds high-frequency angelic energies into your sacred space.
4. **Protection and Guidance**:
   - The Source ensures alignment with divine will, while Shekinah provides the protective and nurturing presence that fosters clarity and peace.

## How to Call Both the Divine Source and Shekinah

**Invocation Example**:

"O Eternal Source of all light and creation, The One who breathes life into all that is, I open this altar in your name and for your glory.
Shekinah, indwelling presence of divine grace,
Fill this space with your nurturing light.
Together, may your energies unite,
Creating harmony and balance in this sacred work.

*Guide and protect this altar,*
*That all acts here align with divine wisdom and love."*

### 3. Archangel Metatron

- **Role**: As the divine scribe and guardian of sacred knowledge, Metatron ensures the ritual's alignment with cosmic law.
- **When to Call**: For rituals involving spiritual ascension, clarity, and connection to the Tree of Life.
- **Invocation Example**:

    "Metatron, divine keeper of the heavenly light, I call upon your wisdom to guide and illuminate this sacred altar."

### 4. Archangel Sandalphon

- **Role**: Acts as a bridge between heaven and earth, grounding divine energies into the physical realm.
- **When to Call**: For grounding angelic energy and connecting prayers with the celestial plane.
- **Invocation Example**:

    "Sandalphon, sacred bridge between the realms, bring harmony and manifestation to this altar of light."

### 5. Raphael (Archangel of the Ritual Focus)

- **Role**: Central to rituals involving healing, guidance, and protection. He embodies the energy of renewal and restoration.
- **When to Call**: For healing or spiritual clarity.
- **Invocation Example**:

"Raphael, healer of the Divine Light, I welcome you to this altar to share your wisdom, healing, and grace."

## 6. Complementary Archangels

Depending on the ritual's purpose, complementary Archangels can be called in:

- **Michael** (Protection, courage, dispelling negativity)
- **Gabriel** (Insight, intuition, communication)
- **Uriel** (Wisdom, grounding, transformation)
- **Invocation Examples**:
    - Michael: "Michael, protector and guardian, stand firm as a shield over this sacred altar."
    - Gabriel: "Gabriel, messenger of divine clarity, open the channels of insight at this altar."
    - Uriel: "Uriel, angel of wisdom and light, illuminate the work performed at this altar."

## 7. Angelic Choirs or Orders

- **Role**: Specific orders of angels, such as the Seraphim, Cherubim, or Thrones, amplify certain qualities like divine love, wisdom, or justice.
- **When to Call**: For a multidimensional infusion of celestial energies.
- **Invocation Example**:

    "Angels of divine love and wisdom, guardians of sacred truths, I welcome your presence to this altar."

## 8. Planetary Spirits (If Applicable)

- **Role**: Planetary spirits can align the altar's energies with celestial influences. For example:
    - **Raphael**: Mercury (healing, communication, alchemy)

- **Invocation Example**:

    "Spirits of Mercury, align this altar with the wisdom and healing of the celestial realms."

## 9. Saints or Ascended Masters

- **Role**: Depending on the tradition, saints or spiritual teachers associated with the ritual's focus may be invoked.
    - Example: **Saint Raphael** (Catholic tradition) for healing rituals.
- **Invocation Example**:

    "Saint Raphael, guide and protector of travelers and healers, lend your sacred energy to this altar."

## 10. Elemental Energies

- **Role**: Represents the four elements (Air, Fire, Water, Earth) to balance and empower the altar.
- **When to Call**: To align the altar with natural forces and ground celestial energy.
- **Invocation Example**:

    "Elemental guardians of Air, Fire, Water, and Earth, I call you to harmonize and empower this sacred altar."

## Guidelines for Central Altar Invocations

1. **Purpose Alignment**: Select entities that resonate with the intention of the ritual.
2. **Symbolic Offerings**: Place candles, crystals, incense, or sacred symbols representing the called entities on the altar.
3. **Words of Welcome**: Each invocation should be spoken with clarity, respect, and intent.

By combining these energies, the central altar becomes a nexus of divine and angelic presence, amplifying the ritual's purpose and connecting the practitioner to higher realms.

# 6. Performing the Magical Ritual or Spell Work

- Execute the central purpose of the ritual:
    - Healing work, divination, energy work, spell casting, or meditation.
- Focus your intent and visualize the desired outcome.
- Chant or recite prayers, invocations, or affirmations aligned with your goal.

# 7. Dismissing the Central Altar Entities

Assuming you have called in the Divine Source, Shekinah, and Archangel Raphael, follow these steps to dismiss them respectfully and ensure the altar's energy is cleared and sealed.

## Step 1: Prepare for Dismissal

1. **Center Yourself**:
    - Stand or sit before the altar.
    - Take three deep breaths, visualizing your connection to the entities as a channel of light, ready to respectfully release their presence.
2. **Gather the Tools**:
    - Ensure that any candles, sigils, offerings, or objects associated with the entities are ready for symbolic dismissal (e.g., candles can be extinguished, sigils removed).

## Step 2: Dismiss the Divine Source

1. **Express Gratitude**:
   - Raise your hands toward the sky, palms open.
   - Say:

     > "O Eternal Source of all light and creation, I thank you for your presence at this sacred altar.
     > Your guidance and power have illuminated this work, and I return to you my gratitude.
     > May your wisdom and love continue to inspire and protect."

2. **Seal the Invocation**:
   - Lower your hands slowly, visualizing the light of the Divine Source retreating upward while leaving a lingering blessing of protection and love.

## Step 3: Dismiss Shekinah

1. **Express Gratitude**:
   - Place your hands over your heart, symbolizing the nurturing and compassionate energy of Shekinah.
   - Say:

     > "Shekinah, divine presence and mother of wisdom, I thank you for gracing this altar with your light and balance.
     > Go in peace, and may your essence continue to guide and uplift this space."

2. **Visualize Her Presence**:
   - Imagine a warm, golden light gently receding into the altar space, leaving behind a sense of harmony and peace.

## Step 4: Dismiss Raphael

1. **Express Gratitude**:
   - Lightly touch or point toward Raphael's candle or sigil.
   - Say:

     > "Raphael, divine healer and guide, I thank you for your wisdom, healing, and protection.
     > Your emerald light has blessed this space, and I release you now with gratitude and reverence.
     > Go in peace, and may your light continue to inspire and guide."

2. **Visualize Raphael's Departure**:
   - See a gentle emerald-green light ascending or fading outward, symbolizing Raphael returning to his celestial realm.

## Step 5: Extinguish Candles and Remove Sigils

1. **Extinguish Each Candle**:
   - Use a snuffer or pinch out each candle in order (Divine Source, Shekinah, Raphael).
   - As you extinguish each flame, silently or aloud say:

     > "I release this light with gratitude and love."

2. **Remove Sigils**:
   - If you used sigils, carefully fold or place them aside, treating them with respect.
   - You may also choose to keep them for future use or dispose of them ritually (e.g., burning in a fireproof bowl as a sign of completion).

## Step 6: Close the Altar

1. **Offer a Closing Gesture**:
   - Place your hands over the altar and say:

     "This altar is now closed.
     May its energies remain balanced and aligned with divine harmony."

2. **Seal the Energy**:
   - Trace a protective symbol (e.g., a pentagram or cross) over the altar with your dominant hand or a wand/athame.
   - Visualize a protective light settling over the altar.

## Step 7: Final Grounding and Gratitude

1. **Ground Any Residual Energy**:
   - Place your hands on the altar and visualize any remaining energy flowing into the Earth, balancing and grounding.
2. **Express Final Gratitude**:
   - Bow slightly or place your hands in prayer position as a final act of respect.
   - Say:

     "With love and gratitude, I close this sacred space. So it is, and so it shall be."

## Additional Tips

- **Maintain Respect**: Treat each dismissal with care and reverence to ensure the ritual remains sacred and complete.
- **Clear the Space**: After dismissing, cleanse the space with incense or sound (e.g., a bell or singing bowl) to fully reset the energy.
- **Record the Experience**: After the ritual, journal about the energies you felt and the results of the work.

This method ensures the entities are dismissed respectfully, the altar's energy is balanced, and the space is left in harmony.

## 8. Dismissing the Quarters

The instructions proceed in the reverse order of invocation, starting with the last direction called (typically North).

### Step 1: Prepare for Dismissal

1. **Center Yourself**:
   - Stand in the middle of your circle or altar space.
   - Take three deep breaths to ground and focus, preparing to respectfully release the energies.
   - Visualize the sacred space still filled with the balanced energies of the elements and the protective light of the archangels.
2. **Gather Tools**:
   - If symbols were drawn in the air (e.g., pentagrams), prepare to trace over them in reverse to symbolically dissolve them.
   - If candles or other items were used to represent the quarters, be ready to extinguish (do <u>Not</u> blow them out with your breath) or remove them.

### Step 2: Dismiss the North (Earth - Uriel)

1. **Face North**:
   - Turn to the North with your hands raised or in a prayer position.
2. **Express Gratitude**:
   - Say:

     "Uriel, guardian of the North and the element of Earth,
     I thank you for your grounding strength and stabilizing energy.

Go in peace, and may your blessings remain as a steady foundation."

3. **Visualize Release**:
   o Imagine Uriel's golden or earthy light retreating back into the distance, leaving behind a subtle sense of grounded balance.
4. **Erase the Symbol**:
   o If a pentagram or other symbol was drawn, trace over it in reverse (starting at the last line drawn) while saying:

   "This symbol is dissolved, the energy respectfully released."

5. **Extinguish Candle or Element Representation**:
   o If you used a candle or another item to represent Earth, extinguish it or set it aside respectfully.

## Step 3: Dismiss the West (Water - Gabriel)

1. **Face West**:
   o Turn to the West and raise your hands or hold them over your heart.
2. **Express Gratitude**:
   o Say:

   "Gabriel, guardian of the West and the element of Water,
   I thank you for your intuition, emotional clarity, and nurturing flow.
   Go in peace, and may your blessings continue to inspire and cleanse."

3. **Visualize Release**:
   o Imagine Gabriel's blue or watery light retreating like a wave returning to the ocean, leaving behind a calm and serene space.
4. **Erase the Symbol**:

- Trace over the symbol for Water in reverse and say:

   > "This symbol is dissolved, the energy respectfully released."

5. **Extinguish Candle or Element Representation**:
   - Extinguish or remove any representation of Water, such as a bowl of water or candle.

## Step 4: Dismiss the South (Fire - Michael)

1. **Face South**:
   - Turn to the South with your hands open or in a power position (hands on hips or palms outward).
2. **Express Gratitude**:
   - Say:

   > "Michael, guardian of the South and the element of Fire,
   > I thank you for your protection, courage, and transformative flame.
   > Go in peace, and may your strength continue to guide and protect."

3. **Visualize Release**:
   - See Michael's red or fiery light ascending or retreating, leaving behind a sense of courage and protection.
4. **Erase the Symbol**:
   - Trace over the Fire symbol in reverse, saying:

   > "This symbol is dissolved, the energy respectfully released."

5. **Extinguish Candle or Element Representation**:
   - Extinguish or remove any representation of Fire, such as a red candle or incense.

# Step 5: Dismiss the East (Air - Raphael)

1. **Face East**:
   - Turn to the East and raise your hands, palms upward, or gesture toward the sky.
2. **Express Gratitude**:
   - Say:

     > "Raphael, guardian of the East and the element of Air,
     > I thank you for your wisdom, healing, and clarity of mind.
     > Go in peace, and may your breath of life continue to inspire and heal."

3. **Visualize Release**:
   - Picture Raphael's green or airy light dissipating like a breeze, leaving behind a sense of clarity and openness.
4. **Erase the Symbol**:
   - Trace over the Air symbol in reverse and say:

     > "This symbol is dissolved, the energy respectfully released."

5. **Extinguish Candle or Element Representation**:
   - Extinguish or remove any representation of Air, such as a feather, incense, or yellow candle.

# Step 6: Final Closing of the Circle

1. **Stand in the Center**:
   - Return to the center of the circle or altar.
   - Visualize the energy of the circle gently retracting back into the Earth or the cosmos.
2. **Seal the Circle**:
   - Using your finger, wand, or athame, trace a circle in the air (if not already created) while saying:

> "This circle is now released, the sacred space returns to its natural state.
> May the energies invoked here remain in balance and harmony."

3. **Final Grounding**:
    - Place your hands over your heart or on the ground and visualize any remaining energy flowing into the Earth, grounding the space.
4. **Express Gratitude to All Entities**:
    - Conclude with a general statement of thanks:

    > "To all the energies and beings who have joined this sacred space, I thank you.
    > Go in peace, and may the blessings of balance and harmony prevail."

5. **Cleanse the Space (Optional)**:
    - Use incense, sound (bells, singing bowls), or a sweeping gesture to energetically cleanse the area.

## Additional Tips

- **Order Matters**: Always dismiss in the reverse order of invocation (North, West, South, East).
- **Remain Respectful**: Treat the dismissal with the same reverence as the invocation to maintain a balanced and sacred practice.
- **Record the Experience**: Afterward, journal about the ritual, noting any impressions or energies you felt during the dismissals.

This structured approach ensures all invoked energies are released respectfully, leaving the space cleansed and balanced.

## 9. Closing the Space

- Clap your hands, ring a bell, or say a closing affirmation to signify the ritual's conclusion.
    - Example: *"The work is complete. The circle is open but unbroken. So it is."*

## 10. Integration and Reflection

- Spend a few minutes journaling or meditating on the ritual's experience.
- Reflect on any messages received or feelings of energy shifts.
- Offer gratitude to the divine and any entities involved.

## 11. Disposing of Ritual Remnants

Disposing of ritual remnants is a crucial step in closing the energetic loop of your magical or spiritual work. Proper disposal ensures that energies are respectfully released, grounded, or sent where intended without lingering or disrupting your space. Here are detailed, step-by-step instructions:

### 1. Understand the Nature of the Ritual and Its Remnants

Before disposal, consider:

- **The purpose of the ritual** (healing, protection, banishing, manifestation).
- **The materials used** (candles, herbs, water, incense ash, offerings).
- **Symbolic significance** of the items (do they carry positive, neutral, or negative energy?).

## 2. Separate and Categorize the Remnants

- **Biodegradable Materials**:
    - Flowers, herbs, fruit offerings, or ashes can often be returned to the earth.
- **Non-Biodegradable Materials**:
    - Items like candle wax or charred paper may need special handling.
- **Sacred or Empowered Items**:
    - Items imbued with energy (e.g., ritual water or ashes from sacred herbs) require intentional disposal to ground or release their energy.

## 3. Choose an Appropriate Disposal Method

**Biodegradable Materials**

1. **Returning to the Earth**:
    - Find a clean, respectful outdoor location like a garden, forest, or field.
    - Dig a small hole and place the biodegradable remnants inside.
    - Say a prayer or incantation to release the energy. Example:
        - *"Earth, I return these offerings to you with gratitude. May their energy be grounded and transformed into blessings."*
    - Cover the remnants with soil and gently pat it down.
2. **Water Disposal**:
    - If permitted by local regulations, pour ritual water into a natural body of water like a river or ocean.
    - As you pour, visualize the water carrying the energy away and dispersing it. Example:
        - *"Waters of life, carry this energy onward, cleansing and renewing all it touches."*

**Non-Biodegradable Materials**

1. **Candle Wax**:
    - Wrap the leftover wax in paper or cloth, and either bury it or dispose of it in a waste bin.
    - If burying, include a statement of intention to ground the energy, such as:
        - *"This wax served its purpose. I now release and ground its energy."*
2. **Charred Paper or Sigils**:
    - Burn completely if not already burned during the ritual.
    - Scatter the ashes in a natural setting or bury them. If not possible, sprinkle the ashes in running water.

**Sacred or Empowered Items**

1. **Ritual Water**:
    - Pour water at the base of a healthy tree or plant to transfer the energy into nature.
    - As you pour, say:
        - *"I release this sacred water to nourish life and ground its energy into the earth."*
2. **Ashes**:
    - Ashes from herbs or incense should be scattered in a meaningful place, such as a garden or crossroads.
    - While scattering, speak your intention:
        - *"May these ashes return to the earth, carrying my gratitude and blessings."*

## 4. Handle Negative or Banished Energy Items

If the ritual was for banishing or removing negativity:

1. **Salt or Salt Water**:
    - Dispose of salt or salt water by burying it far from your home or in the trash. Never reuse salt from a banishing ritual.
2. **Other Remnants**:

- o Wrap items in black cloth or paper before burial or disposal to symbolically contain and neutralize the energy.

## 5. Cleanse Yourself and Your Tools

- **Personal Cleansing**:
  - o Wash your hands or bathe in salt water to remove residual energy.
  - o Say:
    - *"I cleanse myself of all energies, retaining only those aligned with my highest good."*
- **Tool Cleansing**:
  - o Cleanse tools with smoke, salt, or water, depending on their material, before storing them.

## 6. Conclude with Gratitude

- Stand in your ritual space or outdoors.
- Offer a moment of gratitude to the elements, spirits, or deities involved in the ritual.
- Example:
  - o *"Thank you, sacred energies, for your guidance and presence. May the energy released here continue to flow in harmony."*

## 7. Record and Reflect

- Write down the disposal process and your reflections in your spiritual journal or grimoire.
- Note any feelings, signs, or outcomes related to the ritual and its remnants.

## Additional Tips

- **Environmentally Friendly Disposal**:
  - o Use eco-friendly options whenever possible, especially for natural or biodegradable remnants.
- **Cultural or Local Norms**:

- - Be mindful of local customs or laws, especially when disposing of items in natural bodies of water or public spaces.
- **Intentional Energy Release**:
  - Throughout the process, focus on the intention of release, transformation, or grounding.

By respectfully disposing of ritual remnants, you ensure the continuity of sacred energy while maintaining balance and alignment in your practice.

**Final Thoughts on Candles**

**Not blowing out ritual candles** emphasizes the importance of intentionality, respect, and alignment with the sacred energies at play. Each aspect of the ritual—down to how you extinguish a candle—affects the spiritual resonance of your work. By choosing deliberate, respectful methods, you maintain the integrity of your ritual space and honor the elements, entities, and energies you have engaged. **Blowing out ritual candles with your breath is generally avoided** in spiritual and magical practices for several symbolic and energetic reasons. Here's a detailed explanation of why this practice is discouraged:

# 1. Breath as a Personal Energy Source

- **Symbolic Contamination**:
  - In many traditions, breath represents your personal life force or energy. Blowing out a ritual candle introduces your individual energy into the ritual's work, potentially contaminating or altering the spiritual intent that has been imbued into the candle.
  - It may also symbolize asserting personal will over the divine or universal forces invoked during the ritual, which can be seen as disruptive or disrespectful.
- **Unintentional Dissipation**:

- Your breath disperses air randomly, symbolizing chaos or disruption. This contrasts with the controlled, intentional energy flow you've created during the ritual.

## 2. Respecting the Element of Fire

- **Symbolic Relationship**:
  - Fire is one of the sacred elements, representing transformation, purification, and divine will. Blowing on the flame can be seen as an act of disrespect or an abrupt severance of its sacred role in the ritual.
  - Extinguishing the flame with a more symbolic and intentional method, like snuffing, honors the fire element's presence and its purpose.
- **Preserving the Energy**:
  - The flame is considered a manifestation of the energy raised during the ritual. Snuffing it out gently (e.g., using a candle snuffer or pinching it with dampened fingers) allows the energy to dissipate respectfully and slowly, preserving the harmony of the space.

## 3. Cultural and Magical Beliefs

- **Breath and Spirit**:
  - In many mystical traditions, breath is associated with the spirit or soul. Blowing out the candle may unintentionally signal a dismissal or disruption of spiritual energies, which could end the ritual prematurely or unbalance the energies invoked.
- **Connection to Chaos**:
  - Certain folk traditions associate blowing out candles with chaos or negativity, as it is seen as an uncontrolled or thoughtless act. In contrast, rituals demand precision, control, and intention.

## 4. Energetic Practicality

- **Disruption of Ritual Atmosphere**:
  - The act of blowing can scatter ash, wax, or incense smoke, disrupting the physical and energetic ambiance of the ritual space.
  - A snuffer or other method is silent and deliberate, maintaining the meditative and sacred atmosphere.

## Preferred Alternatives

- **Candle Snuffer**:
  - Use a candle snuffer to gently extinguish the flame. The snuffer represents a deliberate and respectful conclusion to the candle's role in the ritual.
- **Pinching the Flame**:
  - For those comfortable with it, dampen your fingertips slightly and pinch the flame. This method requires focus and intent, symbolizing your direct interaction with the fire element.
- **Smothering the Flame**:
  - Place a non-flammable object (like a small bowl or lid) over the flame to extinguish it without introducing breath or chaos.

## Additional Ritual Enhancements

1. **Personalization**: Tailor invocations, symbols, and offerings to align with the specific intent or entity.
2. **Energy Raising**: Before the spell work, perform drumming, chanting, or dancing to elevate the energy if needed.
3. **Sacred Geometry**: Incorporate symbols like the Flower of Life or hexagrams to amplify energy.
4. **Astral Timing**: Align the ritual with planetary or lunar influences for added potency.

5. **Post-Ritual Cleansing**: Cleanse the space again to ensure residual energies are removed.

This comprehensive ritual structure ensures a balanced, protected, and powerful ritual environment. It integrates both ceremonial and intuitive practices, creating a harmonious flow from preparation to conclusion.

# Integrative Healing Ritual: Unifying Body, Mind, and Spirit with Raphael

This ritual invokes Archangel Raphael to unify and restore the physical, mental, and spiritual aspects of your being. By combining symbolic actions, sacred texts, and divine intention, this practice aligns your entire self with Raphael's healing light and divine mercy.

## Materials Needed

- Three candles: one white (spirit), one green (body), one blue (mind)
- A bowl of water (for purification and renewal)
- A small crystal safe for water use (e.g., green aventurine or jade)
- Frankincense or sandalwood incense (optional)
- A copy of the Bible, Quran, or apocryphal texts (choose passages from each if you wish to blend traditions)
- A quiet, undisturbed space

## Step-by-Step Instructions

### 1. Prepare the Sacred Space

**Why:** Cleansing and dedicating your space removes distractions and invites divine energy.

- Set up the three candles in a triangular arrangement, with the green candle in front, the blue candle to the left, and the white candle to the right.
- Place the water bowl in the center and the incense nearby.

Light the incense and walk clockwise around your space, wafting the smoke to purify the area. Say: *"By the divine light of Raphael, this space is cleansed and consecrated for healing. May it be filled with peace, mercy, and renewal."*

Visualize the smoke forming a protective shield around you and the space.

## 2. Light the Candles

Lighting each candle symbolizes the unification of body, mind, and spirit under Raphael's guidance.

- Light the green candle first (body), then the blue (mind), and finally the white (spirit).

As you light each candle, say:

- For the green candle:
  *"Raphael, healer of the body, restore my strength and vitality."*
- For the blue candle:
  *"Raphael, guide of the mind, bring me clarity and peace."*
- For the white candle:
  *"Raphael, guardian of the spirit, align me with divine purpose."*

Raise your hands briefly over the candles as if drawing their light into your being.

## 3. Read from Sacred Texts

**Why:** Scripture connects the ritual to divine authority and amplifies its spiritual resonance.

- Read the following passages aloud:
    - From the Bible: *"He heals the brokenhearted and binds up their wounds."* (Psalm 147:3)
    - From the Quran: *"And when I am ill, it is He who cures me."* (Quran 26:80)
    - From the *Book of Tobit*: *"Raphael said to Tobias, 'Do not be afraid; your prayers have been heard.'"* (Tobit 12:15)

Hold your hands open toward the water bowl, allowing the power of the words to flow into the water.

## 4. Invoke Raphael's Presence

Calling upon Raphael focuses the ritual's intention and connects you to his energy.

- Stand with your hands raised to shoulder height, palms outward.

Say: *"Raphael, servant of the Most High,*
*Healer of body, mind, and spirit,*
*I call upon your divine light to unify and restore all parts of my being.*
*Let your emerald light shine within me, bringing wholeness and peace."*

Visualize Raphael standing before you, radiating emerald light that flows into you and the space.

## 5. Perform the Water Blessing

Water represents purification and renewal, serving as a medium for Raphael's healing energy.

- Dip your fingers into the water and trace the sign of the cross (or another sacred symbol) over your heart, forehead, and stomach.

Say: *"By the water of renewal and Raphael's light,*
*I am cleansed, healed, and restored."*

As you speak, visualize the water carrying Raphael's light into your body, mind, and spirit.

## 6. Meditate on Healing and Unity

Meditation allows Raphael's energy to integrate fully into your being.

- Sit comfortably with your eyes closed, facing the candles.
- Focus on the flame of each candle in turn, starting with green, then blue, and finally white.

Say: *"Body, mind, and spirit, I am whole.
Raphael's light unites me with divine harmony."*

Feel the energy of each aspect merging into a single, unified state.

## 7. Conclude with Gratitude

Gratitude seals the ritual and honors Raphael's assistance.

- Stand and bow slightly toward the altar.

Say: *"Heavenly Father, I thank You for the presence of Your servant Raphael.
May his light remain with me as I walk in strength, clarity, and peace. Amen."*

Extinguish the candles in reverse order (white, blue, green), visualizing their light transferring to your heart.

## Explanations for Each Step

1. **Prepare the Space:** Cleansing invites divine energy and sets the tone for the ritual.
2. **Light the Candles:** The candles symbolize the aspects of your being and Raphael's power over each.
3. **Sacred Texts:** Scripture reinforces the connection to divine authority and purpose.
4. **Invocation:** Calling Raphael ensures his presence and focuses his energy on the ritual's intention.
5. **Water Blessing:** Water acts as a physical medium for spiritual healing and purification.
6. **Meditation:** Focusing on the candles aligns your body, mind, and spirit with Raphael's energy.

7. **Gratitude:** Expressing thanks honors the divine and seals the ritual's energy.

## Advanced Tips

1. **Repeat Regularly**
    - Perform this ritual weekly to maintain balance and healing.
2. **Add Crystals**
    - Place a green aventurine or jade in the water for added healing energy.
3. **Use Sacred Music**
    - Play calming hymns or instrumental music to deepen the sacred atmosphere.

This integrative ritual invites Raphael's divine light to restore your physical, mental, and spiritual health, creating harmony and renewal in all aspects of your being.

# Traveler's Talisman Ritual: Invoking Raphael's Guidance and Protection

This ritual creates a talisman inscribed with Raphael's sigil to invoke his protection and guidance during travels. Combining sacred symbols, scripture, and intention, the talisman becomes a spiritual tool to ensure safe passage and alignment with divine light.

## Materials Needed

- A small piece of durable material for the talisman (metal, wood, or stone)
- A tool for inscribing or marking the sigil (e.g., engraving tool, permanent marker, or paint)
- A green cord or pouch (to carry the talisman)
- A green candle (symbolizing Raphael's light)
- Frankincense incense (optional, for purification)
- A copy of the Bible, Quran, or apocryphal texts (choose appropriate passages)
- A bowl of water (for consecration)

## Step-by-Step Instructions

### 1. Prepare the Sacred Space

Cleansing the space ensures purity and focus for the ritual.

- Light the incense and green candle. Place the talisman material, water, and inscription tool on a clean surface.

Waft the incense smoke around the area, saying: *"By the light of Raphael and the grace of the Most High,
This space is cleansed and made holy for divine work."*

Visualize the smoke purifying the space and creating a sacred boundary.

## 2. Inscribe Raphael's Sigil

The sigil serves as a symbolic and spiritual anchor for Raphael's protective energy.

- Draw or engrave Raphael's sigil (a circle with intersecting lines and embellishments representing his name in Hebrew, רפאל) on the talisman.

As you inscribe, say: *"Raphael, guardian of travelers,*
*By this sigil, I call upon your light and protection.*
*May your presence guide me wherever I go."*

Hold the talisman briefly and visualize it glowing with emerald green light.

## 3. Consecrate the Talisman

Consecration imbues the talisman with sacred energy, aligning it with Raphael's light.

- Dip the talisman in the bowl of water and hold it over the flame of the candle (without burning it).

Say: *"O Lord, through water and flame,*
*Bless this talisman with Raphael's protection.*
*Let it carry your light and shield me on my journey."*

Imagine Raphael's energy infusing the talisman as you perform this act.

## 4. Read Sacred Passages

Reciting scripture empowers the talisman with divine authority.

- Read the following passages aloud:
    - From the Bible: *"The Lord will watch over your coming and going both now and forevermore."* (Psalm 121:8)

- From the Quran: *"Indeed, it is Allah who is my Protector, and He is the best of helpers."* (Quran 22:78)
- From the *Book of Tobit*: *"Raphael said, 'I will accompany you on your journey and protect you.'"* (Tobit 5:4)

Hold the talisman close to your heart as you recite, visualizing its energy growing stronger with each word.

## 5. Invoke Raphael's Presence

Directly calling upon Raphael activates his energy within the talisman.

- Hold the talisman in both hands and raise it slightly toward the sky.

Say: *"Raphael, divine guardian and guide,
Healer of the body and protector of the soul,
I call upon your light to bless this talisman.
May it guide and shield me on every path I tread.
In your name, I travel with faith and peace."*

Envision Raphael standing before you, his emerald light flowing into the talisman.

## 6. Seal the Energy

Sealing ensures the talisman retains Raphael's energy and serves its purpose.

- Wrap the talisman in a green cord or place it in the green pouch.

Say: *"This talisman is sealed in light and protection.
Raphael's guidance is with me wherever I go. Amen."*

Kiss the talisman gently or hold it to your heart as a final gesture of connection.

## 7. Close with Gratitude

Expressing gratitude honors Raphael's presence and completes the ritual.

- Extinguish the candle and incense.

Say: *"Heavenly Father, I thank You for the light of Raphael. May his guidance and protection remain with me always. Amen."*

Bow slightly as a gesture of respect and reverence.

## Explanations for Each Step

1. **Prepare the Space:** Cleansing creates a focused and sacred environment for the ritual.
2. **Inscribe the Sigil:** The sigil serves as a physical and symbolic connection to Raphael's energy.
3. **Consecrate the Talisman:** Water and flame are purifying elements that activate the talisman's spiritual purpose.
4. **Scripture Reading:** Sacred texts empower the talisman with divine authority and reinforce its intention.
5. **Invoke Raphael:** Calling upon Raphael ensures the talisman is directly aligned with his energy.
6. **Seal the Energy:** Wrapping or enclosing the talisman preserves its connection to Raphael.
7. **Gratitude:** Closing with thanks strengthens your relationship with Raphael and acknowledges divine assistance.

## Advanced Tips

1. **Carry the Talisman Always**

     - Keep the talisman with you during travels or in challenging situations for ongoing protection.
2. **Refresh Periodically**
     - Repeat the consecration process occasionally to renew its energy.
3. **Personalize the Pouch**
     - Add herbs like mint or rosemary for extra protective energy.

By crafting this talisman, you create a sacred tool to invoke Raphael's guidance and protection, ensuring safe travels and divine alignment wherever life takes you.

# Ritual for Offering Water to the Earth

This ritual acknowledges the Earth as a sacred vessel for renewal and transformation, aligning your offering of water with gratitude and the cycle of divine creation. By mindfully returning the consecrated water to the Earth, you complete the ritual and express your thanks to the divine forces involved.

## Materials Needed

- Bowl of consecrated water from the previous ritual
- A natural spot outside (e.g., garden, forest, or near a tree)
- A small green cloth or a stone (optional, as an additional symbolic offering)
- A quiet, reflective attitude and intention of gratitude

## Step-by-Step Instructions

### 1. Choose a Sacred Spot

Selecting a natural location grounds the ritual and connects the act with the living Earth.

- Find a place that feels peaceful and connected to nature, such as near a tree, a patch of grass, or a flowerbed.
- Stand quietly for a moment, observing the surroundings and connecting with the energy of the Earth.

Say: *"O Earth, sacred and life-giving, I come to honor you with this gift. May this offering return to you in gratitude and love."*

Place your hands lightly on your heart as a gesture of reverence.

## 2. Prepare to Pour the Water

Setting your intention ensures the act carries spiritual meaning and aligns with your earlier ritual.

- Hold the bowl of water in both hands, raising it slightly toward the sky.

Say: *"This water, blessed by the light of renewal,
Now returns to the Earth,
Carrying the blessings of transformation,
Gratitude, and divine mercy."*

Visualize the water shimmering with the emerald light of Raphael, radiating healing energy.

## 3. Pour the Water

Returning the water to the Earth symbolizes the completion of the ritual and the cyclical nature of energy.

- Slowly pour the water onto the ground, allowing it to soak into the Earth.

As you pour, say: *"O Earth, receive this sacred offering.
May it nourish you as you have nourished me.
Through this act, I honor the divine cycle of renewal."*

Visualize the water merging with the Earth, spreading healing and gratitude.

## 4. Offer an Additional Symbol (Optional)

Adding a physical token enhances the ritual and symbolizes your ongoing connection with the Earth.

- If using a green cloth or stone, place it gently on the ground near where you poured the water.

Say: *"With this gift, I seal my gratitude.
May harmony and renewal flow through all creation."*

Bow slightly as a gesture of respect.

### 5. Close with Prayer and Reflection

Concluding with a prayer of gratitude strengthens the spiritual energy of the ritual.

- Stand quietly, hands folded or open, and offer a final prayer.

Say: *"O Creator of all, I thank You for the blessings of healing and renewal.
Raphael, divine healer, and Earth, sacred vessel,
May this offering bring light, balance, and peace to all creation.
Amen."*

Take a moment to breathe deeply, grounding yourself in the connection between the divine, the Earth, and your own spirit.

## Explanations for Each Step

1. **Choose a Sacred Spot:** Nature provides a grounding energy that amplifies the ritual's spiritual resonance.
2. **Set Intention:** Holding the water and speaking a blessing focuses your energy on gratitude and renewal.
3. **Pour the Water:** The act symbolizes returning blessings to the Earth, completing the energy exchange.
4. **Additional Offering (Optional):** A token enhances the ritual's permanence and strengthens your connection to nature.
5. **Close with Prayer:** Ending in prayer expresses gratitude and closes the ritual with divine acknowledgment.

# Advanced Tips

1. **Perform Barefoot**
   - Stand barefoot on the ground to enhance your connection to the Earth's energy.
2. **Plant a Seed**
   - Add a seed to the offering spot as a living symbol of growth and renewal.
3. **Reflect on the Cycle**
   - Take a moment afterward to reflect on the interconnectedness of life, water, and the Earth's renewal.

This ritual not only completes your spiritual practice but also deepens your connection to the Earth and the divine cycles of transformation and gratitude.

# Sample Incantation for Collaborative Healing Ritual

This incantation combines the names and energies of Raphael, Michael, Gabriel, and Metatron to create a harmonious invocation for healing and balance:

**Incantation:**

*"Archangels of divine grace and healing light,
I call upon your sacred presence this night.

Raphael, healer of body, mind, and soul,
Let your emerald light make me whole.

Michael, protector with sword so bright,
Guard me in mercy and shield me with might.

Gabriel, messenger of wisdom and peace,
Bring clarity and strength that never cease.

Metatron, keeper of the sacred divine,
Align me with the Source, through your celestial design.

By your united power, I am renewed,
By your sacred harmony, I am imbued.
Let your combined energies heal, protect, and restore,
And guide me in grace forevermore."*

## How to Use the Incantation

1. **Recite Slowly:** Speak each stanza deliberately, allowing the meaning and energy of each archangel's role to resonate with you.
2. **Focus on Visualization:** As you say each archangel's name, visualize their respective energy (green for Raphael, blue for Michael, purple for Gabriel, white for Metatron) surrounding and blending with your aura.

3. **End with Gratitude:** After finishing the incantation, pause for a moment of silence to feel their energies, and conclude with a heartfelt "Thank you" to seal the invocation.

This incantation is flexible and can be modified to suit specific intentions, such as emotional healing, spiritual guidance, or physical protection.

# SOURCES

1. Virtue, D. (2003). *Archangels and Ascended Masters: A Guide to Working and Healing with Divinities and Deities.* Hay House.
2. Leitch, A. (2010). *The Angelical Language, Volume I: The Complete History and Mythos of the Tongue of Angels.* Llewellyn Publications.
3. Greer, J. M. (2006). *The Complete Magician's Tables.* Llewellyn Publications.
4. Denning, M., & Phillips, O. (2004). *The Llewellyn Practical Guide to Angel Magic.* Llewellyn Publications.
5. Brand, J. (2015). *Angelic Sigils, Keys, and Calls: 142 Ways to Make Instant Contact with Angels and Archangels.* Power of Magick Publishing.
6. Witecki, E. (2012). *The Angel Compass: How to Call Upon Angels in Everyday Life.* Balboa Press.
7. Virtue, D. (2007). *Archangels 101: How to Connect Closely with Archangels Michael, Raphael, Uriel, Gabriel, and Others for Healing, Protection, and Guidance.* Hay House.
8. Stewart, R. J. (2010). *The Complete Guide to the Kabbalah: Unlocking the Hidden Wisdom of the Tree of Life.* Watkins Publishing.
9. Andrews, T. (1994). *How to Meet and Work with Spirit Guides.* Llewellyn Publications.
10. Conway, D. J. (1995). *Magickal, Mystical Creatures: Invite Their Powers into Your Life.* Llewellyn Publications.
11. Gallagher, D. (2019). *Your Magical Home: The Magic of Hearth, Home, and Family Traditions.* W.W. Norton.
12. Hale, M. (2017). *Practical Angel Magic of Dr. John Dee's Enochian Tables.* Golden Hoard Press.
13. Scholem, G. (1991). *Major Trends in Jewish Mysticism.* Schocken Books.
14. Hart, A. (2006). *The Healing Miracles of Jesus.* Thomas Nelson.

15. Smith, J. I., & Haddad, Y. Y. (2002). *The Islamic Understanding of Death and Resurrection.* Oxford University Press.
16. Long, C. (2001). *Spiritual Merchants: Religion, Magic, and Commerce.* University of Texas Press.
17. Regardie, I. (1997). *The Art of True Healing.* Llewellyn Publications.
18. Harvey, A. (2001). *The Direct Path: Creating a Journey to the Divine Using the World's Mystical Traditions.* Broadway Books.
19. Cunningham, S. (2002). *Living Wicca: A Further Guide for the Solitary Practitioner.* Llewellyn Publications.

## Magazine Sources

1. Learn Religions. (2017, July 15). "Meet Archangel Raphael, the Angel of Healing." Retrieved from LearnReligions.com.
2. Britannica. (2024, October). "Raphael | Heavenly Messenger, Protector, Healer." Retrieved from Britannica.com.

## Journal Sources

1. Sacred Texts. (n.d.). "The Book of Protection." Retrieved from Sacred-Texts.com.
2. Fordham University. (n.d.). "The Golden Legend: The Life of St. Raphael the Archangel." Retrieved from Fordham.edu.

## Online Encyclopedias and Websites

1. Wikipedia contributors. (2024, November 1). *Raphael (archangel).* Retrieved from Wikipedia.org.
2. Catholic Answers. (n.d.). *Raphael, Saint.* Retrieved from CatholicAnswers.com.
3. Catholic Online. (n.d.). *St. Raphael - Saints & Angels.* Retrieved from CatholicOnline.com.

4. Encyclopedia.com. (n.d.). *Raphael, Archangel.* Retrieved from Encyclopedia.com.

## Religious Texts and Scriptures

1. Bible Gateway. (n.d.). *The Book of Tobit.* Retrieved from BibleGateway.com.
2. Sacred Texts. (n.d.). *The Book of Enoch.* Retrieved from Sacred-Texts.com.
3. Sacred Texts. (n.d.). *The Book of Jubilees.* Retrieved from Sacred-Texts.com.
4. Sacred Texts. (n.d.). *The Zohar.* Retrieved from Sacred-Texts.com.
5. Sacred Texts. (n.d.). *Sefer Raziel HaMalakh.* Retrieved from Sacred-Texts.com.
6. Sacred Texts. (n.d.). *The Key of Solomon.* Retrieved from Sacred-Texts.com.
7. Sacred Texts. (n.d.). *The Sixth and Seventh Books of Moses.* Retrieved from Sacred-Texts.com.

## Church Publications

1. St. Raphael's Parish. (n.d.). "All About St. Raphael the Archangel." Retrieved from StRaphaelsParish.net.
2. St. Catherine of Siena Roman Catholic Church. (2018, October 9). "Who Is the Archangel Raphael?" Retrieved from StCatherineRCC.org.